MISSING PIECES

How to Find Birth Parents and Adopted Children

A Search And Reunion Guidebook

By Paul Drake
and
Beth Sherrill

HERITAGE BOOKS
2004

HERITAGE BOOKS

AN IMPRINT OF HERITAGE BOOKS, INC.

Books, CDs, and more – Worldwide

For our listing of thousands of titles see our website
at
www.HeritageBooks.com

Published 2004 by
HERITAGE BOOKS, INC.
Publishing Division
65 East Main Street
Westminster, Maryland 21157-5026

Other Heritage Books by Paul Drake:

WHAT DID THEY MEAN BY THAT?
A Dictionary of Historical and Genealogical Terms

YOU OUGHT TO WRITE ALL THAT DOWN:
A Guide to Organizing and Writing Genealogical Narrative

GENEALOGY: HOW TO FIND YOUR ANCESTORS
(with Margaret Grove Driskill)

NOW IN OUR FOURTH CENTURY: SOME AMERICAN FAMILIES.
A Documentary and Pictorial History of Some Twenty-Five Families Who
Were Settled in the American Colonies before the Year 1750, More than
Fifteen of Whom Arrived Before 1700, and of More than 4000 of Their
Ancestors, Kin, and Descendants.

International Standard Book Number: **0-7884-2534-X**

DEDICATIONS

To Jane, to John, and from their mother with the greatest love and affection to Scott, Ryan, Tyler and Elizabeth and those who will follow them, and from Dad to Paul, Diane, and Cheryl, their beautiful children and their descendants.

Thank you and God bless you all.

Beth Sherrill
Paul Drake

September 2003

Table of Contents

Acknowledgments

We are indebted to so very many relatives, friends and acquaintances that to here name them all would be well nigh impossible.

Nevertheless, for their assistance with interviews we are especially appreciative of Charlotte, Chris, Christina, Dean, Debbie, Donna, Jamie, particularly to Jane, Laird, Len and Mimi, Leslie, Margo, Pam, Ray and Peggy, and to Rebecca and Teresa.

For technical assistance with these contrary, yet so much needed gadgets that we call "computers," surely we owe much to Bethany, James, Joe, and Paul.

To John, for his contribution of the chapter having to with the medical aspects and for his endless encouragement and patience. For the superb editing and help with the manuscript, we thank Roxanne, Leslie, the Heritage staff, and Martha.

Thank you all again, very much. Without your contributions this effort surely would have been impossible.

INTRODUCTION

This book is a formula for success in search and reunion. It is the true story of Beth Sherrill, an adoptee, who after a lifetime of curiosity and with the help of Paul Drake, undertook to locate her birth parents. These materials grew out of a study of the law as it now is, from many interviews with others who also have searched (some successfully and others less so), and the search experiences of these authors.

It is a how-to for those who also would seek birth parents or children who have been adopted in the past. It is expected that from these experiences, whether those were successful or not so, that you will determine your course, set off upon that journey toward reunion, and succeed in those efforts to some degree.

If you have grappled with the law and the adoption system in the past and are yet no closer to the goal of finding your people, or if you have been hesitant to begin a search for whatever reasons, we hope to help you resolve those difficulties. Further, even if you do not intend a search, yet hope to stand on the sidelines and offer encouragement as a search moves forward, these methods, experiences, and the results of others likely will assist you in that station. Finally, if you are one who has resolved that you will in no way participate or assist those who have or are about to set off on such a quest, you will be better able to understand the motives of those searchers.

By design, the system of adoption and the law found firmly in place in most of these United States does not conduce to, encourage, or assist in bringing discovery and reunion. Still though, that same system of laws and regulations will not actively obstruct your efforts to search and locate. The law does not prohibit searches and reunions now, nor has it ever. The result is that if you choose to seek out a parent or a child you may be sure that there will be no adoption policemen knocking on your door to take you off to jail.

For many, if not the vast majority of those involved, adoption is one of the most defining moments of their lives and represents the beginning of an ever-changing series of emotions that continue through life. Just as some adoptees and birth parents do not feel a need of reunion, some carry a deep and abiding desire to find the missing pieces and people that resulted from the facts of an adoption.

Even if you have decided that you neither need nor desire reunion, you must realize that it may come about anyhow. Similarly, the idea that problems will arise only if you are a conscious participant in a search or a reunion brought about by others is erroneous. If someone near you undertakes a search and reunion, you will be affected whether you choose to participate, elect rather to only cheer a searcher on, or to do nothing.

In fact, while the process may affect adoptees, birth parents, and even adoptive parents in varying ways and to different degrees, no matter how you may view the whole matter, searching is a natural, widespread, and almost inevitable outcome of adoption. Searches and reunions, though usually not of the made-for-TV movies sort, have occurred with regularity for so long as adoptions have been in existence.

So, if you are a party to adoption or merely a friend of any member of an adoption triad (adoptees, birth parents or adoptive parents), to deny that such search and reunion efforts might one day come into your life is nothing more than denial of the obvious. Most of all, adoptive parents must prepare for a reunion to occur no matter their feelings in the matter and whether or not they choose to participate, and birth parents and adoptees should anticipate that they well may be found.

So, especially if you are directly involved as an adoptive parent, a natural parent, an adoptee, or a person within the immediate family of any of those, you must consider that possibility, no matter what assurances you may have been given in the past. Further, whether you relish the thought or not, and even if the circumstances are such that you do not foresee that a reunion ever will come upon you, you must be prepared to accept and adjust to the very real likelihood that you will be involved.

Identifying and knowing of birth parents may be as much a part of the identity of an adoptee as the fact of having given birth is a part of every parent, particularly a mother. Just as those thoughts are a part of all parents and all adoptees, changes of attitudes of participants will come to all as a result of maturity and circumstance. Those changes sometimes arrive subtly and slowly, yet others may overtake you with a rush. To insist or pretend that such is not likelihood is to refuse to meet life as it overtakes you.

Throughout your search, whether you choose to use these suggestions and methods or not, you will be the navigator of that journey. You must do your homework in preparation and planning, you must confront problems and make decisions affecting you and others close to you, and you must make a conscious choice to proceed. Though you can not dictate what the results will be, you surely can control how you will be affected by whatever those results.

In most searches the results are most gratifying, though some will fall short of your expectations. Be prepared to glean all the rewards that are present, no matter in what form and with what measure of success.

Thoughts of searching had begun when Mary Elizabeth was a child, and those thoughts had haltingly gathered strength and urgency as the years passed. Present in her mind across all those years was the possibility that her birth mother would not ever want to be found and intended to remain anonymous throughout life.

As you too may have had, Mary Elizabeth bore excessive concern over the views of others in matters of adoptions and conduct of the participants. Her fears that she might be viewed as offensive or callous because she undertook to search, or that by so doing she might be hurtful of others, particularly her adoptive mother, had roots in early twentieth-century misunderstandings, myths, and taboos. It had been the system itself and its regulations that greatly affected the conduct of adoptees and birth mothers, and likewise how many others looked upon such women and children.

Only a very few people had known of and shared the tedious journey of life with Mary Elizabeth, and she had known from the beginning that there were some that neither could nor would understand her true and mature need to undertake such a search and reunion. During it all, being without a clear road map to follow concerning her emotions and expectancies, Mary Elizabeth often had been called upon to rely upon only her instincts in her attempts to resolve her emotional difficulties. You too may have known or may in the future know similar feelings.

Still, those instincts had served her well. She had found herself able to be comfortable and confident about her search thoughts and plans, despite not infrequent measures of resistance, occasional pressures from others for her to cease her efforts, and disappointments that had to do with attitudes of others as to her status as an adoptee. Still she selected a path, stayed that course, and when changes were required she adapted.

All in all, she had chosen the correct path. You too must do the same, all the while realizing that there will not be someone to help you with each and every problem.

Mary Elizabeth and Owen were met by many obstacles and had almost no information with which to begin. Owen, a retired lawyer and genealogist, and Mary Elizabeth, an adoptee, a mother, and one whose professional background was in human services, were able to find her birth mother in less than six months. Finding her birth father thereafter involved only a matter of a few more weeks. Your search may take more or less time, so be patient.

As will you, though occasionally discouraged, they were assisted in the search by many and varied other researchers and members of adoption triads. From those people, they realized commonalties of problems and soon after Mary Elizabeth made the decision to commence her search they were able to develop a tentative strategy for their future efforts. That strategy proved successful, and much of that planning is explained here.

In CHAPTER ONE, "A New Way of Thinking," we will suggest that many of the perceptions you now entertain will not serve you well. Before you undertake even to decide whether or not to search, you must explore within your mind those hurdles that you and society have allowed to exist and continue there.

In the course of our interviews concerning adoption participants, we found that people usually experienced moments of great joy as well as moments of great discomfort. That fact came as something of a surprise and caused us to realize that myths and misperceptions have been permitted to drive adoption and its consequences for decades. Clinging to such unsubstantiated and mistaken beliefs often was the cause of the discomforts that had experienced. Conversely, those who required of themselves that they discard those old ideas found moments of great joy, particularly during their arrival at the reunions.

We have encountered those who were certain that suffering and pain to some degree is necessary and an integral part of the lives of those involved in adoptions. To the contrary, we found that suffering is not a necessary part of the process of bringing about reunions.

Further, we found that change often brings suffering to those unwilling to accept it as a part of life. Both society and expectations are subject to modifications as years pass, hopefully for the better, but never to the pleasure of everybody. Those changes are as difficult or as simple as you allow those to be. Adoption ideas also are subject to change however, rather than those being merely one-time, single, and finite experiences for all involved, such often require life-long adjustments and processes, many of which are very difficult and sometimes heart rending.

In CHAPTER TWO, "A Starting Place," we will examine why and how the principal cause of distress and emotional upset for those involved in an adoption triad often is due to nothing more than the system, its workings, and mistaken notions arising from that system.

Blame and fault may loom as one of the first hurdles you must confront at your starting place. So, spend time looking for blame, IF you must. Know though, that placing blame and finding fault will not be your friends, nor will those add anything of value to your efforts. Thus, to undertake to locate and pinpoint blame is a total waste of time, nothing more.

In CHAPTER THREE, "Who's to Blame?" we begin with a history lesson, hoping thereby that you will gain a broader perspective of the history of adoption and the forces that play upon you, your efforts, and the perception of you by others. Through coming to a broader view of adoption and the process, you will come to realize the inappropriateness of some of the thoughts you now entertain.   From the experiences of others, you will learn to move out of blame and into the world of discovery.

In CHAPTER FOUR, "Why Search?" we will consider some of the reasons members of the triad might have for searching and also will review what should be reasonable expectations when you enter upon such an effort.

Having considered the desires, hopes, motivations, and what should be considered reasonable expectations of a searcher, we next speak to the matter of the pitfalls and impediments that may confront those who are directly involved in a search effort.

In CHAPTER FIVE, "Advice To Birth Parents," we speak to the need to prepare for the likelihood that such parents will locate their child or that the child may find them, often quite unexpectedly. The results of reunions, whether by choice or otherwise can be disconcerting and sometimes quite disheartening. Conversely, there often are rich rewards and heartfelt happiness as a result of such reunions. A birth parent must be prepared for either outcome and for the years of adjustment to that new life.

Found in CHAPTER SIX, "Advice To Adoptive Parents," will be suggestions for coping with the prospect and events surrounding your realization that your adopted child has a sincere desire and intention to locate his or her birth parents. That natural urge will be one as to which you must offer assistance and encouragement, or at least stand on the sidelines and bring no harm to the effort. You will come realize that such a search by your adoptee has nothing to do with his or her love and respect for you, and grows from what may be an almost primordial need.

CHAPTER SEVEN, "Advice To Adoptees," is concerned with the mindset to be developed and the preparations needed if you are to cope with the dragons and discouragement that lurk in your search path.   By understanding and developing those personality features, you will find the courage and motivation to move ahead and will be confident in your capacity to deal with the problems that must be overcome if you are to find your birth parents and the heritage that those parents represent.

Throughout CHAPTER EIGHT, "Needles In Haystacks," and CHAPTER NINE, "More Detective Work," we will consider the tools and methods that have led to successful searches for others. You will be introduced to the assistance to be gained from the public offices and people, the "wheres" that must be visited in person or by Internet and telephone, the records that must be located, and the lawsuits, lawyers, and physicians who may be needed to further your efforts. You will come to know that if you meet "dead-ends" in your search, there will be yet other avenues to discovery, and those are discussed in depth. Finally, there will be expenses, though most can be minimized if necessary. In these two chapters is the factual "how-to" of it all.

CHAPTER TEN is appropriately titled, "Chrysalis." We will encourage you to move ahead with your search, and will suggest that your efforts will bring resolution to many of the concerns that adoption has brought to you. We will encourage you to stay focused on your search and not be sidetracked with other matters that you may be put off until later. The overriding lesson here is that sincerity and a willingness to spend time and money are not a substitute for thought, planning, and gaining guidance from others who "have been there and done that."

Much the same as a moth emerges from its birth cocoon in an altered state, stronger and beautiful, at reunion and beyond you will know that there will be great changes in you and those in your family. You will learn that there will be multiple opportunities to give and receive love, to greatly expand your contacts and friendships, to know of your specific family history, and most of all to know beyond doubt that you are an integral part of a living and breathing family.

In CHAPTER ELEVEN, "The Importance Of Medical History," Dr. John Sherrill, a physician in private practice, will suggest those aspects of your medical history that are so important to you and your descendants. Further, he discusses medical reasons and theories that will be welcomed and much needed by your lawyer and any court that you may call upon order to gain disclosure of your files.

When the authors worked together years ago on an unrelated project, former Senator Anna Belle Clement O'Brian of Tennessee stated it very simply, "Plan your work and work your plan." While you must prepare yourself for a very long search, and hope for a short one, we believe the lessons here will assist and encourage you to develop a plan that will bring a warm and heartening measure of success. If you are to achieve in developing a plan, you must consider some new ideas.

A New Way of Thinking

"...(I)t is right for a gull to fly, that freedom is the very nature of his being, that whatever stands against that freedom must be set aside, be it ritual or superstition or limitation in any form." [1]

This book is about breaking out of a mold and away from some old "rules" by choosing to conduct your life in a fashion other than that which our culture has come to expect of a person directly affected by the adoption system. That choice has to do with commencing a search for birth parents or for a child born to you years earlier, such investigations very often being contrary to the expectations of others, and even those you have for yourself.

Those expectations, inappropriate as such may be for life in the twenty-first century, did not arise from your imagination; rather, those grew out of the system itself and its demands for confidentiality. Understanding the emotional problems that almost surely are intrinsic to the system requires knowledge of some of the history.

The adoption triads comprise hundreds of thousands of American adoptees, the birth parents of those children, and the people who have done the adopting and thereby became "new" parents of those same children. Many of the children who have been adopted are alive as we write, and in addition to the biological parents and adoptive parents, the proceedings of adoption relating to those adoptees affected others. For each of those "placements" there were and almost surely are adoptive siblings, grandparents, and the additional extended families of each of those folks.

---

[1] Richard Bach, *Jonathan Livingston Seagull* (Macmillan Pub. Co., First Avon Printing, NY, 1970), p.114

Our adoption system has been created and often modified in order to benefit homeless and illegitimate or otherwise unwanted children. The system equally has provided some relief to those parents who, for whatever reasons, did not or could not raise their offspring, and simultaneously has provided welcome opportunities for those who sought to create or add to their families by adopting such children into their own homes. Finally, in some measure the system brought solutions to the ever-increasing problems of a government needing to cope with huge numbers of unwanted children.

Those parents who chose not to raise their natural born did so for many reasons, some well considered, some not so much so. Those reasons for which the child was originally given over to the system, no matter of what nature, should not now bring hesitation for you to move forward with a search. Just as some of those birth parents have a desire to again know of their children, many of the adopted children now hope to one day have knowledge of their natural parents, their extended families, and of their ancestry. The years since then have now silently passed, that passing has permitted anyone involved to come to different ideas, and you must now feel free to embrace those newer thoughts. Many of those interested people have undertaken, or at least have given some thought to searching for their missing parents or children.

Therein lies a measure of your strength. You will learn and benefit much from the emotions, efforts, and experiences of those who undertook to search and have been challenged, just as you will be. So it is that in your efforts to find your lost family, whether you succeed or fail, whether you find a happy ending or quite the opposite, and whether you come away enriched or determined that your time was not well spent, you will know that others in our society have traveled the same difficult trails.

Note, though, that a dichotomy is thereby presented to would-be searchers. They must come to know that the very same society that once undertook to protect their interests and see to their well being, now, and by the very same system of rules, poses substantial obstacles in their efforts to search, and even to examine their own files.

How so? Most of those who have made the rules have long taken the position that once an adoption has been accomplished, the records of those proceedings should be closed to everyone. It also has been their view (and now is the law in most states) that short of mutual consent, only under the most convincing circumstances may a court permit adoptive children and their natural parents to be rejoined through knowledge of the contents of those closed files.

It seems that our society has declared, "If you separate yourself from your child, so it shall remain forever more, no matter what." While the debate over the pros and cons of the openness of adoption records continues (and probably will for years to come), this book focuses, not on this debate, but upon how to employ the legitimate methods yet available to you when you have no access to the sealed records.

Of course, the methods open to you, and here discussed, are irrelevant and do not come into play unless and until you have made a firm decision to search. That decision should be and is yours, and yours alone, to make. In making that choice, you will find that some will encourage you and others surely will take an opposite view. Their opinions should and will influence you only to the extent that YOU permit it.

So, while no one can or should tell you whether or not to search, we hope here to assist you in determining when and if you are prepared to do so. If you then decide to make the effort, or if you have already decided to do so, we intend here to provide knowledge of the various methods and practices previously found helpful in such quests.

There is a catch, however. Merely knowing how and where to search is not enough. You will be choosing to follow a path quite distinct from that dictated for you when the decree that brought you into the system was signed. If and when you choose to go down this different trail, you must be emotionally prepared for this, your adventure of a lifetime.

So, while having the mechanical tools quite usually is enough to seek out most long-lost family members, understanding the emotional changes and demands that lie ahead for you is equally important. We will speak to both subjects, and hope thereby that as you proceed across the yet-to-be unknown hurdles, you will have adequately packed your bags of emotional readiness. It likely will be a pleasant trip, but be assured that you will have surprises, though hopefully not too many of those will prove disappointing.

There will be some who will consider the quest you propose to undertake as somehow improper, inappropriate, or even forbidden. When those attitudes surface, consider for a moment how your intentions parallel the tale of Jonathan Livingston Seagull. That delightful story tells of searching for and finding freedom by "changing (one's) level of consciousness"[2] and understanding.

Therein, Jonathan Seagull and others were perceived to be different because of their desire to venture beyond the accepted beliefs and practices of the flock. In order to cope with those differences, Jonathan was required to leave the flock and set upon his own quest for knowledge. While you may not be outcast, you may find challenges along the way. You may have to follow your own path even when it is contrary to the thoughts of others or to the beliefs to which you previously subscribed. In Jonathan's adventure of discovery, the lesson learned applies equally to you: "...you have the freedom to be yourself, your true self, here and now..."[3]

Adoptees and birth parents alike may take comfort from this story of the gulls. As with the gulls, a pattern of life was dictated for you, and yet by venturing forth in a search for a different and more complete world, you too may come to know more of yourself, those of your past, and what it is that you might be.

So, if you are ready to know yourself better, let us begin.

A long time ago, in another society, and in what seemed like a distant world, an attractive blue-eyed, blond haired young woman, whom we will name Barbara, made the difficult decision to give a baby over for adoption. That act of courage in the midst of her desperation made it possible for two people, whom we will call Mr. and Mrs. Kurtz, to have the

---

[2] *Jonathan Livingston Seagull,* Ibid., p. 120
[3] Ibid., p. 112

opportunity to raise a child, even though they were otherwise unable to produce one. Case closed, and everyone lives happily ever after, or so all intended, that is.

The adoption system under which they gained that child had benefited all. Barbara had rid herself of a problem that was beyond her power to manage (or, at least, so she thought), the infant gained a fine home, and the Kurtzes had a beautiful little girl. They named her "Mary Elizabeth." Nevertheless, those who were responsible for the rules had failed to recognize and provide for a critical component resulting from the adoption proceedings that would eventually become apparent to all those good people. And what would that be?

Whether it was through intention, or as a result of an unwillingness or failure to consider the probability that at adulthood many adoptees would desire more information than was allowed by the system, the result was and is the same. The rules of confidentiality very much eliminated the possibility of contact between Barbara and Mary Elizabeth, and thereby made it most difficult, if not impossible, for Mary Elizabeth to learn anything of the lives and the historical and cultural background of her biological family and of their forebears.

Such restrictions are a bit surprising, as well. By so restricting or preventing contacts, the rules imposed upon all those involved literally require that adoptees and their birth parents consider and view their world incompletely and differently than do people not affected by those rules.

However those restrictions came about, there were built into the system mechanisms by which the files might be partially or fully opened. We will speak at some length to those several methods that some of the United States have seen fit to provide. Some have prohibited any access to adoption files, some have allowed essential facts to be extracted by members of the triad, and four of the states have granted almost unlimited inspection of the records.

Moreover, and of great importance to you, if those avenues into the records fail or are unavailable to you, there are other methods permitted by the law by which a search may be conducted without any access whatever to any closed files.

Those perfectly legitimate approaches also were available to Mary Elizabeth and Barbara.

So, Mary Elizabeth might find it possible to learn of her heritage and the background of her parents, and Barbara had an opportunity to undertake a search for that daughter. They both, perhaps, could enjoy and share a new and unique relationship and a greater sense of belonging. So too may you.

Our purpose here is not to lobby, influence legislators and readers, or to provide gunpowder for the conflict between the "closed" and the "open file" advocates. Still though, if these words draw the attention of such folks to changes that might be desirable in order that the emotional needs of such as our Barbara and Mary Elizabeth might be accommodated, we make no apologies.

In keeping with our goals here, we will offer a number of different ways of thinking about adoption and search. Whether or not you choose to follow these suggestions is entirely your choice, of course, but we think these approaches will be as beneficial for you as such have been for others.

There is much to learn by reconsidering old ideas, and also much to be gained by attempting to reevaluate thoughts that one has entertained across a lifetime, especially if they no longer serve a purpose. "The gull sees farthest who flies highest."[4]

Before we undertake further advice, we need to consider Barbara and the situation in which she found herself.

---

[4] *Jonathan Livingston Seagull*, Ibid., p. 86,

A Starting Place

Twenty-six-year-old Barbara worked in a bank in Fayetteville, North Carolina. Not for years had her father been able to maintain steady employment, and he and his family had barely survived from his occasional work, quite usually as a house painter. They took their meals from broken pieces of dishes and somehow managed to keep a roof over their heads.

Barbara had dropped out of school at the end of her eleventh year in order that she might financially assist the family. They lived in a rented second-floor apartment within walking distance from her job. Rendering her life even more challenging, Barbara had been married, divorced, and had a little girl from that unsuccessful union who also lived there with her and her parents.

It was early spring of 1958 and while working as a teller at the bank that she had come to be acquainted with a handsome, well-dressed customer, named Bill, who had dated a couple of her co-workers. One day he asked her to go out with him, and she was delighted to say "Yes." She and Bill saw each other still again, and on the third date he prepared dinner for her at his apartment.

Later that same evening, as the story goes, she felt he took advantage of her, though Bill remembered it to be otherwise. Whatever may have been the whole and unvarnished truth of the matter, the result was that within weeks she knew she was pregnant. She asked herself "How could I have been so naive?" She knew the answer was rooted in her upbringing. She had been raised in a sheltered environment, steeped in fundamental religion, meaning that sex was not a part of life outside marriage; indeed, it was not even discussed. She was quite ill prepared for this world of hers and less prepared for someone like Bill.

Throughout the first weeks of that pregnancy, she spent her days at the bank acting as though nothing was awry and continued in her duties at home as both a mother and a daughter. Even for some period thereafter her life continued as though nothing had changed. She often looked upon the faces of those around her, and wondered how they would react toward her when and if they came to know her secret.

Her feelings often were something akin to panic. She wanted so to hide her plight and pretend that life was as it had been, yet she well knew that within a very few months, if she did nothing, as inevitably as the sun came up, she surely would suffer the consequences of inaction. Her transgressions would be obvious to all and the prevailing Southern winds of Fayetteville would carry the whispers of "illegitimacy" in the form of gossip to and within her circle of acquaintances.

She considered how she was a part of her world. Women did not then enjoy the liberation that they feel today. She lived in a small, conservative, southern community and her parents were devout and strict Southern fundamentalists. By reason of his convictions, her father did not approve of drinking, dancing, or even card playing, and had distanced himself and his family from several other relatives who had chosen to so conduct their lives.

Barbara had no doubt but that if her parents were to learn of this pregnancy, they might disavow their kinship to her, seek to take her daughter from her, and most surely would send her away to live the shame of an unmarried mother. Her desire to protect and care for that existing little girl rendered the likelihood that she could care for yet another almost impossible.

Moreover, she dreaded the ostracism that she thought surely would come from her peers; even from her few close friends. Were those fears not concerns enough, she also faced the very real prospect of being discharged from her employment at the typically conservative local bank. After all, she reasoned, her indiscretion would be so obvious to everyone that the officers at that financial institution surely would end her employment.

By reason of her gender and education, she would then be limited vocationally, and she had no financial means to assist her in whatever decisions she might make. Then too, she believed that her prior marriage would cause all to whisper that she was old enough to, and certainly should have, "known better." She felt certain that "everyone" would know that this child was the product of sex quite outside the bonds of marriage. Stated as bluntly as some would likely say, as they did then, the baby would be a "bastard." Such were the unfortunate products of the intolerant world in which Barbara found herself.

Her thoughts turned to Bill. She knew that marriage to him was quite unlikely, though she would have considered it as a way out of her terrible predicament. He was not the marrying sort and had made that attitude eminently clear to her in the weeks that followed their time together. Her feelings were reinforced as she watched him date others and totally ignore her and her condition after she had informed him that she was carrying their child. She knew that she faced the birth of this child without him and most probably, alone.

Many who so much were a part of her life, and had supported her and watched her grow, would be vividly aware that this child was not a product of a former husband. Moreover, she knew that even if she and Bill were to marry, her mother and father would be embarrassed and unnerved, and the women of the church in which she and those parents had so long been active would be busily counting the months. She was equally certain that they also would whisper, gossip, and gradually end any contact with her, except for those quiet "Hellos" that civility and Southern manners required.

Because of those religious convictions held by her parents and the attitudes of her day, whether as it should have been or not, she was sure that revealing her fearful plight to those parents, or to anyone else known to her, simply was not an option. In her fear and concern and, as it turned out, to her great advantage and relief, she turned to and confided in her family physician.

With a measure of trepidation, mixed with relief that at least she was doing something, she walked into her physician's office. Though in her naiveté she could not be aware of it, the physician had assisted more than one frightened young women with the same problem; many physicians of his day often had done so. He assured her that he would maintain her confidence and send her to those who would see to her well being throughout the remaining months before her delivery.

Saying nothing of the pregnancy, the physician then told her father that he feared that a nervous breakdown was in the offing for her, and for that reason he was prescribing that she go elsewhere and thereby be away from her surroundings until her health improved. While Barbara was relieved by this solution, she knew, at the same time, that her future and the confidentiality she hoped for were not at all assured. Still though, she had no other alternatives with which she thought she could live.

Hardly could she know that throughout those same long weeks during which she was so frightened and worried about being found out, one hundred miles from her, there lived a pleasant, middle-class couple that had been together for years. Very shortly after he had returned from World War II as a brave and decorated soldier, they had married and had hoped to start a family immediately. That was not to be; they had been plagued by infertility and had been unable to conceive and produce a child.

They previously had enjoyed the good fortune of adopting a son, and now sought a little girl. Just as they had been on a waiting list for months for that son, the summer of 1958 found them patiently waiting yet again.

As was expected, the private details of their lives were again examined. Assets were verified, references were checked, and their home was visited to make sure it would be a proper home for yet another child. They were familiar with the process, and would later tell the children that so much did they desire to be parents that they would have suffered almost any indignity or intrusiveness in order to adopt.

For whatever reason (likely through their confidence in the agency) the Kurtzes had asked very few questions about the children whose destiny they were to control at least until adulthood. Perhaps it would have seemed inappropriate, they thought, to ask personal details about the birth parents of their children. More than that, maybe deep down inside they did not really want to know where their children came from, thinking that love and dedication to parenthood would solve any future problems that might arise. After all, they thought, these children would be theirs in every way, just as much as if they had given birth to them.

Whatever the circumstances and no matter who would ever know what about whom, Barbara's moments of indiscretion, followed by her months of concern and regret, were to bring times of immense pleasure for that waiting couple. No one knew that yet, however, and Barbara's thoughts surely were of the moment. Knowing that in no small measure her course in life had been established during that evening with Bill, she began to plan as best she knew how.

It was now but a very short time until her pregnancy would be apparent, and so she needed to hurry with putting her affairs in order. So, the arrangements were concluded by which she would go to another town to live throughout the balance of her term and through delivery.

Barbara later remembered that the day of her leaving was hot, that she had taken her little four-year-old for ice cream, and that her sister had then taken her to the bus station. She had cried as she left, and though she could not know of her future, those were but the first of the many, many tears she would shed.

The bus ride to Asheville was long and lonely, and she was crying still when she reached the facility for unwed mothers. She was such a long way from that small Southern town she called home, and she was SO alone with her thoughts. No matter that she had to leave those she loved fearing their ostracism, criticism and abandonment, they still were part of her home and the familiar was safer than the yet unknown.

She was met at the door by Sister Rose, and recalled that from that moment forward she was treated with the utmost kindness and respect by her and equally by the other nuns engaged there. Barbara recalled that she had thought it strangely ironic that Catholic Sisters, of all people, could so understand and be compassionate of her problem, although they almost certainly had not found themselves in the same predicament.

Then too, Barbara expected to find women of low morals at this facility; she was mistaken. There were none. Women of all stations in life and from fifteen to thirty years old were in residence, and she soon came to consider it a leveling, indeed a very loving experience.

She was given a different name, as were the other "girls" when they arrived. They were instructed to refrain from discussing any details about their lives prior to their stay at the "home." Throughout her several months of residence there, there was no condemnation and, remarkably, she thought, no one even spoke of the obvious. The women were instructed that they should make every effort to leave the entire experience in the past, and to pretend that it never happened.

They were told that they should emotionally prepare themselves to have their newborn children taken from them, to walk out of the door and away forever, and to be actively about their lives just as before. It was to be as though that period of Barbara's life had never existed. There would be no proof to outsiders that it did, she was told, since the records would have been sealed.

Thus, she well knew that when she left that place, there would be no baby with her, she would undertake to be "Barbara" once again, and that same Barbara would return home and to her job, or at least so she hoped. She could not then know how terribly difficult it would be for her to meet those terms and to do what was expected of her.

And so it was, until those few months later when the time arrived for her to "go over," as they called it (meaning to be admitted to the nearby hospital for delivery). Having a baby was not discussed, even then, she recalled.

Her delivery was uneventful. Though it surely was prohibited, shortly after giving birth to her daughter, a nurse in attendance brought the child to Barbara in order that she might see and hold it for a few minutes. She would remember those few minutes with her infant for all of her life that followed.

She examined her tiny feet and hands, reveling in the wonder of creation. She remembered too that she had kissed the child and enjoyed the pleasant new-baby odor. The peaceful thoughts were interrupted by the knowledge that this was only of the moment; this child would belong to someone else and should be forgotten. Then they had taken her little girl from her.

Though she later requested that she again hold the child, she was told that a mistake had been made and that she should not have been permitted to hold her baby in the first instance. And so it was that Barbara never saw her baby again and did not know what had become of her.

This story of Barbara, of her strict parents, of that child born to her out of wedlock and out of sight of her world, and of the family that adopted the child is not at all unusual. For that reason, this tale will serve us in illustrating many of the conditions and circumstances with which any member of an adoption triad may have been, or might still yet be confronted. So, for the moment we leave Barbara and the little girl she gave over to adoption.

WHERE TO START

"(W)e can find a higher meaning for our lives, a spiritual reason we were born to our particular families. We can begin to get clear about who we really are."[5]

For many centuries now our culture has presumed that a mother and father will nurture and bring a young person forward in life, all the while teaching that child of his or her heritage and of the customs and rules of their family circle. However, when birth parents surrender a child to adoption, as Barbara did, that expected and natural process is interrupted, and all family ties are severed. In fact, the

---

[5] James Redfield, *Celestine Prophecy* (Warner Books, New York, NY, 1993), p.131

direction of the lives of all members of the triad is forever changed because of this single decision. How so?

At the conclusion of the adoption proceedings, the lives of the Kurtzes are changed much as are the lives of any parents when a new child is introduced into the family structure. A child alters the dynamics of a family by its very existence, just as its own future and thoughts are very much altered by that same family. The child is destined to become a very different person than he or she would have been had they been raised under other circumstances and with birth parents.

The severance of an adopted child from its birthright brings to the child the status, customs, morals, religious beliefs, habits, and practices, and even mannerisms of the adoptive parents. Advantageous as these values may very well be, such are assimilated to the exclusion of whatever benefits and knowledge that same child might have enjoyed through its own heritage. Not only do these "new" parents provide such training, but so too do grandparents, aunts, uncles, cousins, and those other people within the social circle in which the adoptive parents move and live.

Still more than that, when birth parents choose to surrender a child to adoption, they are neither required nor are they any longer permitted to instruct the child in the customs, beliefs and morals of their own families. The result, of course, is that the adoptees have no choice but to be cut off from their own heritage, rules, and customs of their birth family.

Through that same decree by which the child entered the folds of another family, the birth parents were again at liberty to be about their lives and fortunes. Thereby, they are rid of the obligations of every sort that otherwise our society and its laws would have imposed upon them as parents.

UNWRITTEN PRESUMPTIONS

In addition to the effects and the initial operations of our system of adoptions, there are presumptions that, though unwritten, thereafter are felt at every turn for every member of an adoption triad. These are a) the presumption that the birth mother will be able to abolish or erase the memory of and emotions felt at the birth of the child, and that she will accomplish these requirements simply because she is told to or intended to do so. Next, b) it is presumed and intended that the adoptive parents will have no future interference from those birth parents, and whether realistic or not so, that complete and total separation of the birth parents from their natural child will allow the new family unit to develop without interruption. Finally, c) the system presumes that the heritage of an adoptee will remain unimportant to that child, and that his or her curiosity will be squelched for life as to other than the history and background of the adoptive family.

Even if one assumes that people thought and reacted differently in earlier years, we surely now know that it was naïve to believe that any system of edicts and rules of courts, legislatures, or social agencies could bring about those three results. Though the rules and the law may shape human conduct, the mind often strays from a prescribed course, since it can do so in private. Curiosity is as much a part of the human experience as is memory and it is not in our nature to have that desire to know thwarted by mere words from legislators and social workers.

So, while Barbara (and many other parents of children let to adoption) may make a substantial effort throughout life to conform to the notion that she could and would forget, such was beyond her capability. It was a near certainty that as her deference to the opinions of others diminished over the years, her desire to learn, at least of the destiny of her child, would increase many times over.

As are all of us, a child who has been adopted is born with great curiosity. As a result, there is a high probability that one day, in some measure, he or she will have the desire to know of birth parents, heritage, and history. Were that almost certain curiosity of an adoptee not enough, his or her children, grandchildren and descendants ad infinitum will one day wonder from where and from whom they came. They too will know they had grandparents someplace.

Further, the very fact that such knowledge quite usually is intentionally not included within the upbringing, education, and training of an adoptee, renders that person all the more curious about that missing background information. They simply want to "know" and will not forever be denied.

There is another factor to be considered. The effects upon adoptive parents of having no knowledge of the birth parents, often did, and do yet, give rise to the fear that many of the children to be adopted come with latent, undiscovered, or even concealed defects. Those problems were thought to arise from or having to do with the circumstances of their births and the likely "low" station in life expected of their parents.

Whether or not such beliefs were valid is not now important; perception is validity enough for altogether too many people. The system failed to address the matter of misperceptions, and the adoptive parents were left with their haunting concerns as to such "defects," those occasionally speculated upon by their friends, relatives, and neighbors who also raised questions as to the origin of the child.

Whether based upon reason or not, and while those thoughts and concerns flourished, there was another problem shared by adoptees. The system either ignored or failed to recognize that the severance of adoptees from their biological families, their history and their heritage, could only further accentuate the curiosity that is part and parcel of all of us.

Whether the lack was of forewarning or of insight, many adoptive parents have not been prepared for the almost certain reality which resulted from curiosity and that severance. Having not planned for that probability, adoptive parents sometimes suffer much pain and disappointment over proposed searches for heritage. "And while believing themselves to be doing everything for their children's well-being, they are actually withholding from them the very knowledge they need for their development into healthy adults."[6] Strange, isn't it? While we would not think it at all remarkable for a non-adoptee to study genealogy and seek to know of his or her grandparents, great-grandparents, and

6 Betty Jean Lifton, *Lost and Found* (Harper & Row, New York, 1988), p.8.

still others, and to gain knowledge of the lives of those people, a similar quest by adoptees is not necessarily well received.

In fact, we have come to the conclusion that the desire of the adopted to investigate their own history is very much akin to the desires and motivations that drive all genealogy buffs. In both categories of searchers, heritage is sought, and while, with the adoptee, that desire is piqued by the fact that they have not been permitted to know any facts whatever, in both cases, the goal is the same. They both seek to know simply who they are and from whence they came.

Still, while the two groups are so much alike in their curiosity and desires, there is an interesting, though slight, difference. Most non-adoptees have heard and remember tales and anecdotes concerning their heritage, or at least have relatives who know those facts needed to commence such an investigation. On the other hand, often the totality of knowledge an adoptee has is an awareness that the birth parents chose to surrender that child to the system and to an unknown future. Such is the legacy that adoptees gain from their parents and forebears; surely not the one most of us would desire.

Until a search is undertaken, to the extent he or she wishes to have other than an empty notebook as their family history, adoptees must contrive it; conjure, fabricate, and create it wholly from their imaginings. The psychiatrist, Norman Paul stated it vividly: "...(I)f you look back in time with adoptees, it is like being on the edge of a cliff; there is nothing beyond it."[7] Nothing, that is, except imagination and curiosity. The adoptee often is required to fill in all the blanks in an effort to discover some meaning or ascribe some reason to the separation that has so affected his or her life.

Consider how much easier life might be for adoptees, if from the outset, everyone involved in the process actually believed, understood and embraced the notion that some day those adoptees might have a desire to give rein to their innate curiosity. They could have told the child simply that to go "a-

---

[7] *Lost and Found*, Ibid p.8.

hunting" for their past would be acceptable as part of a complete life.

Rather it is that they have all too often stifled their curiosity for the sake of their own peace of mind and perhaps the opinions of others, attempting "to fit in" and to accept the rules, despite their desires to know more. Incredibly, then, when the children can no longer pretend and have found courage enough to search, they undertake that effort and the world is taken quite by surprise. Surprised, it seems that the child seeks to know who and what he or she "really" might be. What else could we have expected?

OBSTACLES AND HURDLES

Not only will children be ever more curious as they grow older, mothers do not forget their children and adoptive parents must expect that searches may follow as natural consequences of those two absolutes. While the system overlooked those realities, you, the searcher, must not. Just as you may grapple with the emotional hurdles that come from all directions, so too may you be called upon to deal with the roadblocks that arise from the law and rules that govern the system. You may encounter difficulties in finding sources of information, occasional trouble in searching those records, and dead-ends as a result of movements of people from one place to another.

More significant than the difficulties is the approach you will take to address the problems at hand. You must not pretend that those impediments are sufficient reasons for delay in undertaking the search effort. Such troublesome thoughts will affect you and your search, no matter the extent and measure of reality. Still though, difficulty, tedium, and occasional failure should never be crutches to justify procrastination.

As one of the three members of the adoption equation, your capability to deal handily with the problems that attend searches for lost birth parents or their children well may depend upon your willingness to believe and act upon those simple truths. So, know that any or all members of any adoption triad should expect to be met with perplexing, separate, or unique hurdles.

MODIFYING OLD BELIEFS AND IDEAS

"We either make ourselves miserable, or we make ourselves strong. The amount of work is the same."[8]

While the problem areas we have touched upon arise from curiosity and the oversights and misunderstandings within the system and its workings, there are yet difficulties that arise from myths and misperceptions and that will come upon the searcher from all directions. While in the final analysis these too are, of course, products of the system, these difficulties are not from built-in inadequacies, but arise, instead, from old wives' tales, simple errors, or mistaken notions harbored by those around us.

Indeed, popular attitudes, whether by intention or otherwise, have brought about perceptions and perspectives that have not always well served those persons involved in the adoption process. You too likely harbor a few misguided ideas as to adoption. If so, consider that as Castaneda wrote above, the efforts you will make to rid yourself of any of those ideas will be no greater than would be the efforts you would exert to cling to notions of that sort.

As with other adoptees, for lack of an explanation and understanding, Mary Elizabeth developed her own ideas and carried those with her, rather than think of herself as having had no such "real" people. She conjured images of how her other parents might appear and of what station in life they might be; she came to realize that she did, in fact, have those parents out there somewhere. When being about her life with her adoptive parents or her friends she would gaze at strangers, hoping thereby to find features that she recognized as similar to her own. Her eyes were deep brown, and many who shared that feature were suspect.

---

[8] Castaneda and McGraw, *Self Matters* (Simon & Schuster, New York, 2001), p.262

While those products of her imagination served her well at the time, at adulthood those images in no small measure fell away, as did the satisfaction gained from such imaginings. Just as she did, you too now must revisit, reevaluate, and discard any such early notions, consider what the reality of "now" might reveal, and plan to satisfy your need for that reality by seeking out the truth of it all. Those childhood images that can no longer bear the scrutiny of your adult mind must be replaced with fresh images that have the capacity to do so.

The fact that such images can be troubling even to the extent of causing one to shy away from searching for the truth is perhaps best exemplified by the attitude of an intelligent woman who, as an infant, was literally dropped off at a foster home by her sixteen-year-old mother. Even now, she steadfastly refuses to reconsider the matter of that abandonment and does yet harbor deep resentment for that mother.

Despite the wisdom she has acquired from five-plus decades of the experiences of life, she refuses still to entertain the reality that her mother is no longer a teenager with teenage values, and is now an older woman and an entirely different person, with different values than she had that half-century ago. That incapacity to abandon early perceptions has prevented her from searching, even though she has the name of that mother and some information concerning her background.

No matter what your age or position within the adoption triangle, we hope that you, in fact, will undertake to do what that woman seems unable to do. So, be prepared to question all prior beliefs and consider how many changes have come to you during those same years that the person whom you seek has also now lived. Ask yourself if they are based on fact and have validity today or merely involve old perceptions.

In addition to the reluctance that some of us have to consider the likelihood that what people once were, they probably now are not, there is another belief which is equally common. Since labels often arise from beliefs, those labels may well become obstacles to an assimilation of new ideas.

The noun "adoption" is defined as the condition that results from a legal process by which one assumes the parental obligations of another, and the birth parent(s) simultaneously surrender all control and supervision of the child. Unfortunately, that expression and the term "adopted" too often serve as somewhat derisive labels that suggest differences in social status between a child who has been the subject of that process and another child who has not so been. That derisiveness quite usually carries with it a stigma for those children so labeled.

If, as an adopted person, you feel that you are considered or perceived as something less than a complete or whole person as a result of the use by others of those terms, then, once again, you must reevaluate your attitudes. Remember, the difference between you and a person who was not adopted is that your access to your heritage and history were severed and that severance has nothing to do with your character. So, though the labels persist, by understanding the meaning of the words, you should now be able to cast those off as being reflective of your quality as a person.

MYTHS

Myths also often have given rise to emotional turmoil. They can affect the adoptee, the birth parents, and the adoptive parents. One of the more damaging myths is the notion that adoptees are more likely to have problems of social adjustment than will their non-adoptive counterparts. While there are studies to support this belief, other researchers have reached conclusions to the contrary. Whatever the truth of the matter, it is our belief that buying into the notion that if you were adopted, you will have problems greater than others at some time in your life is, first, questionable, and further that idea does not serve to assist you in achieving either your goals of life, nor success in your search for birth parents. , and . If those beliefs are obstacles for you, again you must be rid of such ideas.

Certain issues are certainly pertinent, and can be dealt with effectively. It seems that the principal difference from which other problems arise for the adoptee is the fact that she has been severed, not only from her history, but from her birth parents as well.   The emotional difficulties, which sometimes arise from the permanent loss and separation and the loss of heritage, are the principal distinctions between adopted children and those who are not.

Another of the common myths, perhaps the most onerous of all, is that adoptees are somehow inadequate, unequal or less than whole. As one young woman, recalling her feelings about being given up, expressed it, "I wondered if something was wrong with me; why would someone not want me?"

Though the error in such thoughts seems to us so obvious as to require no further comments, remember too that such myths of inadequacy or imperfection often have led to other inappropriate thoughts. Mary Elizabeth remembers believing that, even though she was happy in her adoptive home, if she were to be "the best little girl she could possibly be" then the birth mother, should she one day come to know the truth, would realize that she had made a terrible mistake.   That birth mother would then decide that she should "...never have given this nice little girl away." These are demeaning thoughts for a child, and should not find any place or meaning in the life of any adult adoptee.

Also damaging to adoptees and revealing of the lack of understanding by some adopted parents or others is the myth that if an adopted child truly appreciated the adoptive parents that child would not search. It has been said that, "If the child loved them and was thankful for what those parents had done, that child would leave well enough alone." Suffice it to say that such thoughts in no sense reflect what really is happening in the mind of the child. Once and for all, everyone should come to realize that searches grow from curiosity about whom and what adoptees are or where life might have taken those children.

As an adult adoptee, you must now know and truly believe that, in all likelihood, the fact that you were given over to the system probably had nothing whatever to do with you or any condition you exhibited. It is likely that the reasons for those actions resided within the personalities, economic conditions, and lives of your birth parents.

You must examine all of your beliefs as an adoptee, a birth parent or an adoptive parent, ferret out the notions that are erroneous, and force those from your thinking forever, all the while replacing those with beliefs that have basis in truth and fact.

Just as myths occasionally bring grief to adopted children and birth parents, so too do such ideas sometimes bring harm to adoptive parents. There exists the destructive myth to the effect that the only reason that an adoptee would search is that he or she harbors some measure of discontent. In other words, there is the notion that a child searches because the parents did something "wrong." It is said that had the adoptive parents been adequate in their parenting, the child would not now seek to replace them.

In fact, and with but few exceptions, thoughts that the adoptive parents were somehow remiss or had inadequately performed their duties simply are not present in the minds of their children. As stated, children search almost exclusively as a result of curiosity as to their origins and do so regardless of the quality of or satisfaction with their relationships with their adoptive parents. Very few are the adult adoptees, we think, who would seek an "unknown" to replace a "known," when it would be so much easier to simply abandon the relationship and any contact with those adoptive parents if it were a poor relationship for example.

One must be ever conscious of the fact that one or both of the birth parents one day may find their way back into the life of their child. Disarming to some adoptive parents is the notion that they will lose their child if a birth parent should come upon the scene or be located and come to be acquainted with the adoptee. As to that, we suggest that there is simply little evidence to that effect. Birth parents are not typically sought to replace the adoptive parents. Most importantly, a bird has wings to fly and will not remain forever in it nest. Similarly, the life skills you have helped your child develop over the years that he or she has been with you, just as with a non-adoptee, will now serve to show them the way as they pursue their goals in life. Though searches and resulting reunions may cause most of those in an adoption triad to reexamine their relationships, whatever affection the adoptive parents have fostered in their child almost surely will continue.

Again considering the birth mother, some myths arise from advice that was given at the time she gave up the child, much of which now should be examined for validity. Perhaps there is no better example than the advice given mothers that the birth of their child can simply be erased from their thoughts and go unremembered in the future.

Even when natural mothers have truly sought to eliminate these recollections, they were unable to completely do so. Many of such mothers have been able to put thoughts of the child aside for perhaps months on end, but eliminate their memory of that event they simply could not do. Perhaps more significant than any concern over their inability to forget, they do not consider failing to do so as any reason to feel remorse or regret. With that, we agree.

Another myth that likely has or will appear in the searcher's path is the notion that if the adoption file you seek is "closed" it thereby is an almost impenetrable barrier. To that too we say, "Simply not true!" That hurdle is not nearly of the magnitude it is thought to be. There are many other and different places to look. That closed file, unreachable though, in fact, it may be, and no matter what it contains, is but a small portion of the total information available to any one with initiative enough to diligently go searching. In fact, as you shall soon learn, Mary Elizabeth was able to locate Barbara without any access whatever to her file.

We will later discuss in detail those many records that are open to you for examination in your efforts to find people and their backgrounds. For now, it must suffice to say that there are and will continue to be public records of many sorts that have to do with the lives of each one of us. Plus, and even if all else fails in your search efforts, you still will have the privilege of seeking a court order that will open that file for you.

Lastly, in your future thinking, you must brush away all ideas that women were "bad girls" or "immoral" simply because of pregnancies outside marriage. Just as in genealogy the rule is that we must never judge ancestors by the standards of our day, when searching for birth parents, again it is not our prerogative to judge others. Consider the fact that an estimated one hundred thousand (100,000) children, more or less, were given over for adoption during the year in which Mary Elizabeth was born and that most were illegitimate.   So, Barbara was not the only woman having sex outside of marriage.   Similarly, we must rid ourselves of the notion that men were irresponsible simply because they sired an unintended child.

In short, whether or not a birth parent is able to forget as advised, and no matter the myths, or how a parent or child may have been labeled or characterized in the past, these are not now important. We must come to know that the many uncomplimentary ideas and negative attitudes that arose during the early and middle decades of the twentieth century should now be relegated to the intellectual trashcan. To our credit, American customs and espoused morals concerning participants in adoptions have undergone profound changes over the decades since then.

WHAT FOLLOWS

Before we leave thoughts of myths, misconceptions, and hurdles arising from the system, we want you to consider the most important myth of all with which you will be faced. Some will suggest that there is something amiss if you search.   We believe it is acceptable for you to choose to search if you feel inclined to do so. By the same token, not wishing to search does not mean there is something wrong with either position. As we go forth with our discussion, we hope that you will perceive either decision as an acceptable part of growth for any member of the triad.

Following your chosen search path may, and likely will, require you to traverse hurdles along the way.   Perhaps your way is blocked by your need to cling to the blame you feel that others deserve for having placed you in a position to feel you have to search.   Read on, as we hope to further raise your level of consciousness as you continue to develop your plan for success.

Who's To Blame?

Many of the emotional difficulties that confronted Barbara, Mary Elizabeth, and the Kurtzes were the results of their participation in a program of compromises; the system of adoptions. One must remember that, while the past is unchangeable and often bristles with potential difficulties and conflicts, much can be gained by exploring it. So too, with adoptions.

By early in the twentieth century the need for society to consider the confidentiality desired by mothers of unwanted children became of critical proportion. Of equal significance and priority were the wishes of usually barren couples to have children and, collateral to that, the ever-increasing number of births of unwanted children who required caring homes and parents. Out of these complex and interrelated needs, an adoption system was created. It brought much good, some difficulties, and opportunities aplenty for those who felt a need to blame others for their problems.

Blame is a powerful word, and one with which we all often must cope, but particularly so for those people involved with adoptions. Before any member of an adoption triad may undertake effective searches, contacts, reconciliation, or reunions, that person must be rid of the tendencies to find fault with others for the difficulties that may have arisen from past operations of the system and the people involved.

A birth mother benefits not a whit by feeling that society, the adoption system, or some man out of her past is blameworthy and the cause of her regrets over having given up a child. Adoptive parents, whose children now seek to know of their heritage, benefit no one by complaining that they are victims of a culture more liberal than that in which they lived at the time of their adoption of the child. Finally, the adopted child gains zero by holding the system, the birth mother, the birth father, or anyone else responsible for his or her problems.

So it is that to the greatest extent possible, all three groups—the birth parents, the adoptive parents, and the children—must put aside fault finding and, instead, come to accept that the facts are as they are, no matter the circumstances, the people, or how strong those feelings. A child was born and adopted a long time ago under rules that were and remain both changing and imperfect, and who did what to whom and when, are questions that should no longer have a place in the thoughts of anyone involved.

Still though, putting such blame from your mind is easier said than done. To the end that you commence to do so, let us consider the past and then examine a few of the more obvious situations in which one might find regret, remorse, or resentment of others. We will consider those engaged in searching, those who are merely bystanders, and those who are the targets of such searches.

For the first two hundred years of our colonies and states, illegitimacy and abandonment of children had been commonplace, were considered a part of every early community, and had been of no great or overriding concern of the powers-that-were. We were yet a new nation struggling to find itself, and the conquering of the wilderness required most of our strength, as well as the attention of vast numbers of people, all to the disadvantage of those unwanted children.

The churches, related families, the kind-of-heart, a few charitable citizens of means, those who needed "help" or apprentices in their homes or businesses, and the law all undertook to find places for those born into poverty or without parents who could or would care for them. Inadequate as were those devices, we were without a government with the means or the inclination to do more.

Then came problems that would demand new and different attitudes and near revolutionary changes. The emigration from the British Isles and the European Continent during the middle and end years of the nineteenth century, coupled with the great industrial revolution, brought very rapid population growth, especially in our larger Eastern cities. The governmental structures of those cities and states were quite unprepared for that huge increase in numbers of people.

With the new residents came even greater crowding, starvation wages, squalor, disease, and even more unwanted children. With those children came a demand for their care or at least for humane mechanisms by which to cope with those most helpless members of our population.

The organization of "Orphan Trains" to carry children from the East to the farm communities of the Midwest was but one of the attempts to solve the increasing problems. By that abortive scheme, the East sought to rid itself of a financial burden that threatened even to break down its social order, and the farms of the vast Trans-Mississippi America hoped to gain inexpensive labor.

"Out of sight, out of mind; send those urchins anywhere you must!" New Yorkers cried, while Nebraska and Kansas farmers were pleased to gain "farm hands" and otherwise unavailable help with their burgeoning families. The problem with that scheme was that it was top-heavy; Midwesterners simply did not need the numbers of children that constantly were on hand to be transported.

By the early years of the twentieth century, just as had the population in the major cities, the difficulties had grown to intolerable proportions, resulting in demands that the legislatures, courts, and those from the then new social sciences address four separate yet very much interrelated questions. All knew that whatever additional solutions might be found, a measure of secrecy surely would be required.

So, first, what should be done with the children, and how might they be protected and confidentiality as to their background simultaneously be maintained? Next, by what devices should would-be and deserving parents be allowed children to nurture and raise, and to what extent did they also require secretiveness? Third, how could confidentiality be assured for birth parents, in order that they escape the stigma that arose from violations of the supposed and spoken morals of that day? And finally, if confidentiality is to be maintained to the benefit of all, for how long should the law guarantee the sanctity of those proceedings and secrets? Difficult questions, indeed, and the answers, equally so.

So then, what could the lawmakers and legislatures do about the protection and care of these unwanted children? They first dabbled in the notion that all persons, with the exception of those immediately involved (birth parents, adoptive parents, and adopted children at maturity), should be forbidden access to all records having to do with adoption proceedings. Understand that the records were open to the members of the adoption triad. Notice that these very provisions seemed to anticipate that some number of birth parents and adopted children later would seek knowledge of and reunion with their birth families; their clans, if you will.

While this approach surely provided no small measure of confidentiality, the problems of application of the rules under the widely varying circumstances, as well as the difficulties in actually maintaining that secrecy, quickly made apparent the need for revisions in the requirements. The legislative efforts that usually followed (though with little uniformity at first) simply closed—"sealed"—the adoption files to everybody, including the parties themselves. All but two of the United States decided there should be no access whatever to those sealed records, except by court order resulting from petition and hearing.

Only if one could convince a judge by "clear and convincing" evidence that the urgency and needs of the parties seeking access justified the opening of the file, would an "unsealing" be ordered. The courts soon came to speak of those who were able to so convince the judges of that need as having demonstrated "good cause" for the request. As we shall see, that standard remains today in those states where, for whatever reasons, orders of courts are yet required in order to gain access.

Within the decades following World War II came ever-increasing demands by children for further knowledge of their true parentage and family history. At the same time, explosive growth in our population continued (one hundred forty million in 1945, and almost twice that number just fifty years later), and rapid advancements in the medical sciences revealed genetic influences at play in an ever-increasing number of ailments and birth defects.

Not only did those discoveries having a promise to improve the health of children provide a ready basis for judges to find "good cause," but many of the legislatures also undertook to provide additional avenues by which specified interested persons might gain access to closed files. Of great importance, most of the "new" mechanisms established by the states did not require petitions to the time-consuming and expensive court system.

There were two categories of these mechanisms. An adopted child who had reached maturity (aged variously eighteen, nineteen, or twenty-one) was granted access to the files quite usually by simple written request to the records divisions of the state. The other, and more common method adopted, was through a system of various "intermediaries."

The goal and task of the intermediaries was to locate a missing parent or child, and thereupon seek to gain permission of that person to be contacted by the parent or child desiring such contact, or to exchange information, each about the other, again through the intermediary. These devices, with variations, are still now widely in use across the country.

Notice that by so closing the records to the efforts of all whom would seek the contents except through those "go-betweens," protection was brought to the children particularly. Thereby, such matters as illegitimacy, abandonment, or whatever other reasons might be revealed in the files would remain as secrets unless and until the parties voluntarily chose otherwise (or, at least, so it was intended).

Through the operation of those rules, since no one could know of the circumstances of her birth, the origins of Mary Elizabeth, and all like her, would not be the subject of speculation and gossip. Her past and that of her birth mother would be sealed away from the eyes of all.

As to the treatment of adoptive parents, as a result of the administration of the regulations by those in the social sciences, standards were established pertaining to the character, emotional stability, financial means, and social standing of those who would adopt children. In addition to these standards, would-be adoptive parents were required to be within rather ill defined age limits and to submit to a regimen of visitations and inspections of their homes by social workers or assistants to the court.

Perhaps most important, those parents-to-be submitted to an examination of their educational, social, religious, professional, and personal lives. Indeed, even after a child had been placed with them on a trial basis, parents knew that their homes would be visited, examined, and re-examined over the months or few years following that placement.

So, during the first few years of Mary Elizabeth's life with the Kurtz family, various social workers from the adoption agency unexpectedly visited their home with an eye to the general well being of the little child. As a consequence, Mrs. Kurtz felt that she was under scrutiny that often would come as a near surprise as to the day and hour of such visits. She felt a burdensome need to have her home and children ever ready for such inspections.

The very nature of those visits, however pleasant the social workers might be, were an intrusion and brought discomfort for Mrs. Kurtz. Though a final decree had been signed for their son, stating that he was "theirs" and by implication that they were "suitable" parents, the visits continued in order to prove to the social agency that the Kurtzes also were worthy of being parents to Mary Elizabeth.

So, the Kurtz family followed the rules, kept a neat home, undertook to keep the children clean at all times, and seldom questioned the timing of or reasons for the visits. However trying for Mrs. Kurtz, she knew that if the social worker went away satisfied from those house calls, there would be a trade-off. Through her efforts, she would gain another child. What a relief it was when the decree was signed, and the Kurtzes knew for certain that Mary Elizabeth also was legally, and thereby truly, theirs.

Parenthetically, notice that by so investigating and screening proposed parents, the child to be adopted also gained much advantage, since the parents to whom he or she might go had publicly demonstrated their responsibility and fitness. It seems probable that many (if not most) of the children adopted under such standards might enjoy benefits that otherwise would have been unlikely in light of what many thought were their "undesirable" backgrounds.

Whether or not true, it was (and yet is) also presumed by parents-to-be that the same thoroughness with which the investigations of them and their homes had been done was present in the other functions of the social service agencies. The truth of the matter was that usually somewhat less effort was expended in investigations into the health and background conditions of the children.

Though attitudes might recently have become somewhat more liberal, during at least the first three decades after World War II, the large majority of adoptive parents did, and yet do, feel that of all people on Earth, birth parents had the least place in the new family unit. So, paramount among the desires of most adoptive parents was that any data gathered by the system concerning them, their homes, and their lives would at no time be made available to any birth mother or father. That requirement of confidentiality by adoptive parents was being met, or so it was hoped.

Just as the closed files prescribed by the system provide a substantial measure of secrecy for adoptive parents and for the children, so too do those also provide for the birth parents. Confidentiality was and remains as important to birth mothers as it is to others of the triad.

Since the earliest times, birth mothers quite usually have entertained the desire that unwanted or unintended births would remain a secret. For centuries, society has made obvious a measure of disdain for women who either give birth to children out of wedlock or for whatever reasons are called upon to "give up" those children. Most thought that surely such women could only be "bad" or "immoral."

Thus, by requiring that the contents of birth records remain confidential, it was thought that these mothers might avoid some measure of the criticism that often came from being in that uncomfortable position. Thereby, or so it was said, those mothers (and also fathers) might be about their lives, believing that their child would be placed in a good home, or at least that they would be relieved of their duties of child-care as required by the law.

Lastly came the question having to do with the length of time that files, once sealed, should so remain. Though much more complicated than the matter appears at first blush, the lawgivers in some states, with the studies and advice of the social workers as foundation, determined that the files should be forever closed. In some few other states, it was decided that the files would be opened to adoptees and "of age" adults within the immediate family. Again, as mentioned, in a large majority of the states it was provided that the files would be opened for intermediaries agreed upon by the parties. The legislators, in two of the United States, (and most recently, in two additional states), determined that the files should be open to adults of almost any degree of kinship, and for nearly any honest reason.

As we shall see, Mary Elizabeth would be called upon to search for her birth mother in North Carolina, which has been said to be, along with Pennsylvania, perhaps the most difficult of the states. How so? North Carolina has seen fit to provide for no intermediaries, registries, or access in any form, except by court order. Thus, though Mary Elizabeth did not know it at the time, hers was to be a very tedious effort.

All that considered, in those many states yet having closed files or similar restrictions, there remain scraps and bits of background information and details that are beyond the contents of the files. Those are known to adoptive parents, to birth mothers, and even, now and then, to children who had not entered the adoption equation till ages three, four, or five, or even more years of age. How could those bits of information also be kept from the world of outsiders?

The efforts to solve that problem took the form of admonitions to all involved to the effect that the whole of the experience was best forgotten. All were instructed that everyone, especially the birth parents, would do well to consider that chapter of life as finished, in the past, and not to be remembered. Indeed, in our story, Barbara came away from the birth of Mary Elizabeth convinced that the baby was gone from her forever, and that she should never again undertake to seek, identify, or contact that child.

Confidentiality was encouraged by society itself. The remnants of the more strict codes of moral and social conduct of the Victorian era, for better or for worse, suggested to the Kurtz family that the matter should be discussed with no one outside the immediate family and the closest of confidantes. Similarly, they and many other adoptive parents believed that they should make no efforts to encourage discussions and questions of background, even with such as little Mary Elizabeth. In fact, the Kurtzes, as did very many families, seldom mentioned the subject at all, simply because in their view it made no difference, and such talk could result in nothing of benefit to anybody.

So persuasive were those admonitions and influences that Mary Elizabeth and many, if not most, of her kind revealed their secret to but few others. In fact, not until she was long married and her own family was well along did she begin to reveal that part of her life to others.

It is easy to see how this complex system of interrelationships filled with conflicting interests continues to create frustrations, hurdles, and prohibitions. It is those irritants that give rise to the tendencies in many of us to blame and to lash out. Those propensities surely also were felt in the Kurtz family, Barbara, and in Mary Elizabeth.

So, let us examine those disruptions and irritants that arise from the system and thereby result in fault finding by each of the participants. As before, we will look first to those of birth parents, then examine the problems peculiar to adoptive parents, and finally, consider the troubles that often beset adopted children as a result of it all.

BIRTH MOTHERS

When a woman comes to know that she is pregnant with an unwanted child, she (and perhaps the father-to-be) is confronted with a series of unusually difficult decisions. Those will not only determine the fate of the child, but also will mold the character of her emotions (and perhaps his) for the balance of her life. The circumstances may be of many combinations. She may be but a teenager, perhaps a widow, or maybe an unmarried mature woman. Then too, whether married, divorced, widowed, or for whatever other reasons, she may be quite unable to assume the economic and (or) emotional responsibility for the child.

Whatever her status, and if unmarried particularly, she may hasten to blame the father; he surely is the most direct and obvious cause! While men are surely also at fault in every physical sense, her appearance during the last months of pregnancy stands as obvious witness to their indiscretion, while he, of course, displays no evidence of the same. If he then goes about his business with little or no regard for her or for the child, she remains to bear the full impact of a set of rules and customs concerning which she had no input and has no measure of control. Little wonder she lashes out.

Further, this mother may feel strongly that she is a victim of her parents, who, in her view, did not train or forewarn her in such important matters of life, as surely it was their duty so to do. Worse yet, her relationship with those parents may not be such that she is comfortable in seeking their counsel during these trying times. She may blame them for not assuming the role of being an interpreter for her in the rules of her world, whether or not she ever provided an opportunity for them to do so. Moreover, this soon-to-be mother may find any number of other people at fault, including even the parents of the father for what she considers his lack of decency, honor, and training.

Whatever may be the truth of all that, during the years after giving the child over to the system, that very act, in and of itself, may be the basis for much of her self-blame. She may have great remorse for not having been stronger and for failing to "stand up" to her world. She well may not recall that she did what she thought best in light of all the circumstances that confronted her and the totality of knowledge she possessed at the time of that pregnancy.

Even society itself may be a target of her distress; after all, it gave rise to the permissiveness that swept her through life to that place. Compounding that thought, she may deeply resent the fact that, while society surely contributed generously to her plight, it then (and now) refused to condone or even accept what she had done. She also may very much blame this same society and its systems for either persuading her to give the child over or for providing the option for her to be rid of it.

All in all, while she may have powerful feelings that others have turned upon or influenced her to her distinct disadvantage, in fact, it is likely that the causes were much more direct and personal. She may have lived through an absence of openness within her community or family, or there may have been no avenues by which she could learn of the risks hidden within her sexuality. Her parents may have insisted that abstinence should be practiced, yet failed to recognize or admit of the powerful sexual urges within the young. And, while earlier there surely were fewer birth control methods, her problems simply may have been indiscretion, poor judgment, or a promise of marriage that she thought reason enough (or excuse, as you will) for intimacy.

Since she is able to derive but minimal satisfaction in finding fault with "society" as a whole, she may feel the need to blame still other and more definable targets. The social workers, the social agencies, and the adoption lawyers surely are visible and readily at hand. The folly of that should be apparent.

While she now might lash out at such people, those each had as their purpose providing some specific measure of assistance, and they may or may not have offered counseling or other advice as a part of those services. Thus, difficult as it may be, she (and perhaps the father) must now admit to her own prominent role in selecting the solution by which she now must live. To blame those workers and agencies for providing a service that she herself sought out and entered upon does not make sense.

In any consideration of the plans, people, and decisions that might now be viewed as having been faulty or without foresight, we must remember that the actions of the social thinkers and workers of the mid-20th century were reflective of the education and beliefs of that day. So, blameworthy as Barbara may feel that those in the system were in the managing of her predicament, we can only suggest that the same people, if confronted with the same problems today, would make different determinations reflective of our present-day thought. To our benefit or not, depending upon your perspective, though such mid-twentieth century ideas often yet dominate, our society seems to be becoming more liberal.

Little wonder that Barbara would resent her world, her parents, or the man who impregnated her. After all, was it not those very people who moved her from being a desirable young and perhaps naïve woman to something quite different, simply because she had gotten pregnant? From those people too had come the label of "bad girl." It was they who had abided by the established moral code, did precious little to guide her through its intricacies, and then declared that she had deviated from it and that she should be chastised for her "errant" actions. The error in her thinking here is apparent, we believe.

As an aside and overview, is it not remarkable that while the bonds between mothers and their children are very powerful, in many cases the unspoken, though ever present, and centuries old, societal expectations are stronger still? Enough so, in fact, that pregnancy has been concealed and the bonds severed, often for no better reasons than that in the public perception pregnancies were somehow "wrong." For many, such as Barbara, their surrender of a child continues to plague them throughout all of their lives.

Though, in the final analysis, it would appear that Barbara and all of those people involved with her directly or indirectly were in some measure blameworthy, the futility of dwelling upon such thoughts is evident. These feelings must be assigned to the past, and honest as those emotions truly are or may have been, such have no place in any plans to search. As must Barbara, having again come face to face with the adoption circumstances that befell her, the birth parent must come to know that who did what to whom, and when, simply are no longer of any significance.

Notice, too, that although mothers such as Barbara might remain in some measure "undesirable" in the eyes of her world and society, the process of adoption did succeed in saving her from that label and also surely, did lift Mary Elizabeth, up and out of that morass of stigma and gossip. In so doing, it provided the child a route by which to be spared the criticism that so often was part and parcel of that earlier period; it gave a baby a new life and identity. To that extent, the results were wonderful for everybody, including Barbara.

BIRTH FATHERS

Some of the men who now or in the past have been named as the father of an illegitimate or unwanted child may have suspected that the claim against them is false. Then, if a search by such as Mary Elizabeth, whether intentionally or not, again gives rise to that question of paternity, the man may feel no small measure of resentment. Nonetheless, we think a discussion of that paternity question and his concern are outside the scope of this work. We can only suggest to any man who believes he may have been erroneously so named, and again now is said to be the father, that there are adequate tests available of which you may avail yourself. Similarly, those tests may also serve to establish with some certainty that a man indeed is the true father.

So, whether as to paternity or any other aspect of adoption, the adoptee's contemplation of a search has no place for blame, and surely should not be delayed because of concern that the putative father may or may not admit to that fact.

BIRTH PARENTS AND THEIR SPOUSES

If you were not married at the time of the conception of a child born to your present mate, and particularly if that birth took place years before you met him or her, the appearance at your door of a birth child of that mate, about whom you had no prior knowledge, surely will be a surprise. Upon first thought, that event well may bring a measure of anger or resentment.

One couple found themselves in a situation where the husband had sired a child before having had any relationship with his wife-to-be. After years of marriage, that child, all grown up by then appeared at their doorstep. Their marriage was tested to a considerable extent, since the wife had treasured the thought that she alone had been the mother of his children. Both realized that whatever misunderstanding and heartache his actions had brought to the marriage, that child was in no way the person at fault.

Our advice to you, as a birth parent, is that you must dig deep within your soul in an attempt to understand the hurt your spouse may feel. From that soul searching and your affection for your mate, you must find the words necessary to assuage his or her fears about your loyalty. Similarly, the wife in the above example must be aware that the conception and pregnancy is over, done, and completed, the child has appeared, the father can in no way change any part of the past, and she should commence the emotional task of putting the matter behind them.

So, no matter a relationship prior to the time that a couple and a child became acquainted, that "new" son or daughter is in some measure a part of his family, and in decency must be treated accordingly. Further, whatever feelings you may have concerning the turn of events should be kept between you and your spouse. They should not involve the adult child who has sought your spouse. Remember that child did not choose to be conceived, nor did it choose to be born to your mate. Likewise, the child having played no part in its conception, an adoptee's action of now should not be viewed as wrong. Moreover, seeking a parent should be considered as quite appropriate for an adoptee.

If there has been marital infidelity, the issue may be even more tedious, and one that will require much attention and discussion by you and your mate. While the resolution of such problems is beyond the scope of this work, we do insist that the child was not the cause of these difficulties, and whatever discussions you may have with your mate should not involve that innocent person. Moreover, in none of your meditations over the matter should your judgment and opinion of the child be influenced by reason of the relationship between you and your mate or any relationship of your mate with another person.

Importantly, remember that it likely took much courage for this child to confront the challenges of a search for you. Thus, your approach should be one of open-mindedness and willingness to meet, and only later should you evaluate the merits of the child as a person. To seek to blame the child for any role in the whole matter is grossly unfair, and should be a subject of serious soul-searching.

ADOPTIVE PARENTS

Concerning adoptive parents, we think there are three significant factual situations, any of which frequently gives rise to the urge to find fault with others. The first is regret by one mate that the other apparently was infertile. Next, there is that blame often directed at the social agencies for what seem to have been their failures to discover health, personality, or physical defects in the child before adoption. Finally, there is a measure of resentment often felt by parents who blame the system for making it possible for the child to vent its curiosity and seek out his or her birth parents.

As to infertility, especially in the earlier years when the sciences were unable to detect that fact, either the husband or the wife might blame the other partner for that physical inability to permit his or her genetics to be carried forward. In fact, whether it was he or she may not now be ascertainable. How so?

Throughout history, and during most of the first half of the twentieth century, it was thought that if a man was able to sexually perform, it almost surely was the woman who was infertile.   And so it was that it was she, albeit often erroneously, who was the target of undeserved resentment. Now, of course, we know better, and so all of those moments of distress are in the past, just as are the circumstances of conception for the birth mother.

For those who yet entertain some measure of blame over infertility of your mate, we think it futile for us to attempt to dissuade you from those ideas. Only you are able to see beyond that physical impairment and look to the other characteristics for which you chose that person. Moreover, once the adoption was accomplished that very same mate may well have been and now be a superb parent and father or mother.

Most importantly, incapacity to pass to another generation your own genes by reason of infertility in your partner is far, far from the end of the world. Your manners, customs, beliefs, moral standards, and even the political, philosophical, and religious thoughts that you hold dear are passed through love, nurture, upbringing, and teaching, and surely not by the mere act of conception.

Finding fault with the system, when the child brings disappointment, physically or otherwise, though totally distinct from the fertility question, is very common. As to any placing of blame that you might lodge against the system by reason of its failure to reveal or ferret out potential for disease or disability in the child, you must realize that there was generally no intention by anybody to cause harm to you or the child.

Operating by the dictates of their time, though we may not like it, there were mistakes. Oversights were and are human, but more than that, those workers of just fifty years ago did not have the tools or staff to learn what now might be easily ascertainable. Further, the capacity of science of that former day to make predictions and prognoses concerning future health and physical condition was much less than today. Recall, if you will, that the physicians and families who just one hundred years ago stood helplessly by as children died of "whooping cough," "flu," "strep throat," and "blood poisoning" similarly wished that they had more knowledge and different tools by which to predict.

Just as our automobiles and airplanes have vastly improved over those same decades, so too have the sciences and our understanding of human behavior. Whether through oversight or lack of knowledge, adoptive parents must now realize that the system did and will continue to solve the problems, still yet it has fallen short from time to time. So, just as we do not measure the efforts of the past against the standards of today, we also must not place blame for what we now view as failures of foresight or prediction resulting from earlier ideas of adoption or lack of knowledge in the sciences.

Finally, adoptive parents came to believe and understand that this same system would provide safeguards to prevent disruption of their lives and the lives of their children by birth parents, and also were assured that there would be no mechanisms by which the child might seek out natural parents. In short, the same mechanisms that assured confidentiality for the birth mother supplied adoptive parents with ample reason to believe that once the adoption was concluded, their lives also would move on, uninterrupted and without interference.

Human as it was to have done so; it was and yet is unrealistic to rely on such provisions of confidentiality. In the best of the affairs of man, secrets are not kept for lifetimes.

Thus, no one should be blamed because of methods and operations of the system that permitted such breaches. While that system gave rise to the notion that the book was closed, the child became that of adoptive parents, and the past was behind them, those were not always to be. Though the participants in the system were not made aware of that distinct possibility of breaches in the wall of confidentiality, that lack of awareness also is now as deeply buried in the past as it is unchangeable.

So, at adoption, all parties enter into the relationship with assurances and beliefs in mind, all of which grow out of the system and its imperfect rules. The fact that at adulthood a child may undertake a search with an expectation of some measure of success serves to undermine or weaken those earlier assurances and that fact also may not be pleasant for some adoptive parents. Still though, since a decision to search is nowhere forbidden by the law, everyone generally, but the adoptive parents particularly, must come to understand that while the system may be imperfect, it is NOT the source of a child's desire to search.

The thought may arise that if the system is not a legitimate target for blame, then the child must be dissatisfied, unappreciative, or ungrateful. If parents entertain such notions, then we think it not at all remarkable that they should vent anger or apprehension at any suggestion of a search. Even more so is blame likely to be lodged against the child if it is suggested that those parents should somehow assist with, or at least be receptive to, that investigation.

There are other emotions that may arise and cause adoptive parents to object to any search efforts. They may feel threatened if they anticipate that "their" child might come to have affection for such newly discovered birth parents. Indeed, the threat of divided allegiance by this child they have so long nurtured and prepared for life may be the most powerful of their fears. Simultaneously, that concern may be heightened if the adopted child exhibits enthusiasm at the prospect of finding or meeting the birth parent. In such an event, and surely not arising from love or affection, the adoptive parent must realize that exuberance arises from curiosity and the "rush" that comes from a successful effort.

The child well may feel, and the adoptive parents must come to believe that feeling love for additional persons does not diminish a child's existing love for its adoptive parents, or for anyone else for that matter. As human beings, we have an unlimited capacity to love and be loved, and so to appreciate and to have deep affection for one person is not to have a lesser affection for another.

Whatever love and respect you have previously shared with your adopted child surely will continue without abatement, no matter who else may enter the life of that child. So, while your child, upon the discovery of a birth parent, may need to carve out bits of time from you and all others in order to further that new relationship, that need will have nothing to do with the depth of love you feel, each for the other.

Unfortunately, there also is a tendency to blame the fact of adoption for any actions of the child that are perceived to be "different" or beyond what would be expected from a birth child. Such thinking suggests that an "adopted" child carries with him or her, a propensity to do the unusual. Since it surely is not unusual for a child being raised by its biological parents to seek out family history, similar efforts by an adoptee should not be viewed as remarkable. To view such actions as out of the ordinary is to, again, consider adoption, not as a process, but as a label distinguishing such a child from other children.

Without realization of what is happening, insidious self-blame and feelings of failure may powerfully affect adopted parents. If so, it may yet remain for those parents to search deeply within their own thoughts. Thus it is that if you have such emotions, you must come to know that just as there is nothing improper when an adoptee searches, you are in no way to blame because he or she does so.

So, probe deep into your thoughts and in so doing maintain the utmost of intellectual integrity. Even though we think that you surely should not be, if you thereby yet perceive yourself to be at fault, you must confront those ideas, correct such errors, and be on with your life.

Finally, and importantly, after an honest appraisal and understanding of all possible sources, including the system itself, you well may come to the realization that no one is guilty of any action as to which you should be placing blame or finding fault. When and if you come to that conclusion, then frame your future thoughts accordingly and be prepared to face whatever comes from the search efforts.

SHOULD THE SEARCHER BEWARE?

To the extent that a searcher may be someone other than the child or birth parent, and should the person being sought wish not to be found, that latter might now target that detective-of-sorts. After all, the thought of an adoptive parent or a birth parent may be "Is this stranger not someone who is taking advantage of an imperfect system, all to the detriment of the family that I have created and now cherish?"

Likewise, just as any member of the triad should be ready for what may come, so too should the searcher be prepared. It is likely (and should be) that the independent investigator enters into the effort well knowing that not everyone involved will view him or her as a hero. Notice, too, that as with all members of the triad, regardless of his or her expectations in that matter, that searcher did not design the system and almost surely has done nothing further than utilize the sources available to everybody with energy enough to do the same. For having used those sources and taking advantage of the loopholes in the system, he is not blameworthy, and to find fault with him is to "whip a mule that ain't the one pulling your wagon."

THE ADOPTED CHILD

The method by which our rules of adoptions may be changed is through acts of the legislatures and courts after advice from those who know of the social sciences and understand the political pressures at play. So, a few words are appropriate concerning members of the adoption triad, especially adoptees, who dedicate effort and time to proposing changes in the law and the system concerning those features they find disagreeable, especially concerning access to files.

As to the efforts of those people carrying the banners for change, though they usually have legitimate and honest views and purposes, we offer neither comment nor advice. We do suggest that, for your purposes here, what they say or do not say, and where they do or do not lobby, are of no importance in your search. So, if you have the desire to be heard politically, keep those activities separate and distinct from your search efforts; your views may serve only to antagonize some of those very people who otherwise might assist you.

Adoptees surely are not exempt from the category of those who place blame in the system and others involved. Further, perhaps their reasons for doing so are the most valid, since they had no part in any of the original decisions that now so very much affect them. Indeed, it may be said that of the members of the triad, those children who are the victims or beneficiaries, as the case may be, of the system, have a greater number of perceived reasons and targets for blame than do any other of the parties.

We think it likely that the requirements by most states that adoption files remain sealed are the most annoying of the regulations encountered by adoptees. The thought prevails that within those files lie solutions and answers for most problems. After all, does not the file contain the names, addresses, stations in life, educational background, physical descriptions and material concerning the health of the birth parents as to which the searcher is most curious? Would not the addresses there found make possible an immediate reunion by which all of the anxieties of years might be dispelled? And the simple answer to both questions very often is "No."

As we have discussed, the adoption system was reflective of the time, place, and attitudes of the day. For better or for worse, as we have said, it was thought appropriate in most states that the files remain closed. Most important of all, and as you must come to realize, no matter how complete or how lacking in evidence your file may be, if it is closed you can not learn what is there, short of a court order. Fighting city hall will accomplish next to nothing.

So, and as we shall see in the chapters dedicated to the actual mechanics of the search, while important information is almost always to be found in those files, most simply do not contain that measure of completeness expected. In addition and of which we shall speak in the chapter entitled Chrysalis, much more than gaining a list of names and addresses must be accomplished in order to bring about reunions that have any chance of being fulfilling. So, while enjoyable to examine, that old file may not be the pot of gold that you expect.

Like many adoptees, you may blame your birth mother (and father), particularly; for having removed you from those very sources from which we all can learn of our heritage (that "severance" was discussed earlier). At one time or another, we all wonder from whence we came; what religion, what national origin, what physical features, and what happenstance of life combined to create the person we now find ourselves to be. The very process to which your birth mother gave you over has made that inquiry a very difficult one. In short, you were cut off from your clan, and it surely is somebody's fault, or so you think.

All that said, there are avenues other than through that file by which you may reach the facts you need. So, while the system that resulted in closure of the files also may to a measure be blameworthy, be done with thoughts about closed files, just as you must with all other urges to find fault. Again, in the mechanics chapters, we will discuss these alternative methods by which you may gain much of the same information. Enough for now, of laws and closed files.

Some adoptees feel that the act of having been given over to the system by the mother can only be considered as evidence of her rejection of him or her. After all, even though at birth she was surely your "mother" in every sense, was she not the very first person to walk out of your life? Even your "very own mother rejected" you, or so you may feel.

You may believe that in an almost callous fashion, and surely through no choice of your own, you were turned over to a machine-like system, after which that parent (or parents) was free to walk away and put you from their minds. Through all your years until you came to adulthood such questions were almost without answers, and so there remained with you the ever-haunting question of how she, or they, could have done such a thing. Such thoughts may have given rise to your need to place blame upon someone, the birth parents being the likely target.

But wait, you should now realize that she might have been almost powerless to do otherwise. Perhaps the culture within which your mother lived was even stricter than you can imagine. Suppose she was an older married woman, or even a widow, whose sole indiscretion resulted in that pregnancy. Suppose she fell ill and had no means by which to care for you in any way. What if she was in love or even engaged, found that she was pregnant, and then was spurned by her lover? Imagine that she was raped, and was so embarrassed that she told no one.

Not the least of her reasons for having given you over to the adoption system may have been extreme parental pressure.   Uncomfortable as is the thought for us, the number is legion of parents of mothers-to-be who have encouraged adoption for their grandchildren simply because the term "illegitimate" might be applied to those immediate descendants.

So, are we apologists for unacceptable conduct? Not by any means. Nonetheless, we do suggest that sexual activities were, and remain, a vital and unavoidable part of our very being, and access to what few contraceptives there were those years ago was difficult at best. Then too, the event of your birth those years, probably decades, ago is a fact and can not be changed in any way, and your mother may carry a measure of regret for her failings that is well nigh to being an ongoing horror for her.

You must realize that she likely did the best that she felt she could do, given all the circumstances. In short, unless and until you find yourself in a similar position, and thereby are able to fairly judge her conduct and her reasons, you must maintain a willingness to forgive the very human actions and mistakes that may have taken place long ago.

Dedicating your efforts to finding or ascribing fault is a waste of time. Much better that your energy now be directed to learning the truth of the matter. We suggest that when you do accomplish a reunion with your birth parent (or parents), "why" will be your first question, and she (or he) may well have a better reason than you can now even imagine.

THE EFFECTS OF WORDS

As the great Mr. Justice Holmes said, "A word is not a crystal, transparent and unchanging. It is rather the skin of a living thought, and its meaning may vary greatly with the context and time in which it is found." We think this thought should guide us all in our use of the words "adopted" and "adoption."

Because your birth parent(s) for whatever reasons chose not to raise you, you fell under the purview of the system of adoption, and with that assumption of duty by those who had charge of that system the words "adoptee" and "adoption" became applicable to you. As we mentioned earlier, properly applied those words describe a process and a legal result, and thus are quite neutral. Nevertheless, though the process itself oftentimes has had results that are truly remarkable in goodness, these terms too often have been used derisively or to describe or imply inappropriate character or background of any of those involved.

Unlike some, one woman of whom we know grew up hearing her adoptive parents say that she "was adopted" or "You are adopted." In her case, the term "adopted" became a brand, rather than a mere description of the manner in which that child became part of that family. It would have been much more understandable for the child if the words employed had been such as "We went through the process of adoption to have you" or "We adopted you." No matter the meaning intended, the thought that remained with the child even to adulthood was that somehow there were notable differences between her and other children. Of course, the difference was the way by which the child came to be a part of the family.

When those phrases were used time after time and year after year, that adoptee could do little else than to be conscious of differences between her and her peers without perhaps knowing how to ascribe the correct meaning to the words. Children, we believe, have the desire to be viewed as "the same" as their friends, and the result of feeling different because of a label may later bring feelings that someone is to blame.

That brand, or label, through its use by anyone, is inaccurate. Unfortunately it is more detrimental if the term becomes a convenient way to explain away shortcomings, intellectual or physical inabilities, or the lack of some specific prowess or "talent" that the child might exhibit. Upon the occasion of a parent (or anyone else) using the expression "...adopted child," or "Well, he's adopted, you know" to explain away some mischief or lack of aptitude, again the child feels as though he or she has been distinguished from his friends and peers; that, even though their conduct might be identical.

Said another way, our lack of certainty as to what traits are inheritable and the convenience of using the child's behavior as an excuse for placing blame, both render the word "adoption" a catch-all reason for unexpected conduct of any sort. If we could one day know the entirety of our characteristics, abilities, and talents that come to us from our ancestors, we could not any more use the fact of adoption as a dumping ground for ills and aberrations that our children might display.

The result is that by the use of those words, blame rightly due elsewhere is overlooked or ignored by others. Sadder still, is the reality that the adopted child comes to believe that such is the truth of the matter. The adoptee, having heard blame or weakness ascribed to them repeatedly, may come to resent and harbor ill-feelings both for those who put that child in such a vulnerable position, as well as for those who, whether with malice or not, simply did not choose their words carefully.

Equally implicit in the use of those labels is the notion that your parentage should be scrutinized or is suspect in some measure. Why? For no better reason than that you came into this life as a result of conduct by your birth parents that then was viewed as in some measure unacceptable. As a result of that supposed undesirable conception and birth, the label "adopted" was imposed upon you, the results often being that even you may now and again question the value or worth of your natural parents, and yet be powerless to investigate those matters or even to know those people. Still again, feelings of undefined inadequacy are not far away.

So, since you are "adopted," it is likely that you will be viewed by some as having arrived with "baggage," some of which they presume to be "bad." While it is not uncommon for all parents to take credit for being "fine parents" when especially others note accomplishments and good deeds by you, unfortunately, it is handy for adoptive parents to hide their own blameworthiness by crediting your failures to the fact that you are adopted.

Take the time now to consider whether or not such has occurred in your life, not in an effort to place blame but to decide for yourself what being adopted REALLY means. You must consider how the use by others of the words "adopt" and "adoption" has affected you. The words are not good, bad, or somewhere in between, and are not a measure of you as a person. Realizing how you have allowed labels and your perception of such to affect you is the first step in your process of change. How you come to view yourself is a choice that you must make and occasionally reevaluate. Consider that, while others may have used those labels in an uncomplimentary fashion and you may have come to assimilate those notions, you need now to relegate such ideas to the past. Always be willing to leave labels behind.

In review, we have seen adoption records, once open, then closed, identities concealed, and a child's family ties severed, all serving to set the stage for several generations of frustrated adoptees and birth parents. We should remember that it is much easier to create families biologically than it is to do so by mere operation of law. So, though beneficial in so many ways, the business of adoption has created problems, and the very nature of the differences in the needs of the parties rendered some of those problems very difficult of solution. The issues that are not easily solved give rise to blame.

More importantly, whether it is with the system itself, one or more components of the process, or any of those people with whom you have been involved as a result of an adoption, all ill feelings must be set aside. While you may be one of those so adversely affected as to have ample cause for resentment, allowing such emotional wounds to fester can only bring greater pain, and surely will serve no purpose in your search efforts.

No matter what the complexity of the problems or pain anyone might have experienced, the system did often succeed. Recall, if you will, that the mechanism brought little Mary Elizabeth to the Kurtz family, removed her from an environment that might have carried the stigma of illegitimacy, and made it possible for Barbara, her birth mother, to be about the task of putting order into her life.

Adequate as that system was, it did not contemplate the fact that curiosity would overtake many that would be involved. So, let us move on to a consideration of that curiosity and many of the other reasons for which people undertake to search.

Why Search?

*"Sometime in your life you will go on a journey. It will be the
longest journey you have ever taken. It is the journey to find
yourself."*[9]

As mentioned in the chapter "Who's to Blame?" we know
that in the past illegitimate, unwanted, and abandoned
children often had access to considerable information
concerning their origins. While throughout the last half of
the nineteenth century there was an ever-increasing sense
that secrecy as to those facts should be secured and
maintained, until then that attitude was not widespread.

As the desire for secrecy increased and knowledge thereby
became more difficult for adoptees to gain (and for all others,
for that matter), the curiosity to learn of their history did not
diminish proportionately. Then too, the on-going and
increased interest by Americans in genealogical research
served to pique that curiosity.

We all have a rich heritage and historical background of
ancestors, some brave, some weak, some successful, some
that knew abject failure, some who were long-lived and some
not so, and we all had an occasional "black sheep." Adoptees
since the middle of the twentieth century have been
foreclosed from establishing their connection to any of those
fascinating people and events, are excluded from all patriotic
organizations of descendants, and can and often have strong
feelings of emotional emptiness and a desire to know. The
result is that the increased numbers of people affected by
adoptions that seek to learn of their children or of their own
genetic past and ancestral heritage should come as no
surprise.

---

[9] Sarah Ban Breathnach, *Simple Abundance* (Warner Books, New
York, NY, 1995), p. "February 24"

Today, there are as many reasons for a birth parent, adoptive parent, or a birth child to search, as there are personalities of those who do so. These reasons range from idle curiosity, through a deep desire—almost a need—to know of one's past, to an immediate and pressing need for medical background.

Except for the need for medical information that might prove helpful for any member of the triad, we suspect that few of the reasons for searching are felt equally by all of those potential participants. As to those medical matters, science now tells us that as a result of those who went before us we are born with decreased resistance to or tendencies toward various ailments, weaknesses, and debilities. Who does not know of a family in which numerous members over two or more generations have suffered from the same or similar illnesses or birth defects? To the extent that we do so inherit, all members of any adoption triad would benefit by learning and passing along knowledge of such inherited characteristics.

Once again, we feel that the experiences of Barbara, the Kurtzes and Mary Elizabeth will aid in understanding a few of the several forces that often lead to a search. In the course of the research for this work, we found it to be truly remarkable, though perhaps predictable, that among adoptees, birth parents, and adoptive parents there are so very many identical and shared ideas and emotions.

Remember, Mary Elizabeth was given over to adoption in late 1958. A decision to search is not created in a vacuum, and it surely had not been so for her mother, Barbara. As that mother contemplated undertaking to find that daughter abandoned those decades before, she realized that over the long years she had developed an increased capacity to deal with her moments of deeply rooted remorse and regret. We feel that in some fashion, regrets also are transformed into motivations for search, and to that extent, these have value.

Barbara's journey—the process of coming to peace with her thoughts—had been an inner struggle and at times had been most difficult. It was a beginning of the healing process, she thought, one of the benefits being that she was more comfortable with the prospect of a search. Indeed, we think that such peace of mind, if not a prerequisite surely is desirable from the standpoint of your own emotional health and comfort.

WHY A BIRTH MOTHER WOULD SEARCH

Barbara remembered that she had left the hospital without seeing her little girl again. She had returned to the "home" to gather her belongings and, at once and in time for Christmas, she returned to Fayetteville and to her family.

The nervous breakdown story had been plausible enough, it seemed, and her parents and friends had not mentioned the matter of that "nervous condition" again. Although she remembered her life prior to the birth as having been pleasant and enjoyable, after her return she often cried and found difficulty in resuming the life she had led before. She could not then know the extent to which her future life also would be very much changed.

Still though, being with her first little daughter brought to her a degree of comfort, especially since she had the feeling that by giving up one child she had managed to remain with the other. But what a sacrifice she had made.

Over the next few years, her feelings of sadness continued, and rarely did a day pass without thoughts of the pretty little child she had surrendered to God only knows whom. Much as a mother whose child has died must mourn, so too did Barbara often grieve over the loss of that, her second daughter. In her struggle to put an end to those punishing recollections, and as she had been instructed to do, she undertook to relegate the whole of the regrettable events to the past.

So, Barbara moved on with her life. She married again, then she, her daughter, and the new husband moved far away from her town and from her past, she hoped. Still though, and despite the new surroundings, a decent husband, and more children, the memory of that baby left to those social workers back in Asheville proved to be much more difficult to erase from her mind than she had ever anticipated.

She had told no one, of course. Though in hindsight she suspected that it would have been emotionally beneficial to have confided in someone—rather a catharsis, as it might have been—she also knew that there had been no one who she had trusted enough to tell that deepest of secrets. Even these years later, she felt that her judgment had been sound, and to have done otherwise might well have brought harm to her baby, herself, and to others of her family. As Barbara then thought, one must be prepared to keep some secrets for a lifetime.

Barbara gradually came to realize also that it would have been next to impossible for her to give up that child, had she not been assured that the whole of the episode would be accomplished in the utmost confidence. She had been told that upon her signing of the agreement of release that she would never see that child again, and no one would learn of what she had done. Though that was, indeed, the way it had been for the years that followed, her memories remained.

She sometimes felt as though she had made a deal with the Devil himself, a trade-off that forever bound her. She felt that by that trade, she had taken the path of least resistance; it was easier to give away the child and the privilege of ever seeing it again than to have stood before the scorn and financial hardship that would have resulted from undertaking to raise it. No matter those feelings of guilt and the fact that life might have been different had she chosen another course, she felt that she had to live by her bargain, and had no right to intrude into the life of that child and its new family.

Though much of her concern about the attitudes of others had subsided as she had grown older, she yet reasoned that if she were to tell anyone, even though near four decades had passed, she would have gained nothing from the sad memories and long silence. How so?

It might be that the perceptions of all who knew of her past would be the same as those would have been had she revealed her pregnancy when it occurred. Despite the years of pain resulting from the loss of the little girl, she yet might be called upon to endure the criticism and stigma of having been a "bad" woman who had abandoned her child. She would have suffered for naught, or so she reasoned. Her secret would be "out," yet she would not have gained the daughter she gave over to adoption.

And so it was over many years following that birth, Barbara often and silently had wondered and speculated about the appearance, education, and activities of the little girl. Particularly was that so on that daughter's birthday and during holidays when families traditionally gather together. Empty and regret-filled feelings regularly came upon her during family reunions and similar gatherings.

As did Barbara, upon such special occasions birth mothers of adoptees find that their joy of the moment is often, though briefly, interrupted by thoughts of their missing child. Even though they are in the company of family members and are enjoying the occasion, they have awareness that one of their children is not present.

Nor in times of distress or disaster can those mothers call or speak to anyone in order to learn of the well being of their child. Particularly may such anxiety occur when the mother has had other children; either before or after the child she surrendered, and thus fully understands the depths and complexity of her feelings.

Despite the adoption process, the rules, and the admonitions from the system, at special times there remains a need to gather everyone together who belongs with you. In fact, that child, though now adopted away and into another family, still belongs in thought at least, as do any other children of that birth mother. Such emotional linkage exists, albeit diminished by the passage of years, and to deny those feelings is difficult at best.

Such events, emotions and memories sometimes also serve as a vivid reminder for some parents that they one day may consider searching. Lurking in Barbara's mind, and likely in that of other such mothers, is the deep concern that adoption and its results may have brought unhappiness or even harm to their child.

She realizes that, for better or for worse, she quite literally and irretrievably gave the future of that child over to unknown strangers. She relinquished, not only the physical child, but also gave up her capacity to protect or to lend direction to that child in its journey through life.

One mother told us of her concern with news, no matter from where, of a disaster or tragedy that had affected many people. Whether as to our children or other members of our family, in the event of catastrophe, we at once attempt to contact those family members, yet this woman, though she yet had those same desires, was unable to do so. She knew of no place or person who would know of the safety of that daughter. She could not telephone her, and could do nothing more that silently worry over whether or not the child might have been involved. This mother could only hope that she was yet alive and well and had not been hurt or even killed by any of such calamities.

So, worry may arise from not knowing of disaster or even of everyday injury. Concern may also come to a birth mother when she realizes that she has a medical condition of which she had no knowledge at the time of the birth of the child she gave over to adoption.

Barbara found herself in precisely that category. She had come to know over the years that she was at a substantially increased risk for cancer. Through those painful experiences, she came to know that her strain of that terrible scourge could be successfully treated, if discovered early on. Out of her natural concern for her children and their descendants, she felt regret by reason of her inability to convey medical information and a warning to the missing child.

That birth mother, who told us of her of concern with disaster, also told of her need to draw her missing daughter near to her. Even after nineteen years of separation and knowing nothing whatever of that child, she yet had a desire to assure the daughter of her continuing love.

Though we suspect that the vast majority of mothers understand such feelings, it remains difficult to determine the basis for such life-long affection. Whether such emotions are primordial, instinctive, or, instead, result from the phenomenon now spoken of as "bonding" during pregnancy, we can not say, nor do we need to speculate. Whatever the source or reason, that love or affection very often provides the motivation and initiative necessary to move one to a search.

Searching often assists a birth mother in resolving lingering questions that arose from her decision to give up a child. As a result of such searching and discovery, she may (probably will) find that the choices she made those years earlier caused no harm to the child and, rather, brought a greater benefit for all. Better yet, and to her great pleasure, she may learn that her child achieved a happy and satisfying life, became a reasonably well-adjusted adult, and even advanced to responsible positions in business or the community. She also may discover in this now grown child the excellent parent she had once hoped to be, on and on. The possibilities are many. Reward enough for any parent, we think.

We believe that the motivations from which a birth father might undertake to search very often are the same as those that drive birth mothers. Still yet, there is an additional reason that may not be uncommon; fathers may want to share whatever property they have accumulated with their progeny. Many men, whether or not they have dedicated their lives to their work, all to the neglect of children and family, give thought to providing for others as they approach their elder years. Finally, while we cannot be at all sure, it may be that fathers have some primordial urge or desire to know of those who will carry forth their genes. Whatever the reasons, there are those fathers who do seek, just as do mothers.

There may be one very powerful and remaining reason to search that applies to birth mothers and birth fathers alike. If either one had no other children in life, the urge to effect a reunion with that only child, might be very intense. Either parent may feel a need to find that one child through whom their lineage and history will be continued through the generations.

Whatever other reasons there may be, it is enough that a parent has the desire to search for a natural child. Satisfying the need within is entirely acceptable, however your journey of discovery does require, at each and every step along the way that you consider the lives, happiness, and emotional welfare of all whom your efforts will affect.

WHY ADOPTIVE PARENTS SEARCH

A few words as to searching by young people are in order. It is not our intention to encourage minors or immature young adults to undertake such investigations, nor do we pretend to be in a position to advise adoptive parents or other friends or family members as to whether or not they should search in behalf of such young people. Those decisions are within the domain of the adoptive parents, and it is they alone who have the knowledge necessary to measure both the strength of their relationship with that child and also the capacity of the child to cope with the emotions that well might arise along the way.

As Barbara worried and wondered over what had become of her little girl, she could not know that the Kurtzes were busy with daily life and the upbringing of Mary Elizabeth and her brother. She was a healthy, well-adjusted child, and had experienced no difficulties in adjusting to her new home and situation in life. Further, as far as the Kurtzes knew, while she was yet a youngster, other than for a few questions she posed, she seemed to have little or no interest in knowing of her birth parents.

Why, then would adoptive parents like the Kurtzes ever consider searching for Mary Elizabeth's birth parents, or at least assisting Mary Elizabeth in doing so?   There are perhaps three reasons.

The first and most common of those reasons has to do with the appearance of medical problems that might be attributable to genetics. Such a willingness to assist or to search may arise when your child, having reached an age where the results may be carefully weighed, asks for help with or undertakes a search for birth parents. Finally, though not common, some adoptive parents have an honest and genuine interest in knowing of the natural heritage of their child.

If you believe that your son or daughter has demonstrated medical symptoms that might be traceable to his or her family background, your first step is to consult your physician. He will know whether or not the likelihood of an inherited tendency or debility is sufficient to justify the effort you propose to undertake. As we have said, searches may be time consuming and, unless you personally do the investigation, the effort will involve some considerable expense. So, before you decide to move ahead, take the advice of the physician as to the medical need, yet follow your own heart as to your need to continue the efforts.

As mentioned, the most common reason for you as an adoptive parent to undertake to search is that the child either has requested that you do so or that child has sought your assistance with his or her search. However, there are considerations other than that mere request, the most important of which are two in number.

Whether or not you as the adoptive parents are prepared to have a stranger in the form of a birth parent on the emotional periphery of your life must be answered. The other, and equally difficult question, is whether your child is emotionally mature to the degree necessary to manage what might be total rejection by the birth parents, a finding that either or both of those parents are dead or are of less than desirable character, or lastly, the possibility of utter failure in the search effort.

While we later will discuss problems that may loom on the horizon as the adult child considers a search and the potential results, for now we feel that if you have answered "yes" to both of those questions, then consider moving ahead with the effort. All parents have an obligation to help their children find fulfillment, emotionally, intellectually, and socially. So, if after full consideration you find your child mature enough and yourself emotionally prepared to accept the reality that your child has another parent, and you feel that you can guide or at least accompany him or her through unexpected discoveries, pleasant and unpleasant, then proceed.

While adoptive parents are often somewhat curious about the lineage and birth parents of their child, quite usually that interest is not sufficient to lead to a search. Moreover, we suspect that if that were the only reason why you would seek out a birth parent, then, since you can have no knowledge of what may be uncovered, we think it ill advised to do so. While mere curiosity is sufficient for a child to seek birth parents, it is not reason enough for adoptive parents to do so.

Still though, if you find that need within yourself sufficient to send you off looking, be oh, so careful with the feelings of everyone involved. The past may be painful.

REASONS WHY AN ADOPTEE WOULD SEARCH

The story of Mary Elizabeth, with experiences of others known to us added, will serve well to illustrate some of the thoughts an adoptee may have about searching.

Mary Elizabeth remembered that as soon as they believed that she was able to understand, the Kurtzes revealed to her that she had been adopted. She was told that she had not come from inside her mother's tummy. She was unable to comprehend where she had actually come from and had come to believe that she had fallen from the sky. Though she did not then quite comprehend, it all became clear to her little mind when she watched the movie, "Dumbo." Just as the stork had delivered the baby elephant, she suspected that the stork also had brought her.

It was not until later that she would come to understand that she had grown inside another woman; one who was not the same as the mother she had known all of her life. She was told that her birth mother had loved her enough to give her away. That confused her. What had happened to that other mother? If she had really loved her, then why had she not wanted to keep her?

She thought that she had been given up because she had done something wrong. And why shouldn't she think that; no one knew to tell her otherwise.

As Mary Elizabeth grew to maturity, so too was she able to probe more deeply in her mind. Who and where had she been before the adoption? What were the appearances and stations in life of her birth parents, and what were the circumstances that caused her to be surrendered over to the system, and following that, to Mr. and Mrs. Kurtz? What were the characteristics she had inherited from those parents? How would she have been different if she had not been placed for adoption? The questions were too many, the answers too few.

Of all her concerns, the one that grew with every year that passed was "Why should I not know the truth as to the whole of it?" While she realized that the Kurtzes had related what few facts they had been told, she could not understand why those scant bits of information should be the end of the story.

Having realized that they were unable to answer her questions, by her teen-age years Mary Elizabeth no longer made inquiry of Mr. and Mrs. Kurtz. Mary Elizabeth's curiosity about her heritage and about those other parents appeared to cause Mrs. Kurtz some considerable emotional discomfort.

So, simply stated, and unlike everyone with whom she was close, Mary Elizabeth had no idea from where she had come. The Kurtzes had not been able to help, she knew of no one else who could, and she had no other link to the past. Her world and her history began only within herself and her imagination.

Mary Elizabeth created scenarios in her mind, in order that she might fill in the gaps, and also to explain why she had been given up and rejected. She often mused as to how nice it would one day be were she to learn the truth of it all. As those thoughts came, she knew that only through time and effort on her part would the answers come, or perhaps those would not come at all.

Further, the words "You are adopted," told her something about who she was and also revealed to her that she was "different." Perhaps it would have been helpful to her if she had been able to share her unique thoughts and concerns with someone. However, she felt that speaking of such matters to others, especially those who had not been adopted, would be inappropriate, a betrayal, and a breach of the peculiar code of ethics that had been taught to her by the Kurtzes. Accordingly, she did her best to seek her own counsel and in silence attempted to make sense of her mysterious beginnings.

Whenever thoughts of her adoption resurfaced, as those often did, frustration came. Of whatever character and whoever she was, that first mother was real, and unless she had died she was out there someplace. But where?

So, Mary Elizabeth grew up, finished school, married Mike, moved off to their life together, and then came her first son. It was remarkable to her when that boy was born. It was then that she came to the stark reality that until the first moment she looked upon him she had never known anyone to whom she was related "by blood" in any way.

Although that infant was the extent of her knowledge of her family at that moment, she knew that there were other relatives out there, perhaps many. But for that moment, at least, she thought, "My life, my lineage, and that of my children begins with me."

The next eye opening reality that came upon her was when that son, at age three, was diagnosed with a brain tumor. Though her first concern was for his life, she also was seized by the thought that it somehow might have been an inheritable trait that had come from her unknown family. Was that illness the result of a genetic problem about which she would have known if she had been in contact with her birth parents? What of her plans to have several more children? Would they be so afflicted? The boy survived, more children followed, and though the question of what her genes carried that might one day affect those who came after, to her relief all were healthy and intelligent.

As with most children, and family members proud of their progeny, Mike's relatives were quick to claim as theirs most of the features of the children of him and Mary Elizabeth. Since none of those people were related to Mary Elizabeth, there were no answers as to what each child had inherited from HER side of the family. There could be no maternal Aunt Jane who was musically talented and whom the daughter "took after" and no Cousin Jim, on her side, whose nose and mouth were identical to that of any of her boys.

Still though, Mary Elizabeth could claim their brown eyes. Each one of them had been born with eyes of that color, just like hers, and no one in her husband's family shared that color.   All the while she knew there surely were other similarities with her ancestry, undiscovered as those yet were. She so much wanted one day to know of her "blood" relatives, and to claim many of the features of the birth parents she knew to have once lived, even if not now.

Do adoptees like Mary Elizabeth wake up one day and decide, "Gee, it won't rain today, so I think I'll go hunt for my birth parents?" While this might be the reality for some very few, for many, including Mary Elizabeth, their curiosity began at the moment they were told that they had been adopted and it then grew, thought by thought.

For adoptees, that need to search has been hidden for years, just beneath their level of consciousness. Then, when someone else mentions an ancestor or some genetic factor in their own background, the curiosity of the adoptee, and with it the desire to search, surfaces, is pushed aside for lack of time or knowledge, only to resurface still again.

While the interest in searching is often heightened by a marriage or the birth of a child, the age at which one actually should undertake such an odyssey, more than from any other factor probably should have to do with the emotional readiness of that individual. Though we do not always know why, some person or event of life will cause that inner voice to demand an audience. That voice will no longer be silenced or ignored, and to quiet it we can only resolve to do something about the need to know.

We sometimes feel the need to justify our desire to search by saying that we need medical information or that we need genetic information, or more emphatically, that we have a right to know. For Mary Elizabeth, the reason to search she found most compelling was simply that her need was an inevitable consequence of having been adopted.

Though we insist that you do not need a reason to seek out the truth of it all, there are several that may apply to you. P. D. Eastman's story for children entitled, *Are You My Mother?*[10] is a delightful tale about a baby bird that has fallen from his nest and sets out in search of his mother. In the story, the bird says, "I did have a mother. I know I did. I

---

[10] P. D. Eastman, *Are You My Mother?* (Random House, New York, NY 1960) p. 37

have to find her. I will. I WILL." As with many adoptees, for the little bird, it was the knowledge of the existence of a mother that demanded a search for her.

During his journey the little bird asked everyone and everything he came upon if that creature or object was his mother, since he knew nothing of her, every object was potentially she. To his disappointment, each responded, "No, I am not your mother." But unlike in the tale of the baby bird, adoptees (Mary Elizabeth included) cannot interrogate total strangers about motherhood.

Adoptees, as did the little bird, undertake searches as best they can under the circumstances. They go about their lives carefully observing and measuring the features of others, especially in public, seeking to identify some aspect or characteristic of those strangers as being similar to their own. For the want of knowing what else to do, in frustrating silence they are required to carry forth their futile examination of strangers.

Since adoptees have no visual means of connecting with those other parents, many times they create a mental picture of them; imagination has to suffice for reality. In their minds, adoptees take certain of their features and create another person whom they think would resemble that missing parent or link in our lives.

Locating those parents one day will at last provide a means of replacing the fantasies with real people. At long last, by that discovery, you will see someone who appears to you to carry some of your same features, shares your walk, your hair color, your height or your eye color. You may finally be able to see rather than continuing to wonder from whence you came. You no longer need fantasies about your birth parents, as they will then be in every sense "real" for you, as real as your adoptive parents surely are.

You may find that some of your imaginings now bring a smile. What little girl has not dreamed of being a princess? Surely awaiting you were beauty, fame, riches, jewels, beautiful dresses and fancy tea parties. As an adoptee, you were free to maintain that image so long as there remained no birth parents to prove otherwise. Pleasant as those memories were, the discovery of those parents will bring you to a new reality filled with real people and real stories.

Reason or not, there also are events that bring us to the beginning of our journey. Perhaps you have been exposed to a doorway of opportunity in your life through which you must move before it closes, just as it was with Mary Elizabeth. Or it may be that you have witnessed the success of another adoptee that has successfully completed a search. Or perhaps it was a chance meeting with a relative who encouraged or inspired you to move ahead with the task. Perhaps a friend, interested in genealogy, told you of their very interesting ancestors. Whatever the prompt, you found within yourself the fortitude, confidence, and resolve needed.

Your encouragement may not arise from any of those external causes. Instead, you may long ago have formulated a plan intended to be put into action at that point in `life when time and financial freedom so permitted. It may be that those restraints are now gone, and you feel free to move ahead.

Perhaps you will search because you cannot do otherwise. You may have achieved other of your goals that previously had prevented you from dedicating the thought and concentration required, or it may be that new information has enabled you to better know where to begin. Perhaps recent changes in the law of your state, significant or insignificant as those differences may be, have now made your task a bit easier. Maybe, your station in life or newly gained "free time" has caused you to no longer have any excuses.

There is still another and highly subjective reason for searching. That, in the last few years, has been described as "finding yourself." While this suggests that you are on a course that will bring you to a greater understanding of who and what you are, for the adoptee there is an added dimension to that journey of self-discovery.

Finding yourself requires that you know what is missing. As are we all, you are the product of the genetics passed to you when you were conceived, yet because at adoption you were severed from your history and biological family you have not had the luxury of exploring those most fundamental roots.   Further, you also are the product of the family in which you were raised, even though you well know that there is some part of you that is very unlike that family.

Just as are the manners, customs, morals, education and training that came from your adoptive parents rightfully yours, so too are your features, physical being, and yet unknown history.   That part of you has passed across a thousand generations and is yours and your birthright, just as are those aspects of your personality that came from your adoptive parents.

As you search for and find others, so too will you discover yourself.   The adventure will bring you full circle, to your origins, and back again to you.   However, the "you" will be different from before.   So, your quest for that vital and integral part of your very being-the finding of yourself-is reason enough for a search.   Finally, and no matter the other reasons, you may simply feel that in the long run you will have a better life because of your journey.

Be aware, however, that whatever your reasons or lack of the same, as you begin, throughout your search, and afterwards as well, you doubtless will be asked "why" by some people.   Providing an explanation to them may be an important and difficult step not only for increasing their understanding, but for yours as well.   In other words, explaining may help you to articulate why you must search. Tell them whatever you choose, or tell them nothing, but remember there is NOTHING wrong with you because you search.

However, except for your family and others very close to you, we believe that you need not justify or defend your desire or the actions that grow out of that need. If you are unable to articulate a more compelling reason than "I just need to know," then that should be sufficient for anyone. One adoptee who was being assisted by a social worker in her efforts to find her birth parents told of the great relief she felt when that social worker said, "You don't have to have a reason to search."

So whether you are seeking "authenticity," "closure," "wholeness," hope "to find yourself," or have the desire to find some connection to the past, is unimportant.   However you choose to label your effort, it is worthwhile, and it surely is your privilege to be about it. You cannot begin to know how a search may affect your life, but the journey is time well spent.

No matter how firm your resolve to make the journey or how demanding your reasons are, advice gained from the difficulties of others will assist you. Further, hereafter we will discuss searching from the perspective of each member of the triad in an effort to increase the understanding of all members.

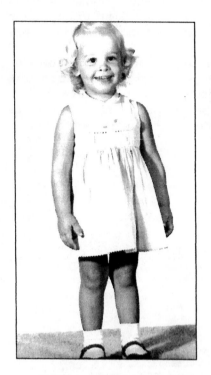

These photographs show the remarkable resemblance
between Beth at age 2-1/2 and her father Carl at age 2.

Advice To Birth Parents

"No one can make you feel
inferior without your consent."
-Eleanor Roosevelt

Over the years, the remorse and difficult memories and feelings of being unworthy resulting from giving up her child had diminished for Barbara. Time heals, though slowly and incompletely.

She early had learned that she could be more comfortable if she would be careful to leave those past actions neatly tucked away in the recesses of her mind. Little by little, and knowing well that she could not alter that past, she had come to resign herself to her life as it was and to her plans and hopes for the future.

Nevertheless, she frequently thought of that "little girl" even though more than forty long years, a lifetime almost, had passed since she had given the child over to those unknown strangers. Barbara often wondered, "How much did that girl resemble her other children? Where had she ended up? Had her birthdays and holidays been pleasant ones?" Had those other people, whoever they were, proved themselves able and willing to love and care for that little girl for all of these years?

Since Barbara had other daughters, she surely knew the strong love and deep, perhaps even primordial, feelings shared by a mother and her children, and she wondered if that child had sensed any of those mysterious bonds. Over it all, the thought occasionally and rather abruptly came upon her that she had always had within herself enough love and affection to share with yet another child and another and another still. Despite such disarming thoughts, she knew that it was too, too late for such a lifetime of sharing love and affection with that one little girl; that child she had given away now was in her forties or, God forbid, might even be dead.

Barbara had concerned herself with what others thought of her and had lived her life accordingly. She tried to be "good" in the eyes of all, and had never revealed even a hint of that episode of her life; not even to her past husband or her only sister, and even her parents had died with no knowledge of that saddening event. Even though she believed that she usually had succeeded in her efforts to carry herself to be a total lady, still the memories persisted. She was often called upon to remind herself of the adage, "To err is to be human."

In addition to the usual hurdles and challenges of marriage and of raising a family, there had been emotional problems for her, as well. Her ways of dealing with those had not been the best ways. She knew that she had sabotaged her personal growth so she could at times remain in that numbing state of denial about her past.

As she grew older, thoughts of the daughter she gave away were becoming more frequent, and no matter how she tried, she could no longer put those thoughts out of her mind. She wondered if giving that daughter up for adoption had brought harm to or been terribly unfair to the child, and she prayed that it had not. Over the years, she also had known a measure of guilt for having maintained this secret and also for having sought to put the child and the conditions of her birth in the quiet past. So many regrets.

Something within her had changed so much so that it frightened her, and she felt anxious as she thought about her plan. Barbara knew that she had to weigh her own need to tell someone against her fears that to do so might bring even greater pain to her than that felt for the concealment of it all. Should she now risk gathering support and assurances at the expense of providing an opportunity for those around her to ask what may be very uncomfortable questions about her past?

What would the future bring? Would she ever see that child again? Would that child want to see her after she had given her away? Would a search bring the birth father into her life once again, allowing him another opportunity to reject her? Before she could think about searching, she knew that still another task was imminent.

Now she was again married, and to a totally kind and good man. George was different than most men she knew. His business had taken him to many places and he had developed a broad perspective of life. He was tolerant, understanding and oh, so patient with her.

As a result of his love and acceptance of her, she had found the courage to approach her demons. It had not been easy, living with the blame, guilt, and shame that had accompanied her over the long years. Though those painful feelings were uncomfortable, they were familiar. She had come to wonder how she could ever part with those.

Her other children were adults, and she and George were alone one particular evening. Barbara's thoughts had been particularly troubling for a few days, so with fear and trepidation she resolved to tell him all, no matter the consequences.

With trembling voice, she told him the story. Of fear when she learned she was pregnant out of wedlock, of the man who was unwilling to assist her with her difficult decision, and of the beautiful little girl she had given up for adoption. George remained calm, supportive, and understanding, traits that for most take years to develop and, for some others are never learned. Despite feeling like that "bad girl" from her past, she hoped that he would love her anyway.

Her hope was realized. The emotions she had tried desperately to keep hidden for so long begun to overwhelm her. Though she could share this secret with no one else, what a relief she felt at being able to share it with him! How important his loving acceptance of the situation would be.

Though fortified by his quiet acceptance, she was unprepared for what followed. George arose from his chair and returned a moment later with the telephone. He said, "There will be no more secrets in this family. You need to call the children." Wisdom and understanding that few possess, surely.

Panic came over Barbara. Telling George had been difficult enough, but telling anyone else had not been part of her original plan. How could she tell the children after keeping these secrets from them for all of their years? What would they think of her now? How would her mistakes now affect THEIR lives and her vital relationships with them? She wondered if they would still love her.

She had tried to be a good role model to her children. Would they think that she had deceived them? She knew that very few children consider their parents to be perfect, but how many children would understand that their mother had failed to ever mention and had given away one of their sisters? And beyond those concerns, what would follow? Would she risk the love and support of her family only to find a stranger who would have nothing to do with her or worse?

Though similar concerns may be at play for a birth father, surely Barbara, with her secret, is in the company of many other birth mothers. The fundamental—the core—question that she and all others like her must address sooner or later is whether or not she is ready to face the challenges of bringing the past back into her present and somewhat predictable life.

In answering that question, we feel you should follow your own Guiding Star; do as YOU know best for you, and not any less for that missing child. As you feel confident in so doing, open all the doors you can, all the while remembering that so long as you are kind and honest, you are not responsible for the feelings of others, only for your own.

As was Barbara, you must also consider exploring the past in order to move forward. Without coming to grips with the emotional hurdles that have been accumulated over your years, moving forward will be difficult. It will be as though driving with the parking brake engaged. These re-considerations may be accomplished at any time during your search preparation or effort and likely will continue throughout your efforts and even long beyond.

Moreover, even if you do not plan to search, as a birth parent you should steel yourself to the possibility that some day you may be found by that child. Whatever planning and thought you now dedicate to those old problems may be vital to all following an appearance of that long missing child.

Your journey of emotional preparedness first begins, as it did for Barbara, when you realize the need to share your secrets with those close to you. Upon that realization, you next must give careful and long consideration to those difficulties and that discomfort that you may bring upon others through such revelations. Those will have to be resolved as you move forward.

Next, you must again give thought to the decision those years ago to give up the child, how it may have affected that child, and also of the role played by others when you made that choice. Finally, and equal to the incongruity of deliberately seeking the painful past are the fears that you may not be able to cope adequately with the future that awaits you. Those fears also must be conquered.

Just as we all would be, Barbara was unable to consider all of these problems simultaneously. So, let us investigate each of those, just as she did.

WHOM TO TELL AND HOW TO TELL THEM

Once Barbara has made the decision to search, probably the most pressing and immediate problem for her (and for most women) is a consideration of the feelings and reactions of her husband, George, upon learning of that birth those years before. All women who have faced this prospect know her concern and fears as to his response. Fortunately for Barbara (and Mary Elizabeth), she and George were able to cross that hurdle.

What if you are the father who is preparing to search? The same advice is applicable to you, but we will continue with our story of Barbara.

Pretend that she is you. If you have previously revealed that birth to your mate, you have a distinct advantage, and you need now but tell him that you are prepared to move ahead with a search. But suppose he has no notion of the existence of the child.

In attempting to speak to that tedious prospect, we suggest that most marriages will fall within two categories. One, where you and this man have had an understanding relationship over the course of your years together, and you each have at least occasionally confided in and sought the help of the other.

The other category is where the marriage or relationship has been or is somewhat strained from time to time, and is held together in considerable measure by the existence of children or by some other facts of their lives together. So, in which group did Barbara and George belong? Her approach to her mate concerning this secret will be very different, almost totally unique to him, depending upon that single answer.

Still though, while his support and understanding surely are the desired results, no matter what, Barbara had to reveal the truth of it all to George, even if she told no one else. Why? Because, if he does not understand, she yet must make the decision as to whether or not to begin a search, and if he does or will understand, her decision is a much easier one.

So, in which group do you and YOUR mate belong? If you are our Barbara, we feel that you must tell him, and do so in a straightforward, honest and caring fashion. (Here is the one place where the situation may truly be difficult and complicated.) You here must seek to understand the needs of the male manner of thinking, and if you find you cannot do so, you must at least seek to bridge the gap between the two of you.

Having revealed the birth, our advice would be to at once continue on by telling him, as best you can, why you have been unable to talk about it, why you have had to keep it to yourself these years, and why you were so very afraid to speak out. (He may need the reasons, every one of those.)

If it is true with you, you might reveal how you were advised those years ago to totally put the experience from your mind, and you attempted to do just that. IF it is true, you also should tell him that your regrets, pain, and loss weighed so heavily upon you that you thought yourself unable ever to articulate your feelings to him or to anyone else on earth. And you felt rightly or wrongly that he too should be excluded from knowledge of that event. If, in fact, it is true, reveal to him further that you feared that upon learning of that birth he would think less of you or come to believe that you were and are not truly his.

Perhaps none of these were and are your reasons, but this recital of the thoughts of others may have served as a reminder of your own motivations during those very difficult days and weeks of your life. So, search your soul and seek to uncover those true reasons that drove you to those years of secrecy, especially as to your mate.

If, after all your thoughts, you are unsure of your reasons for having kept the whole matter to yourself, then that is all right too. Simply reveal to him that you do not know why. Tell of the rush of confusion, concern, and fear of the unknown upon learning of your pregnancy. Go on to relate that you truly do not now know what your thoughts were at that time or in the years since then, and that it well may be that you now would respond differently, especially if you then had the confidence in him that you now feel.

Be certain that he will need assurances that you did not ever intend to be deceptive. You may choose to relate to him, in the simplest of terms, that it was concern for your relationship with him that led you to these measures; you simply did not want to hurt him in any way.

In all likelihood, he will want to know about the father of this child, but at the same time, he will need reassurances that he is more important to you than ANY man, especially the one who fathered this child. Be guarded; chose your words carefully, and tell him no more than he truly needs to know. Perhaps more than at any other time, you now must be perceptive of his needs as your life-mate. Your reassurances in the matter will help to ensure his receptiveness to your need to search.

You will need to be able to draw upon the strength of your relationship with him to carry you through the search. While the day may come when your needs to find the child are foremost in your thoughts and purpose, that day and time is not now.

If he objects, and yet you are firm in your desire to search, you may be called upon to exercise more tact and diplomacy with him than ever before. Still though, and despite his objections, no matter how threatening of your happiness, the decision must be yours, and you must make it in light of both the pleasures and the consequences that might arise by reason of your choice. In that deliberation and decision, remember that you likely know him better than anyone else. But, you also know yourself better than does the rest of the world.

Now, to the question of how you might best cope with the difficulties in revealing the truth to your children. Remember Barbara? She had seen to a measure of religious training for her children. She had been herself, rather active in her community, or at least involved in the activities of her mate and her children. Over the years, she had maintained a solid and communicative relationship with them. As do virtually all parents, she had made mistakes and used those as a basis for advice and forewarnings.

She had discussed the perils of pre-marital sex with her children, and she now must tell them that her advice as to that difficult matter, as with all of her other explanations of life, arose from the experiences of her past. She needs to now remind the children that our status as parents does not render us exempt from error, both now and in the past.

Hopefully, when you are called on to have this discussion; you will have paved the way for such openness and confession. If not, you must proceed anyway. Why? You are in the process of preparing not only yourself, but also those around you for a reunion. You need, at the least, their acceptance, and at the most, their support, encouragement and reassurances.

Whether you are telling a son or a daughter or both, approach this as an opportunity to teach them still another lesson of life. In all instances, be candid and forthright.

Throughout your explanations with the children (and all others, for that matter), you must remember and remind them that your pregnancy those years ago, with all the attendant problems, is not now the issue. Whatever the causes or reasons for that event, and no matter who had a part in the decisions then made, the children must understand that you now need and want to search for that other child. Many have found that their children, more than almost any other people, best understood their desire to search for this missing member of the family.

Perhaps those in your life are threatened by this revelation or by your search and you are afraid you will lose them. Could your request to be reunited with one of your children be oppressive in any way? You are not asking for the moon. All you ask of them is possibly their support. Surely that is not too much to ask.

What if one or some of your children object? You must decide if their desires in the matter are of greater significance to you than is your own desire to locate that missing child. Perhaps your child may not perceive you as other than their mother and may not see you as a person, a woman who feels the need to do something just for you.

So, then, whom else will you tell? It has been our experience that most women have decided not to tell their parents about the child they gave up and any decision to search for him or her, whether or not those parents had prior knowledge of the child's birth those years before. Still, you alone must decide whether or not to include them among those who are to know of your effort. Of those women who have chosen to inform their parents, most have waited to do so until the child was found.

You will need to make this decision, depending entirely upon whether or not you feel they will be receptive or at least not be a deterrent to your efforts. We suggest that the support of your parents, or lack of the same, should not be the decisive factor as to whether or not you undertake a search. It is not their lives that are likely to be drastically affected; it is the lives of you and of that missing child.

Similarly, whether or not to discuss the matter with your clergyman, siblings, confidantes, or good friends are decisions you alone must make. The fundamental question to ask yourself is, "Whose business is it?" The answer again is yours to determine.

However, in any of the situation described, the advice of a counselor, skilled in matters of adoptions may benefit you and all others involved, particularly when difficulties. We believe further discussion of therapy is beyond the scope of this work. Perhaps you should consider a support group, since they likely will understand the questions that confront you better than anyone known to you. Consider also that your close friends are or may be that support group, particularly if one is not available in your area.

So, carefully consider with whom you will share your plan, if anyone, and pick only those who will encourage or help you. You need NO discouragement at this time in your life. Be very selective, and in that selection note also that those folks, just as you, must maintain total secrecy while you search. Why? Because almost certainly you do not want that child to learn of you before you have completely prepared for a reunion.

JOURNEY INTO THE PAST

The business of adoption is preempted by a single decision. It is surely this decision that brings you here. As a birth parent, it is also likely that more than enough emotional baggage remains with you today because you decided years ago to give a child over to the system of adoption.

Attempting to forget that time of your life, you probably buried many feelings and emotions. Excavate, if you are able, those feelings you had as you made your decision to give up your child. Go back in time to the moment you knew you were pregnant (or when you discovered your mate was pregnant). Try to remember what you were feeling as you began the process of deciding whether or not to keep your child.

For your sake, you should begin a journal, a very personal journal where you will write down your most private thoughts. It is our hope that with this journey into the past, you will see how your decision and thoughts thereof have affected your perceptions and continue to impact your approach to the future. It has been said, "We write not to be understood, but to understand." And so it is for you. Though time-consuming, whether emotionally or otherwise difficult, it is our view that you will benefit greatly through such efforts.

It is important to try to recall your thoughts of yourself, of others and of the world in which you lived during those days when you pondered the decision to give up your child. So, let us consider some of the questions since your answers may reveal to you the reasons for which you did what you did. You will be well served if you take the time needed to now consider these questions and critical issues.

First, consider for a moment the magnitude of your decision. You likely had no idea how much this one choice would so vastly affect your life and no less, the life of your child, not to mention the lives of many others. Consider how the course of the life of that child and all of her descendents turned on the effects of that decision. It not only affected where and with whom she would live and altered who she would become, but it changed her children and their families forever. It was the most significant decision having to do with Mary Elizabeth's life and perhaps Barbara's, as well. Speaking in terms of cause and effect, everything else and every other decision you have made paled in comparison.

You must prepare yourself for the reactions of the child whom you seek, be those pleasing to you or not so. They had no choice or say in the decisions that were to affect the entire balance of their lives.

For the many who have lived with the feelings of having been given away by the first person that knew them, they will want to know why the keeping of them would have been so difficult. They must now know if they themselves were the reason, or if their surrender to outsiders, instead, was by reason of other and very powerful influences and circumstances. Perhaps the child was the manifestation of violations of a number of the rules of the society of her time. For these reasons and for the reality of curiosity about one's past, you should be prepared to consider this question of "why" whether you plan to search or are the one sought.

Without doubt there were many factors that brought your decision those years ago. No matter those reasons for having done so, or the fact that at the time those seemed valid and sufficient cause to you, or were at least acceptable, think through those again and prepare to set those out early in any relationship that may be renewed. While doing so; let us suggest some further matters for thought.

As you think through the past, do you now feel that you were a victim, prevented from being able to keep your child, or powerless to control the situation? Should someone else really be blamed for the decisions you were constrained to make? Or do you think that you were provided several solutions, and that you chose the one alternative that you then found the most tolerable?

While outside forces may indeed have been very powerful, you must again consider the steps you took in gaining help, legal or otherwise and which, if any, of the suggestions of others influenced you. In all such matters you must be honest with yourself as you differentiate those choices made by you from those made by others.

Continue to look to the past as you remember how things were then. Did your pregnancy compromise your standing in a particular religious or social setting? Was your decision affected by economic concerns? What pressures did you feel concerning how others would view you, whatever your choice? Of what or as to whom were you afraid? Perhaps it was that society (the neighbors, the women at church, or your co-workers) would discover what you had done. Or perhaps you were afraid that you would disappoint your parents. We suspect that your decision was influenced to a great extent by many of those around you, some without your realization.

As a result of any compromise you may have made for the sake of someone else, have you now or then felt a measure of guilt as a result of giving over a child to maintain the status quo? Trying to be perceived as being good in the eyes of all is a heavy burden for anyone to bear. For Barbara, she had believed that she had violated the rules of her society, and that the exposure of that breach of the rules would have rendered her a social outcast.

Who helped you make the original decision? Why did you confide in that person (or persons) to the exclusion of others? What other facts must you now consider in order to prepare yourself to disclose the secret to the ones from whom you withheld the facts initially? Remember that some of those folks will need to know why you so withheld the truths of it all.

For better or for worse, you were and remain a product of your own society and time, and any or all of those concerns mentioned were reasonable thoughts of the moment, no matter your choices made as a result of those pressures.

If you kept the secret from your parents, in order to have a long term reunion with your child you will soon need to prepare to or reveal the discovery of the child or his or her discovery of you. Again, by telling your parents and siblings and some others of the truth, you will experience a great relief and a healing unequalled in your life.

You may have been able to avoid telling certain other people those years ago, and yet now find that you feel an obligation to clear the air with those people, whoever they may be, and thus commence many relationships all over again. In short, we firmly believe that should you search or be the person found, continuing to keep secrets from those close to you must cease. If you think you have explored the above areas sufficiently, next consider the father of your child.

Perhaps your child was the result of an unfortunate liaison, a one-night stand, or even worse yet, a rape. If you are the birth mother, you were the one who had to solely bear the physical stigma of a pregnancy that required two to conceive. Some circumstances may have indeed been beyond your control, yet you were the one left not only with a critical decision to make about the child you were left carrying, but also with the emotional scars from the incident.

Force yourself to recall the nature of your relationship with that father. What if rape or incest were factors? What part did he truly play in your decision, if any at all? How do you now feel about him? Perhaps you are angry with him or you feel that he rejected or rebuffed you or you have no thoughts whatsoever as to that man. Perhaps you have felt much resentment because he was able to walk away from that situation to which he equally contributed. Perhaps both of you made the difficult decision together. On the other hand, perhaps you experienced dual losses because you lost him as well as your child.

If given the opportunity, what would you wish to say to the father of your child? Perhaps you hoped that you would never have to see him or even hear his name again. Perhaps you should write a letter, which you should not plan to mail, telling him how you feel about the decisions he made, with or without you. We hope thereby that you will become more comfortable with your thoughts as to his role in that whole experience. We think that as a pre-requisite to a search, if you have not already done so, you must come to grips with your concerns and memories of him. Once again, this may be a place where you need to consider counseling.

Much of this consideration will be the material of your discussions with that child. Whether you relish the thought or not, upon reunion and almost without exception, adopted children will have a deep and natural curiosity about that sire and who and what he was.

Enough questions for the moment. For many, it has been safer emotionally because you have not been required to think about so many issues. If in fact, like Barbara, you were assured that your actions and child would remain strictly confidential, and that you should forget that you surrendered a child. If you believed this to be true, you likely carefully avoided confronting many of these matters. You are not at fault for so relying.

Still though, the truth is and was that secrecy could not be assured, and any mother who felt that her secret was safe, now must presume quite the opposite. The stark reality is that if you are a birth mother who surrendered your child, you should expect to be found. It is for this reason that we have suggested you review the past as part of your preparation for the fact that you may be discovered. However you feel about it, the past is part of who you have become, you can not bury it, and you must not allow it to prevent you from moving to the future, yours and that of your child.

In an ideal world, a mature unwed mother would not be ashamed of being pregnant to the same extent that she was just three decades ago. She now very often may love, care for, and raise her child by her own means and within her circle of supportive family and friends. But for Barbara and many like her, the society of her day failed to offer that support. Times have changed, albeit hardly perceivable at times.

While we realize that the future may reveal that those you did not tell might have helped and not had the attitude you feared, your decision was nonetheless based upon your interpretations of the situation at that time. You must recall that it was you in no small measure that limited the participation of others in your decision-making, and thus it is that you might feel constrained, as mentioned, to answer to those who were excluded from such knowledge.

Though we charge most women with the responsibility of having made their own decisions, often however, because they were so young or because of extreme outside pressures or influences beyond their capacity to cope, for all practical matters they had no choice in the decision. You may be one of the women who confided in her parents, hoping for wisdom and guidance in making this difficult decision, only to be faced with an ultimatum that you simply must not consider keeping your child.

Regardless of the circumstances, as you decide to share your secret to some extent, you may have certain hopes of or expectations in others in whom you now feel you should confide. In an ideal world, those who we might now tell would assure us of their love.

We know of a birth mother who found her grown daughter. She then came to the realization that for their sake and her own, she must reveal that reunion to her parents. Though she had excluded them from knowing of her pregnancy when the child was born those years before, she now had a deep desire and need. She wanted them to accept the child as one of their own, even though it was by this time nineteen years old.

She needed her parents to tell her that their love would continue as before. She hoped that they would understand that at the time of the birth she thought they would in no way welcome this child. It was not her desire ever to be deceptive, rather it was her need to protect those parents that caused her to exclude them from knowledge of the impending birth.

In our less than perfect world though, you are bound to feel remorse and regret. Despite those feelings, you must face the realization that the mistakes of the past cannot be undone. The decisions made by you and by others took place in another time and under rules that to a greater or lesser degree differed from now. As you develop a plan for your search, realizing that you were born into a different set of influences and attitudes will arm you with the emotional strength necessary to face the challenges having to do with that search, especially as those relate to attitudes toward births outside of marriages.

So, the rules now are a bit different for most. The greater permissiveness of today allows us to discard many of those old and more restrictive requirements of society. If those old ideas are to be discarded, though, you must CHOOSE to do so and thus find freedom to move ahead.

As you, the birth mother, again consider those earlier times, in addition to addressing your feelings about the father in a letter, you will do well to make a list of your disappointments and regrets. That small effort, though it will take some time, will cause you to truly THINK about what it was that happened to you and the child. Place on that list everyone, dead or alive, whom you feel rightly should share the blame by reason of any part that person played in the event. Notice that if you too should assume some of the fault, then do so, and add your own name to that list.

Blame anyone you wish, but in the final analysis, whether you were influenced by your parents, your friends, pastor, doctor, or the society in which you lived, if you were an adult, you are the one who is ultimately responsible for the consequences of that decision. On the other hand, if you were yet young and immature, and you feel someone else is responsible, you still need to be prepared to bear the weight of your choice, no matter how unfair that may seem.

In the final analysis, it was you who gave over the child and thereby set into motion every one of the consequences down to even now. Had you not given up your child, there would have been no adoption, no adoptive parents, and no need for a search.

You must commit yourself to such self-examination, and no matter who deserves blame you must prepare to address these issues with yourself, perhaps with the child, and possibly with others after reunion.

Then you must move beyond those thoughts; the destructive feelings that someone else should be blamed for circumstances in the past, or at any time. Remember, you are no longer about the business of living in the past; you must begin to concentrate on the choices that you are willing to make available to you now and in the future.

You need have no remorse for having been required to live under a different set of rules since you are no longer bound by those rules. Just as you likely were responsible for the choice to give up a child, so are you now free to choose how you perceive yourself, how you view and interact with others, and with what attitude you will approach future challenges, all in light of the standards of today.

Next, you must move beyond presuming that your decisions in that other distant day and time have rendered you now of weaker moral fiber. Though you must explain your reasons to some, whatever those may have been, you have no duty to and should not attempt to excuse your conduct. Most importantly, life does not require that you again suffer pangs of regret and conscience.

You should charge your family with loving you regardless of their feelings related to the issue at hand. You should consider that the child you gave up likely will view your decision based on her more progressive thoughts and beliefs, and you have the right to expect that of all others. We do not suggest defiance of the ideas of others, but we do suggest that you have no further duty to answer to anyone for the past. Enough!

Let us move now to Barbara and her memories of her child's father. Unlike others who may not have unpleasant memories, Barbara did. Still, she dare not allow those thoughts to interfere with what may be a good and lasting relationship with her/their daughter. While she has no idea where the father of that child now is, or even whether or not he is yet alive, the thought that a search for her "little girl" might bring him into her life once again may be unsettling. Nevertheless, as did Mary Elizabeth, an adoptee knows that some male was her father, and she may well hope to gain knowledge of that person, just as she wanted to know of her mother.

It is because of the desire that likely resides in your child that you now must prepare to give your child his name or some means by which to find him, should she choose to do so. Remember that she experienced none of the pain that he may have brought upon you, nor should you impose that upon her.

Your entire relationship with that father those years ago is a matter of being honest with yourself and with the child. We believe that for some a very difficult dilemma is posed if you do not truly know who the father was. In that event, you now must choose between either revealing that you had sex with more than one man at the time of the pregnancy or of devising a devious scheme of untruths or half-truths in order to prevent your child from knowing that truth. It is our belief that Victorian morals should not be a factor in deciding how and what to tell about the father, and so it is that still again, you should be truthful.

In the course of this writing, we interviewed a birth mother who had told the daughter she gave away that her father was indeed a certain individual. Almost contemporaneously with that, she told another child of hers that the father of the adopted daughter instead was yet a different person. Notice that these circumstances brought to the adopted daughter the stark realization that short of paternity tests she can never be absolutely sure of her sire.

Whatever was the truth of that matter, the mother cannot now retract those words. The damage is done, the words having been spoken. We are reminded of the expression, "You can not unring a bell." So, the truth, whatever it may have been, likely would have been better.

You must consider the consequences of your actions, if through any remarks you cause that child to seek a man other than the true father. If you should choose to conceal the truth, be aware that science has advanced to the point where a man accused of being the father may readily prove that he is not.

EXCEPTIONS

In our view, there is but one set of circumstances that may require secrecy. That is incest. We think that all other knowledge that you may have of paternity should be revealed to the child, if that child seeks to know, though perhaps to no one else.

In matters of incest, you must decide whether or not any good could possibly arise from a revelation of the truth. Anticipating that the answer likely is that no one could benefit from having such knowledge, we think you must decide for yourself whether you should reveal the facts.

But our suggestion begs the question; so what do you say in the alternative? It would seem that only by stating that you do not know who the father was can you avoid subsequent questions. It is difficult for us to advise that you be less than truthful, however we think that the consequences of revealing the truth in such pregnancies might be so damaging to your extended family and posterity that this may be one secret that will require retention.

What about rape? No one with any decency would blame a woman for a rape. No matter his punishment for the crime, though, or his life thereafter, he is the father of your child. The truth of the matter may be very unsettling for you even in the event of date rape. Remember the letter we suggested you write to him? That was the place to vent your feelings, not now when your child asks for his name. She deserves to know the truth regardless of the emotional hurdle you must cross to be able to reveal that paternity.

One of the women interviewed revealed that she had become pregnant as the result of a date rape, was unmarried, had borne and raised the resulting daughter, yet at no time had she revealed to the child the nature of that conception. She simply could not bring herself to do so. As the child arrived at adulthood, her curiosity was heightened to the point that she wanted, not only the name of the birth father, but she also was insistent that she meet him face to face.

While in the event of a rape, women are justified in seeing to criminal charges, this mother chose otherwise for reasons that we think are not within the purview of this book.

Clearly, this woman had ample reason to bear the burden of emotional baggage. For this mother, the wound inflicted by the man had scabbed over, but the prospect of coming face to face with him caused that wound to reopen accompanied by much of the pain of those 20 years before. Little wonder; she had raised the child without any assistance or even word from him, and the deep resentment and anger she felt for him again came to the fore.

Nevertheless, and most admirably, she not only gave the name of the father to her child, but she said nothing to discourage her then grown child, and a search was undertaken. The father was located in a distant state and because of the daughter's trepidation at the thought of confronting her birth father, the daughter requested that the mother accompany her to a first meeting. Though this mother's mind was flooded with fears, intimidation, and deep concern over the outcome, she subordinated those fears and hesitations to her desire to support her daughter's vision of reunion.

In that reunion, she and the daughter were most successful. Still though, the mother had been called upon to overcome deep adverse thoughts and fears that she had silently carried with her across the lifetime of the daughter. Though she had hoped and so set her course as to never again lay eyes upon that despised man, she had risen above those feelings, changed that long intended course, and had been willing to sacrifice her wishes, needs, and comfort to the end that the child be fulfilled.

Some time later, she found herself able to discuss the circumstances surrounding conception with her daughter. Noble or foolish? Was there another way? The answers are difficult. Whatever her choices were, she chose a course, and though it might have been very different, that course resulted in a satisfactory relationship for the daughter.

SEARCHES BY BIRTH FATHERS

As to searches by birth fathers, unlike with a birth mother, the first question that arises in the mind of the birth father is "Am I, in truth, the father of that child?" If for any reason, he thinks he is not, then as suggested medical science has developed adequate tools to make that determination. You need but consult your physician who will surely know of such tests. All men should remember that there is no reason why a child should be imposed with the burden of proving paternity, and that in all decency that obligation falls upon the man so charged.

A birth father must also consider what that birth mother might have said about him since that child will probably have found her first. If you are that man and your child or the birth mother are either together or have enjoyed a reunion, then you may expect that some measure of the mother's feelings toward you have been imparted to the child. If that mother views your conduct as reprehensible you should not expect that the attitude of the child would be much different, at least at first. However, it is the duty of the searcher to enter into such a search with an open mind, as much unfettered by preconceived notions as possible.

We know of one son who was mature, accomplished, and very successful, and who set out to locate his birth father after having been raised by his mother. Though that mother had (and perhaps rightly so) nothing good to say about the father, she might have admitted of the possibility that perhaps his character had improved as the years mellowed him, as it does us all. Nevertheless, he persevered in his search.

The story ends well. Though he entered upon the search with some indifference across the years, the numerous contacts that followed brought to the son a measure of compassion and understanding for the man who brought about his birth. Similarly, the father was much rewarded to know of his accomplished heir and new friend. At the death of the father, the son came away knowing that there had been reasons for the absence of those many years, and that those former difficulties could and should be left where found, in the deep black of the past.

If on the other hand, the birth mother and the child do not know each other and the child is unaffected by her stories of you, as a father you now have a duty to realize that the mother also may have mellowed over the years. Any stories you tell the child must be tempered by the reality that with age comes differences in attitudes.

Thus it is, and without exception, that you must approach that child in absolute and total honesty about what you have done and your reasons for so doing; as a father, such honesty is an absolute duty of yours, no matter how painful or self-deprecating. Your child has been without you for many years and though it may not have been your fault he or she may well blame you for that estrangement. So be it.

As with all others of us, your life was dictated by the rules of your generation, however tolerance for men who do not see to the raising and well-being of their children has not increased appreciably. Though it may seem callous, if you impregnated a woman and then left the scene, no matter the reasons, that child has ample reason to blame you.

So, as with the birth mother, we suggest you search your soul, make a complete and honest list of your reasons for having not cared for and been with that child, and if the blame is yours, assume it, and prepare to relate it when you must.

IN REVIEW

In review, whether you are the father or the mother, it is time well spent revisiting the past to understand the decisions you made, how others influenced that decision, and the effects it had upon you, your child and the many other people through the years. Though you must deal with self blame and blame of others, for better or for worse, our society has become more permissive and it is within this frame of reference that you must decide who is blame-worthy and who is not.

So too must you judge yourself, not by the rules of 1950, but by those of the twenty-first century. One hundred years ago, it seems that society was less accepting of a child that had been born out of wedlock, and yet it seems obvious that we should judge our children under the rules of our day. Some of the rules and attitudes by which a birth mother was known as a "bad girl" in 1950 simply do not apply now. Nevertheless, revisit those views of the past and prepare yourself for the questions you will encounter by those important to you, including your once adopted child.

In our day, it is necessary that you also undertake the business of extending forgiveness and of setting aside blame you have placed on others. We think such an adjustment of attitudes is very much a part of your preparation for reunion.

Forgiveness is a difficult concept, and we believe that you must forgive and abandon whatever bad feelings you have for others, not for their sake but in order that you may free yourself from painful past moments. More often than not, you forgive others for your own sake.

Remember the list you made of those, including yourself, whom you felt worthy of blame? It is now time to overlook or put aside the actions or inaction of everyone on that list, and equally also of yourself. The point of this exercise is to move out of the past with your thoughts and into a future where you are free and no longer bound by thoughts of blame, guilt or ill will. Whether in the future or now, you hold the key to allowing yourself to replace the inaccurate and unhealthy thoughts and beliefs with those that are more appropriate and conducive to your emotional health.

As we have mentioned earlier, a choice was made years ago and who did what to whom is no longer important. Your feelings of regret, remorse, or resentment have no place in your life if you are to undertake the efforts required of you. You need to begin the process of repainting the canvas of your life in order that it conform to how you will view it in the future.

FACING FEARS

As a birth parent, along with the challenges of returning to the distant past to the time when you gave your child up for adoption, you have hopefully now realized that while you can not change the past, you are able to alter the effects it has upon you. When the portrait of your future is painted, how will it appear?

Will you be the woman in the background, hiding behind her husband, children and others in her life whose needs she allows to supercede her own? Will you be the man pictured alone because he is unable to form or maintain attachments in life? Will you be a meek woman cringing with fear, frustrated and overshadowed by society and the figures in your life to which you, even as an adult must still look for guidance? Will you be the man shown amidst a huge gathering of people because he has decided it should be that way, or will you choose to be the woman in the picture shown basking in her abilities and ready to face the world? Which will it be?

Whether you are man or woman, birth father or birth mother, the choice really is yours to make. And you alone must make that choice.

As you explored the past, what images remain? Were your thoughts of yourself, confused by the prospect of leaving your infant child with unknown others in exchange for continued acceptance within your social circles? Perhaps in that past you were limited in your choices by the restrictions of that society. Perhaps in the recent past, you have been limited and frustrated by the closed file. Perhaps your fear of rejection has painted you into a corner, there to gain refuge from your fears of seeking out your child.

Some of the images you have painted, albeit mistakenly by reason of ignorance or fear, you can now begin to paint over. In the past, the canvas of your life was cluttered, clumsily drawn because the rules made it impossible to for you to depict your past in any other manner. Your palette may have been limited, and being yet young you were constrained, as you would have been if you were painting by number. Someone else decided for you the colors you would use and the pattern you would follow. You felt it necessary to stay within the lines, the boundaries of those who held domain over you. And so it was, and because you could not do otherwise, you followed the rules.

As discussed earlier, those constraints are no longer at play. You are now at liberty to paint as you choose, with an unlimited choice of colors and with a new design in mind.

Still though, you must choose to do so; you must pick up your brush and commence the task. Painting that new picture signifies facing your fears. Determination is your brush; with it changes can be made.

Some of the most confident of people have fears, but the difference between such frightened folks and those not fearful is the capacity they have developed to deal with those fears. Have you been amazed at the capability of some people to assume great risks?   Risks are measured through the perceptions of the risk taker. You now have before you a risk. Will you run from it or will you embrace the challenge and face it down?   It can hardly be doubted that you minimize that risk by continuing to prepare yourself for it.

Look for the reasons why you have allowed fears to creep into your thoughts. While some of those likely are realistic and healthy, have you allowed yourself to be ruled by other fears that nearly paralyze you from further action? Asked a different way, when you think of searching for that child you gave over to the system, are any of those fears destructive of your incentive to move forward?

So, what are those fears? Is it revealing or recalling the past that prevents you from taking the next step forward? Are you afraid of telling your spouse? Your children? Your parents? Do you fear the probability that your friends, past and present, will learn of your search, look askance at your efforts, and ask embarrassing questions concerning your motives?

Whether any of these concerns are barricades to your efforts or there be still others, you must address and defeat each such hurdle. You must ferret from your inner self any and all causes for hesitancy, and address each, one at a time.

A few more paragraphs having to do with your inner thoughts are appropriate. As you commence your search planning, you should realize that no matter where you fall in the triad, you almost surely will experience emotional highs and lows.

Exemplifying that fact is the true experience of a birth mother who successfully undertook to find her daughter. She had given birth at age twenty, given up the child to adoption, later married the natural father, had another child by the same man, and across the following eighteen years had discussed the birth and that first child with not one person, not even her husband, the father of her child.

Those nearly two decades of suppressed and deep feelings came to the fore of her thoughts quite unexpectedly while she was attending a religious event. She was being attentive to the happenings there and had no awareness of her deep regard for the child. Quite abruptly and much to the concern of the parishioners seated near her, without intention and to her complete surprise, she burst into tears. Through that deeply emotional experience, she succeeded in replacing the long years of pain with feelings of utter peacefulness. That few minutes of release provided for her the strength and resolution needed to find her child.

Similarly, for Barbara an admission to her family and the feelings of cleansing that those confessions brought gave her the strength to search. Over the decades she had spent much energy and subterfuge in hiding her thoughts, feelings, and emotions. Releasing those emotions through discussions with her immediate family permitted her to go forward, at last free of the fear of exposure.

So, listen carefully to your inner self and its requests that you search. If you will but close your eyes and listen, that conscience or soul, or whatever it may be, will reveal your fears to you, and by helping you understand yourself, will aid you mightily in defeating those concerns. Sit quietly by yourself and try such self-examination. We think you will come away knowing more of the nature of the fears and concerns and be better armed to conquer those.

We again suggest that a sincere effort to articulate a problem with precision will provide for you most of the solution to that difficulty. So examine very carefully with us some of the fears that we think stand in your way. In addition to the fears of which we spoke, consider the following.

We think that your most dominant fears are those of rejection and of failure. We believe those two fears to be quite distinct, each from the other.

The components of rejection arise out of our desires to please others, and also from our concern that we have fallen short in the past. A birth mother may feel strongly that by having given up her child, she will be rejected. After all, some think, "I should not have gotten pregnant, and when I did I should have cared for and raised my child." At the very core of this problem is that we do not feel that the rules of society have changed enough, or that the influences of society have yet rendered our conduct acceptable to the world and especially to our child.

Because we think that is a dominant thought in the vast world, we are afraid because we simply do not want to once again be stigmatized and to relive memories of those events. Since we do not know if that child will be willing or able to cope with the past, we can only fear that prospect of rejection.

In keeping with those fears, you likely have or will steel yourself to the possibility that the child may not want to know or associate with you. We urge you to accept that many adoptees have wondered who their birth parents were, and will at least want to investigate the possibility of future pleasant relationships, no matter the past.

As desperately as Barbara needed to know of the well-being of that little girl whom she could not raise, she also feared that that child would not want to have anything whatsoever to do with her. Just as she had rejected that child, so too was she afraid that the child would now reject her. Birth fathers are in the same position, especially where the birth mother places the blame for the whole of the event at his feet. We believe it is obvious that such concern for the possibility of rejection can serve only to defeat your search.

Sure, you might be rejected, but what have you lost? Rather than facing failure, is it safer to make no efforts to succeed? Of course not! Adopt a pragmatic approach. If rejection is in the future, so be it. You will be rewarded by whatever you learn and will gain closure concerning who and where that child is and has become.

Akin to the fear of failure is the fear of success. You may be confronted with and be called upon to deal with quite unknown, new, and difficult circumstances and will be required to cope with such. Though you may perceive your present life to be one of uniform mediocrity, you also may imagine that your present life is better than what may come. You may fear that the introduction of those people into your life will be a Pandora's Box. While that may be a realistic fear, you must remember that to be found at the bottom of Pandora's Box was Hope.

CONFIDENCE IN YOUR ABILITY TO COPE

How do you bring yourself to believe that whatever lies at the end of your route, you will go there still? One thing is for sure, if you do not undertake the risks, you will never know.

You must resolve that whatever the results, you will accept the consequences, since at the least some of your decades-old questions will have been answered. You must resolve that the effects that will be visited upon you will be insignificant and outweighed by the benefits of finding the child, or at least learning something more than you now know about her life.

As to that most powerful of fears, that of rejection, you have and will be able to conjure up ample reason for assuming that your past actions rendered you undesirable to the extent that you should not—can not—move ahead. As to that conclusion, we can only say that you have a duty to yourself and to your child to understand that it matters almost not at all who or what you were.

The child's need and hope for success in a search may be equal to your own. Further, and just as you would, soon after reunion your child may desire and need an apology of sorts. Along with that apology or very soon thereafter he or she also might need a simple explanation for your actions that so affected that child for his or her entire life. Finally, your child may need words that reveal your realization that the problems experienced by him or her are every bit as significant as any of your own.

You will not be able to convince everyone that what you are doing or have done should now be considered acceptable. Again, not all problems can be set right to all people, and some ill feelings may remain. We only suggest that you must NOW reject such ill feelings as hurdles for your search. Do not allow others, no matter their place in your life, to sabotage or undermine any plans you have formulated.

POTENTIAL OBSTACLES

Notice that a lack of sufficient funds is too often used as an excuse for inaction and as a crutch to shore up a decision to delay. In fact, as revealed in the chapters having to do with the mechanics of a search, there is no reason to spend great sums, and many have successfully searched with only a minimum of resources. The matter of a shortage of extra disposable sums is really but one more escape from your fears. You may have to move more slowly than otherwise, but virtually everyone can afford to do a search with a little budget planning.

Also lack of extra time is not a reason for delay. Even if it is minimal, a search requires a determination of what sum of money may be used over what number of months, and calculating that amount of time you can extract from your other projects and duties. We say simply that we all find time to do the things we really want to do, and that money is a manner of spending what you can and no more.

Moreover, you can no longer use a lack of know-how as a reason for procrastination. This little book in your hands deprives you of that excuse.

Then again, that your yet undiscovered child may be of a different station in life is no reason at all. No matter the social position in life or the affluence or lack of it now enjoyed by either you or that child, you must know that whatever measure of such either has is quite without importance. Would you decline to associate with any other member of your family because they have more or less wealth and recognition that have you? Over and beyond that concern over station in life is the possibility that your child may be found so undesirable or repugnant that a relationship is intolerable to you. In short, your search should have nothing to do with money and status. In that regard, remember that not all children turned out well, and some not at all.

What if you do not want to be found? Have you not yet remaining a duty to provide knowledge of that child's medical and ancestral history? Those facts can in NO way bring harm to you, and yet may be of the utmost value to the child.

Then too, a picture or a memento would be nice as gifts. These small gestures, you owe to your child.

In addition, it may be that your child will refuse to have any relationship whatever with you. The life of that offspring of yours may be full, complete, and quite satisfactory, and he or she simply may choose not to include you. Only by presenting yourself to that offspring gently and with humility, can that child make any decision whatever about you and that may be immediate or otherwise.

So, upon your appearance in the life of your child you likely will learn whether you will be accepted or rejected or somewhere in between. Your own actions and display of understanding of the child's fears and concerns about you will do much to determine the course of that and future meetings. Just as your actions led to the separation, so too almost surely will your actions determine the course of the future and of any continuing relationship that is created.

Finally, there are yet a couple of other important thoughts to remember. Even if you succeed and develop a cordial and affectionate relationship, you should know that it might never be one of mother and child, except to you. You must realize that your child simply may not want another mother. Having been raised by whomever else, that child may have no emotional space for still another "Mom." Your child likely addresses another couple as "Mom and Dad," and you should be happy that such was his or her destiny.

Do you hope that your child lived a full life? If so, you should continue to want the best for them, no matter your future relationship.

Enough negatives. We have suggested those possibilities in order that you are prepared. Do not be discouraged, for the most likely result is that you and the child will find some measure of solace, closure, and enjoyment in the reunion. Most have so found, and have gone on then to develop casual relationships in which both feel secure in who and what they have and are, and are able to continue with their separate lives, greatly enriched by the whole experience.

So, you have a child with whom, until now, you have not been in contact for many years. Though he or she often has occupied your mind, until now you have not had the freedom or the courage to add him or her to your life's story, to your canvas.

Though separate and distinct, adoptive parents have problems not unlike your own. Perhaps understanding the problems attendant upon adoption by other than birth parents is deserving of explanation.

As a young child, it never occurred to Beth that she bore no resemblance to her brother, who also was adopted.

Advice To Adoptive Parents

Though being a parent is not an easy job, the Kurtz couple was happy with their young family. They changed diapers, wiped runny noses, bandaged knees, and stayed up late at night when their children were hungry or sick. Later they had incurred the added expenses of braces, medical bills, and a college education. They had dedicated much time, energy, and no small measure of financial resources to the upbringing and maintenance of their family and had faced them many responsibilities that such efforts demand. And life was good.

Throughout the years Mrs. Kurtz gave thought to Mary Elizabeth's birth mother, yet it was not as though that woman of the past could in any way be another mother for Mary Elizabeth. At the same confusing moment, she was well aware that her daughter and her unknown origins had come from this woman. When the Kurtzes thought about the matter at all, they did their best to forget that those responsible for Mary Elizabeth's birth might yet be out there somewhere walking about.

It was foregone, or at least they assumed, that the unknown woman who had surrendered Mary Elizabeth had given up all duties and privileges of motherhood. The world of that woman, whoever she was, doubtless had become very different from what it might have been had she acted as Mary Elizabeth's mother. How much she had affected her own life, those of the Kurtzes and surely that of Mary Elizabeth was beyond the imagination.

Having never met her, Mrs. Kurtz did not know of her nor did she have any desire to do so. Though she could not imagine how anyone could do so, Mrs. Kurtz felt strongly that the woman had relinquished all rights to be a mother to this child whom Mrs. Kurtz had grown to so cherish. This was but one of the events and circumstances that Mrs. Kurtz always would have difficulty comprehending.

Regardless of that extent of her understanding or the circumstances of that past, Mr. and Mrs. Kurtz were Mary Elizabeth's parents now. By whatever twist of fate or good fortune, they had been the ones chosen to raise this child, and for that, they were most grateful. All that said, still yet Mrs. Kurtz occasionally felt a bit threatened by that woman of no face or name, that woman who had given up so very much.

Birthdays were emotional times at the Kurtz household, and Mrs. Kurtz sometimes wondered about the birth mother's thoughts with the passing of those days. Then too, she also was ever conscious of the stark reality that she had not been the one to carry Mary Elizabeth to term and then exalt in the wonder of the birth. It sometimes hurt that many of her friends and relatives had done so, yet she had not.

Though she avoided dwelling on such hurtful thoughts, Mrs. Kurtz was ever conscious that her child had been born to another woman. And in her most private moments and darkest dreams she feared that someday, if she was not ever vigilant that unknown person might return to claim this beautiful daughter. As a result, she held Mary Elizabeth closely through all of her activities, watching her as she played, and cautioning her many times about talking to strangers.

As Mary Elizabeth matured, she seldom mentioned her ongoing desire to know of those other parents. Though when she asked, Mrs. Kurtz assured her that if she wanted to search when she was older, it would be acceptable to do so. Other than that, adoption or her status as an adopted child was seldom discussed.   Any questions regarding the information that might have been given to the Kurtzes had been settled long ago; there had been none. Occasionally there had been speculation about the origins of some specific trait inherited by Mary Elizabeth or by her brothers, yet there was never any thought given to a plan to find the answers.

Mary Elizabeth relegated any actual search she might undertake to some day in the distant future, yet with little hope that such a day would ever be a reality. More than that, Mary Elizabeth had believed that such an effort well might prove intimidating, threatening, and perhaps even harmful for Mrs. Kurtz.

Moreover, for Mrs. Kurtz the question was to arise more than once; "Why should those other people in any way be involved in the life of MY child?" After all, she reasoned that those birth parents were nothing other than nameless beings that conceived, delivered, and then abandoned little Mary Elizabeth.

Though she did not—perhaps could not—realize it, Mary Elizabeth was, legally, emotionally, and in every way, her child, and Mary Elizabeth had the same deep feelings about Mrs. Kurtz truly being her mother. Indeed, both had developed a bond and love that could never be compromised or diluted by others.

Mrs. Kurtz was not alone with her feelings—those fears of losing her child. It is our hope that others such as you and she will learn how to better cope with those troublesome feelings and not feel threatened by efforts your child might make to search. Even further, we feel that an attempt at understanding this need is as much a parental duty as is the need to deal with any other desire of the child. What then was there for the likes of the Kurtzes to ponder and come to understand?

During her years as an adoptive parent, Mrs. Kurtz did not seriously consider that one day Mary Elizabeth might reveal a powerful desire and need to search, and since the records in the state of North Carolina remained closed, such a search would be impossible. We should all consider that adopted children may one day join the ranks of those who have had a desire to seek out the very people who, by giving them over to the system, made it possible for you and other adoptive parents to have children as your very own.

No matter your feelings over the years, for many adoptees knowledge of birth parents is and will continue to be an integral and necessary part of being a complete adult. Unlike now, the climate of the day when you gained this child may have been such that adoption seldom was discussed. It simply then was assumed, erroneously, that maternal bonds were severed by the birth mother when she gave up her child.

Not so now. Choosing adoption means being a part of the adoption triangle forever and ever, amen.

Further, or at least some adoptive parents and social services agencies often believed, it might prove confusing, even bewildering, for an adopted child to later come to know more than one set of parents, especially if the child became aware of those additional parents early in life. Serving to encourage that view was the fact that very little information was given to adoptive parents at the adoption event. There usually was but slight suggestion that the biological beginnings of any adoptee involve folks other than those parents who adopt them.

One additional factor was and sometimes is yet at play. In order to assist in accomplishing an erasure of the past, for many years the social services, public and private alike, made some effort to match the physical characteristics and ethnic backgrounds of adopting parents with those of birth parents. Once again, thereby, the hope was that a child would become integrated into the new family as effortlessly as possible, especially since questions of differences in appearance and size might prove tedious or even embarrassing to the child, particularly during their early years. And, given the circumstances, those efforts very often were beneficial.

Taken together, these attitudes, efforts and methods often caused adopted children to be most hesitant to ask questions about origins. Further, and as with other adoptive parents, a result of those forces may also have been that you truly may have had no realization even that your child was curious. That lack of awareness may have caused you to be surprised by your child's seemingly sudden interest in searching for her long missing birth family.

Notice then, it usually is not the interest of these children that is new. Rather, it is his or her newfound courage to reveal that curiosity that is the most telling. The revelations of such as Mary Elizabeth that they now want to know of, or that they have completed a search for, and have found those "parents" who conceived and delivered them may cause you and any other adoptive parent to seriously ask, "What did I do wrong?"

You were, in some measure at least, naive in presuming that perhaps if you gave enough love and worked diligently at parenting, this child of yours would be so happy and contented that she would never think about that first set of parents, much less seek to search them out.   Now, and suddenly, or so it seems, she is informing you that she is one of those adoptees who very much needs to investigate and locate those missing pieces and people who have some place in her life, even if only minimally.

Or, indeed, perhaps she has already accomplished a search.   At this point, you must know that you have done nothing wrong to cause this, nothing at all.   The events and changes your child has undergone or is now undergoing are an almost inevitable end product of the whole of the adoption process.

It well may be that you are either reading this material because you now face the reality of a search, or you consider one to be eminent in your future.   If so, it well may be that you feel threatened, threatened by the fear that your efforts over the life of your child might now go unrecognized.   And in fear that the very woman (and man) who walked away from the duties you so happily undertook again will step into your world and steal away something of the relationship you have developed.   On the other hand, perhaps you do not feel threatened; you merely seek an understanding of the process in an effort to be supportive of your child.

Still though, you may be comforted in knowing that to the extent you have provided your child with the elements by which he or she is now a loving and decent person, her love and respect for you will not be diminished by these new discoveries.   We think that your understanding of this fundamental fact is critical to ridding yourself of any concern over the place those birth parents might come to occupy in the life of your child.

Further, you must realize that your relationship with your child is not contingent upon the child's relationship with other people.   So it is that your mutual respect and love developed over the years will not be reduced merely as a result of any search effort.

In the balance of this chapter, we hope you will come to understand some of the reasons why your child would have a desire to search for his or her birth parents. Next, we will encourage you to work with this need of the child, just as you have worked through other problems and issues in the course of her upbringing, all the while realizing how you must avoid emotional traps along the way. Third, we will urge you to carefully consider how you must handle your own emotional needs. Lastly, we will discuss how you can assist with a search through documentary material and memories you might have retained.

UNDERSTANDING THE NEED TO SEARCH

We believe that by coming to know more of the thoughts of your adopted child, you will more easily come to understand why he or she MUST search. To that end, accompany us to an imaginary family reunion, the type of ordinary reunion familiar to most of us. Let us there seek the thoughts of an adoptee.   As you read, think how these thoughts and experiences might contribute in bringing a child to the point of searching for those reunions unique to adoptees and their birth families.

So, you are attending our reunion. It is at the "old home place" on a Southern, July afternoon. Upon your arrival, loving and familiar faces greet you, and smiles and hugs are the rules of the hour.

A pleasant breeze is blowing, and you hope there will be enough ice to go around since it is sure to be a hot, hot afternoon. A buffet has been set up just inside the garage, and the tables are heavy with home-cooked food that you are sure will be delicious. The sights and smells delight your senses.

You fall in line with several cousins with whom you shared your childhood, and you all help yourselves to plates-full of food. After lunch, and because you could not eat another bite, you all move to lawn chairs under the shade of the old trees. The babies are being passed around, held, and rocked by the women who are catching up on the latest family news and gossip. The men are off smoking and lying to each other about big fish and deer, war, politics and whatever else men talk about.

As expected of kin, you all share old jokes and favorite stories of well-remembered family members now gone, some illustrious and some sure-enough reprobates. The children are running through the yard, playing games in the barn, and the dogs are barking, as dogs do when children play. You hear a child in the distance say, "Oops!" as a baseball lands near you, too close for comfort. But no admonishment is given because such things are an expected part of a reunion.

More than memories are being shared. The most important emotion that permeates the thoughts of the participants at your family reunion is a satisfying feeling of kinship. You feel welcome because you are one of them. You are comfortable there and the peaceful feeling of belonging is a powerful one.

Imagine now, instead, that you are attending such a lovely gathering, and but there is a difference. You are there as an adoptee, an adoptee of one of the members of this pleasant family. You pause for a moment to look around at the loving faces of those with whom you have grown to adulthood. Suddenly, as it has so many times before in your life, you recall that you are not really kin to anyone there. No person present is a relative other than through some operation of the law. You were selected to be a member of this group, while the others present became members by virtue of their birth or through marriage to someone born to this family. Your membership, unlike those bound to the group by genetics, did not arise from that source, and to you, the difference seems to be a glaring one.

Save for your relationships with your own children, if you have any, you have NO known biological family there or anyplace else. Though no one realizes it, for a moment, the conversation and laughter are absent for you; you seem frozen in time. Your lineage and theirs are different.

Though quite aware that you are most welcome in the group and perhaps comfortable and happy with these people, you remain cognizant that you are not truly a "card-carrying" member of that family nor will you be, ever. You are an in-law in your own family and you feel some measure of estrangement.

That feeling of not quite belonging is recurring, nagging, and in the midst of the fullness of your busy life, it reminds you that there are aspects of your being that simply remain unknown to you. You know that those present do love you. Yet, no matter how sincere the love and companionship shown by these people for you, the void remains; there is no biological connection. Such thoughts leave you with the often forbidden, yet familiar feeling that one day you will have to go hunting for those missing pieces.

You wish that you too had a family heritage to share, a family that stretches beyond your recollections of just these people. You truly need to enjoy common features and personalities and a family history of which to be proud, just as do these people. You are grateful for and often relish what you have, but a part of you needs your own heritage, not a borrowed one.

And, indeed, while many at such a gathering do look, walk, talk, and smile alike, any similarities you have with any of these folks have been learned, not inherited. After all, as you so often remind yourself, you were ADOPTED into this family. There was some legal hocus-pocus and you then were declared to be one of these people. That seems so strange, sometimes!

Probably few, if any, of those present have any awareness of your silent thoughts, and most have given little or no thought to the fact that you have no biological ties to them or any known person. Only other adoptees can truly understand that you do so much want to resemble someone and to feel that you are an integral part of some biological family group. You need a family into which you were born and not one which strangers selected almost at random.

You often wonder why you were not wanted, instead, by your own people, and why you could not have remained as a part of that natural group, whoever they were and yet are. Enough family reunions of your biological family have gone by, you feel, and enough time has already slipped away and you now wish to be included.

That such thoughts occur to a greater or lesser degree in adoptees is a certainty. For most of us, heritage is ever present and taken quite for granted, but for most adoptees, it must be earned through search. Such is the way it is.

WHAT TO DO

Let us return to reality. Now that you have been exposed to some of the inner thoughts of an adoptee, are you willing to commence in your efforts to understand your child's need to have her own reunion with that "other family," her birth family? It is our hope that you will want to learn more of those thoughts. By so doing, you will reach that level of comprehension that will permit you to fully appreciate that your support, or at least your acceptance of a search, is of the greatest importance for you and your child.

That understanding is critical. Just as other important aspects of rearing your child have been challenging, reaching the decision to help her (or him) is only as difficult as you allow it to be. As it may have happened in the past, once again placing the needs of another ahead of your own will be the gift you need now to give.

So, continue with the acceptance and encouragement of her activities, just as when she ran track or sang in the church choir or perhaps when she graduated from school. Support her just as you did in the past when she took the necessary risks and succeeded in efforts that required dedication and strength on her part. This new challenge must not be approached any differently than in those other hurdles of her life.

You also should understand some of the qualms this daughter likely has concerning this search. The risks are great for her. The road of search may be long and tedious, and while great pleasures may be and often are experienced by all, more than one disappointment is likely to be encountered along her path. She is displaying no small measure of courage in undertaking such a search, and you must applaud her for her efforts.

In the upbringing of your children, you likely sought to instill ambition, courage, and fortitude, and you must here continue with that support, no matter your preferences in the matter. You should admire her tenacity and steadfastness in this task, just as you did during her youth when she undertook other difficult problems. Remember that you are the one who gave her this needed measure of courage, so now you should help her harness that virtue without fear.

Searching often presents an adoptee with as great a challenge, if not greater, than anything she has done before. While, at those earlier moments, earning an "A" in calculus, hitting a much needed foul shot, or reaching a high note seemed terribly important, those now pale almost to insignificance when compared to this endeavor. Indeed, her searching well may place her emotional stability at risk to a greater extent than nearly all other prior efforts.

So, there is much to consider. Even though you likely told your child that you had chosen her, it may well have occurred to her that to be chosen equally revealed that before that choice was made someone else had given her up. It also may have come to her mind that another child could have been chosen instead. No matter if you picked her from a line up, or if some person such as a social worker selected her for you, she may have taken the view that she came to your home purely as a result of the "luck of the draw." It is your task, not to salve over those notions, for it is too late for that, but to realize that those may have been disheartening thoughts for the child, and your encouragement and love are again needed by her.

Thus it is that, whether by providence or otherwise, she is your child, is devoted to you, and does not wish to bring harm to you by her search or its results. It simply is that a most powerful desire from deep within her being literally demands that these efforts be made. As to her motives and desires to search, we believe that it should be apparent to you, and to all others involved, that your daughter would not expend such time, effort, and money for the sole purpose of causing you grief or discontent. In NO way should an adoptive parent infer that the child is unhappy, disappointed, or discontented. Then too, that parent should realize that the decision was not made in any effort to hurt or displease the mother and father who raised the child after the birth parent(s) did not or could not nurture and care for that child.

You may be called upon to understand still more. Your child, regardless of her maturity and responsibility (or any lack of the same), may be unable to articulate why she has this powerful need to search other than to say, "It is something I must do." If pressed, she may list several reasons, though we feel that it is not necessary for her to list any at all. It is enough that she feels a need to do so.

Having birth parents is part of an adoptee's identity. Just as the members of your extended family known to you have been and now are an integral part of your life, birth parents and their place in life are an important part of the puzzle faced by the adoptee. Moreover, just as you seek to know and appreciate your direct ancestors and their lives, so too do adoptees need to know of those who came before them.

Whether or not she speaks of the matter, she also may be grappling with how the missing pieces of her life will fit together. She may be very aware that while finding her birth parents will close a long chapter of her life, those discoveries also will introduce a completely new one. She will need to reconcile her life as it now is with what it may be in the future, regardless of the extent to which the search may be successful.

How she fits in her world may and probably will change dramatically. She may suddenly find a rich heritage, and realize at long last that she has a part in the great play of history. She will, finally, find herself able to see beyond herself and her own experiences when she looks backwards in time and will be in a position to allow her children to share the same benefits.

She may wish to ponder what she might have been had she been raised by those other parents. Incidentally, she will find no answer to that question. She will decide that not only is her heritage a vital part of her, but that she also is the product of her own past experiences, which includes you, and which will not change. Be receptive to new thoughts that surely will be a product of this search.

There are still other challenges that may come to your child. One of the more difficult of those is the belief that the birth mother might choose to reject her yet again. Consider that your child may well feel that adoption, though appropriate and even necessary at the time, was an act of rejection.

In addition to the other challenges facing your child, it may take a greater measure of persistence and determination for her to attempt to find that parent who once decided he or she did not want or could not keep her. While it may be that the birth parents have loved your child, they may not have wished for a reunion. It may also be that the very existence of your child will embarrass that birth mother and she may very much prefer to keep that birth from her friends and family.

You must attempt to help your child understand that rejection is not a reflection upon her, but is a by-product of her birth mother's past inability or unwillingness to cope with the situation. If you can find it within yourself, you can encourage the child by pointing out that perhaps society has changed enough so that it now is acceptable for those parents to be receptive of her.

However, you both should know that it might be that the birth parents would allow unresolved issues in their own lives to interfere with a reunion. But significantly, you should guard against giving any indications that you might in any way reject her because of her search and incorporate that belief into your thought process.

Do not presume that your child will find such rejection. The birth mother may have hoped for a reunion only to have been unable to bring it about. The birth father may not have known of the birth of your child, and now may welcome her into his life. You must not now feel intimidated by their desires and now is surely not the time for you to reject her.

Your child may need your help in another matter. While she hopes to find a real person, she may search for years only to find nothing more than a headstone. She would then have been denied any contact with the physical presence of the woman who held the key to a gateway of experiences. She is the one who could have explained why she gave up your child, perhaps identify the natural father, and turn the initial act of rejection into one of pleasantness and love. So much healing might have occurred from her spoken words.

Your child then may need to adjust her thinking and create an innovative approach scenario as she makes plans for further searching. Perhaps you will need to salve over this disappointment. While the other door has been closed, she continues to have many possibilities regarding the existence of siblings who may be out there, the history of her family, their stories, their successes and failures, their joys and sorrows. Another need not follow one disappointment, and she should be encouraged to continue with her search.

Realize too, that the adoptee may have other fears that you can not know. Suppose the parent is of the lowest station in life, or is of a character that a measure of pride will not be possible for the child. Suppose the parent is in prison or is mentally ill.

It would do you well to consider that if the search is successful, the person she has located will almost surely have an extended family that may or may not welcome her into their fold. The same applies to the spouse of the person she has located.

Any of those results are distinct possibilities, some of which the child may have considered, even if but briefly. It may be that your encouragement is very important to the child you have so well raised, educated, and with whose problems you have until now sought to assist.

Awareness of such concerns should not constitute a reason to avoid a search. Instead, such cognizance should serve to prepare you for the challenges that may confront your child. If you already have a loving, supportive relationship with her, there is absolutely no reason to allow the search and its attendant problems to become an obstacle to the continuation of those same good feelings you have built over years. So, be available throughout the search to offer support in whatever fashion and to whatever extent she needs it.

If the extent to which the bond with your child is marginal, the same thoughts yet apply, though the challenges may be greater for both of you, probably due in some measure to your strained relationship. No matter the sources of your apprehension or to what extent you have allowed those to affect your relationship, these must be set aside, at least for now.

In all of this, our message remains.   In order to accomplish a winning strategy and to cope with what cannot now be predicted, you should make every effort to focus on and anticipate the needs of your now grown child. Though your feelings are important of course, this is not the time for your child to feel constrained to focus on those.

Perhaps your assistance will neither be needed nor requested. Your support and approval in this matter yet may be critical.   Your efforts to understand the search process and some of the effects that may be visited upon your child's thinking and emotional well being will aid in increasing your capacity to help with whatever the needs of your child may be.

Finally, if the long missing parent is found and reunion is brought about, even minimally, you may again be required to broaden your perspective.   By so expanding your understanding now, you will stand more ready to adapt to whatever results might come about.

TRAPS TO AVOID

During our interviews with those involved in adoption triads, we found some recurring difficulties—traps— experienced by both adoptive parents and children. Leading among those, perhaps, is a failure by many to realize that an adoptive child may literally feel a true need to search. And that need may not be set aside, stifled, or satisfied simply because you suggest that the whole idea may not be beneficial to anybody involved. In short, whether you think a search is a good idea or not, your child may have a deep-seated desire to do just that.

This is a moment of choices and decisions, just as have been so many times in the past. You can, through subtleties and innuendo, make your child uncomfortable about that need and thereby sabotage her efforts before the search is even under way or, in the alternative, you can realize that there now is a new and perhaps even pleasant adventure ahead for you and the child. Considering the reality that the child truly does feel that need to search, the overriding thought for you now should be that there simply are no satisfactory reasons for you to put your feelings ahead of her desires.

It is up to you to evaluate the whole of the matter, but in so doing, don't deceive yourself. You and you alone must make the critical decision as to whether or not your actions and attitudes will deter this desire of hers, or instead will benefit and long be remembered as pleasant by the child who is now and should remain as one of the most important beings in your life.

One of the least recognized, but very important traps for you to avoid is your own basic need to be accepted in the future, just as you were in the past. As with all of us, changes in the attitudes of those we love or respect are tedious to comprehend and accommodate. Rejection, in even the slightest way, is even more difficult for us. Beyond the everyday fears we all may have regarding our appearance or personae, the fear that one day, and perhaps soon, you may be rejected in whatever ways you have conjured up, by either your child or even by the birth mother, may be very difficult for you now.

In addition to fear of rejection we all hope that our conduct and actions are and in the future will be found acceptable, even if not laudable, by all within our circle. That desire within may cause you to have a measure of fear that this search by your child will cause others to decide or suggest that you have not done as you should have done as the mother of your child.

One adoptive father said, "If the well-being of your son or daughter will be served by this (search), then there is no reason not to support him or her, unless you have fears that you haven't done enough as a parent." To this we say: the parent has not been born who has not made mistakes in the rearing of a child, and your errors of the past quite likely are not greater than those mistakes made by any other parent. And in the matter of such common errors, it makes no difference if the child was adopted or born to you, your mistakes quite likely would have been the same. So, realize that this is neither the time nor the place to dwell on past mistakes of judgment, and surely not a time to contemplate fear or rejection for having done so. Face your fears, most of which are products of only your imagination and be prepared to move on.

Similarly, you should not dwell upon the fact that other adopted children, even others of your own, have NOT searched or planned to do so. All children are different, as you long ago learned. Just as was your duty, you saw to it that your child grew to be an independently thinking individual, and an upstanding citizen who would and could manage her own life. Surely, you now do not feel nor hope that your training and her achievement of those goals should be set aside.

Equally dangerous to your mental well being and a satisfactory relationship with your child is allowing yourself to dwell upon the idea that your child should have only one set of parents. Such notions are but a mask, we think, to hide the fear that by searching, differences between your family and that yet unknown family will be brought into focus and reveal that somehow you will not measure up. To this we say, we all are who we are and have been, whether rich or poor, of high station or low, in the public eye or not, or somewhere in between. The introduction of yet one more household into your child's life will not alter greatly what really has been and is your life.

Anxiety also may arise from what you suspect your neighbors and friends will think and say about the whole of the matter. We say that—if ever—this is a time when you must shift your focus from the views and attitudes of other people, whoever they may be, to the needs of your own family, to yourself, to your spouse, and particularly to this child who needs to search.

More than that, it even may prove necessary to come to the defense of your child. The questions before you surely are: Do you become the victim here, or will you be seen by all as a loving, understanding mother? How will your life story be told; did you help, and do so earnestly, or were you guided by those who really knew nothing about you, your child, and the needs and peace of all your family? So, approach this trap just as you have other problems where you have been successful or effective; if you have sustained your family through difficulties before, this surely is not the time to change your course.

There is more. You must avoid the guilt trap laid in your path by well meaning others who use words such as, "How could she do this after ALL you've done for her?" "Has she been unhappy lately, she seemed so contented? "You seemed to have had such a good relationship with her." "Oh my, without you there is no telling how she would have turned out." Such comments probably indicate an initial reaction of surprise and perhaps a need to empathize with you over what they perceive as a betrayal, an ungrateful attitude, or rejection on the part of your child.

These comments, well intended or perhaps otherwise, actually reflect their lack of understanding regarding an adoptee's desires to search. Depending upon the individual, you may or may not attempt the task of educating them, however you must avoid allowing such comments to negatively influence your relationship with your child. Above all and ignoring such comments if necessary, you MUST constantly be aware that her need to search almost certainly has nothing whatever to do with the quality of your parenting now or in the past.

This search is about her and about an important component of her life that has been kept from her, even sealed away in a file somewhere, to which she has had no access. To understand, imagine for a moment that there are many secret and important details of your life that strangers have locked away from you and to which others have access, but you do not. It is that scenario she now faces, and likely has since before even you knew of her compelling desire to search.

Another trap that threatens to hold you is the thought that your child is struggling with the fact of having been adopted, and it is that which requires her to search. We think that if you have such concerns, now is surely the time to discuss that matter with her. It has been our experience that a search is about adding to one's experiences of life, about meeting others who have roots in a family different from the one you have known, and about finding one's true place in a world that may vary from the experiences she has had to now. Indeed, some searchers have come to a feeling that they have been most fortunate for having two families.

On those rare occasions when you gave thought to those long unidentified parents, you may have come almost to feel that they do not exist. Having likely never seen nor been acquainted with them, or at least having had but a brief relationship many years ago, in your mind they have no reality now. You must avoid such thoughts. At the very least, visualizing them as individuals quite capable of receiving your good wishes and even your love enables you to transcend the notion that their worth was altered the day they walked away from your child.

You must soon come to understand that your child's birth parents, as are you and your family, may be very much alive, working, and going about their lives together or separately as best they are able under their own sets of rules, life's works, and standing in their community. Indeed, just as they may be very different in so many of their views and goals, those folks might, instead, be much like you.

In truth and in fact, your child's birth mother (and father) may be people who you could come to enjoy and who just might be a distinct benefit to your child in ways not now realized by you. It may be amusing to note that you are the parents of the sibling of those not yet discovered- the siblings or half-siblings to your child. While she may have been raised with siblings in your family to which she is related through adoption, in another family she may have other siblings related to her biologically. Choosing to make these other family members a part of your life may be quite enriching to you and to all of those involved.

MANAGING YOUR NEW EMOTIONS

"No passion so effectively robs the mind of its powers of acting and reasoning as fear."[11]

In your efforts to cope with this new and perhaps unexpected effort by your adopted child, you may have a flood of feelings, some from years ago, some new as the days pass. This choice by your child again may give rise to those old feelings and fears that you suffered as you ventured into the strange world of adoption and its requirements. You may have regrets over your infertility or that of your mate, that having been no small factor in the decisions that led to your adoption of this child who now seemingly will betray you. After all, you think, that birth mother surely would have known that you were unable to do what she could do; have a child.

She could, and yet you were unable to pass on your inherited traits and features, your mental agility, and your talents that might have come from those before you. Those factors alone may cause you to feel that there may be a bond between your child and that other woman out there.

Honest as are those feelings and fears, as we have mentioned, it is the experience of virtually all researchers that you will not be replaced as a result of the discovery of another parent. More than that, interviews tell us that the other mother will not likely seek to undermine your years of work and sincere efforts to do well by this child.

However, what if the birth mother has decided to express her displeasure regarding the upbringing of your child? All of you must be willing to move beyond the past, recognizing that the actual issue may be masked by criticism. Water under the bridge is not a good excuse to end this particular journey.

We also hope that all of the parents come to better understand that giving birth provides a bond quite different from those that result from years of mutual experiences.

---

[11] Edmund Burke, ed. Richard Shea, *The Book of Success* (Rutledge Hill Press; Nashville, TN 1993), p. 154

More than that, though, when you attempt to place blame, in the case of the adoptee, it is particularly difficult to distinguish responsibility for certain traits based on genetics or environment. It has taken the efforts of both sets of parents to make THIS child what she is today. But, in the end, personal growth, healing and closure are more important issues than winning the argument.

Of further note is the responsibility your child must now assume for the outcome of her adult life. While answers to the nature vs. nurture debate are difficult to find, there is an added component to personality. Once your child has become an adult, she assumes responsibility for her life and her actions. While she may be faced with difficulties of both the past and the future, the strength of her character is now up to her. Regardless of who wants to blame whom for the mistakes made in her life by either set of parents, her future is in her hands now.

Equally important for you to remember is the reality that as human beings our capacity to love and be loved is not finite. When you cultivate a new and trusted friend, must you discard an old one to make room? Of course not. Said another way, our ability to have deep affection for others has no bounds; we all have plenty for everybody. So it is, that you can rest assured knowing that your child can love more than two sets of parents.

We hope that by now you are looking your daughter's search and possibility of reunion squarely in the face. Your child has decided that now and perhaps for once in her life, she needs to be in control of her adoption and all it entailed. Equally, she wants a reunion of her own. As she undertakes her journey, you may also find it necessary to join with her and commence your own pilgrimage.

So then, how do you do that? First, decide what is bothering you. Are you afraid? If so, of what? It may be that you feel assailed from many directions. You may have concern that the whole of the adventure—and surely, that is what it is—will be uncomfortable for you. However, as with all problems, it is but the small parts of the whole that will be troublesome. As the adage goes, when you look at the forest before you, you must be able to see the trees.

To so discern the parts of the whole, take the problem apart, sort those parts, examine each, and ponder those smaller issues in your own way, just as you have done with other complicated tasks. If upon consideration you find that you will be able to cope with each if and when it arises, then you have seen the trees in that forest and you are able to move ahead through those. Above all, do not borrow trouble from the unknown future; many of what you now consider to be difficult possibilities simply will never come about.

You may come to realize that you have not been honest with yourself. Perhaps, deep inside, you are saying, "Should those who once chose to give this child over to an unknown future have the privilege of stepping back into the world I have created, assume a place in the life of my dear child, and so benefit from my efforts and sacrifices? One mother said with a slight, yet stern smile, "Why should those strangers be allowed to step back into the picture when I have already washed diapers, wiped runny noses a thousand times, bought five hundred pairs of shoes, and paid for braces and college?"

Then too, perhaps your child has been particularly challenging to raise. Again, you ask, why should those who had precious little concern those years ago now enjoy the benefits of my having assumed half a lifetime of often trying and difficult parental duties? Selfish attitudes on your part? Perhaps, but honest ones, nonetheless. We can only suggest that those duties you undertook were for the child and because you chose to do so. Though that parent of the past may benefit to some measure, it is the child and her future life and family who have been so advanced by your work. That birth mother will benefit no more than any other friends and associates that your child has or will develop.

You may have a deep and abiding fear your relationship with your child is in jeopardy. Or, you may feel betrayed; thinking that she is now being disloyal to you. You may feel threatened by the mere fact that she is searching. Perhaps you fear that the yet unidentified birth mother might try to assume your role or might diminish your position in your child's life. Or worse, yet, you fear that your child might prefer that her birth mother take your place. You may suspect that her natural parents could somehow emotionally steal this child away. Could they now be of great wealth, while you have but little? You may wonder if you could have done something differently in the past such as to delay, if not prevent, this proposed search.

Troublesome thoughts, indeed, however the cold hard response to all those questions is, "Being replaced is not how it works." When such fears arise, try to remember that your relationship with your child is not contingent upon her feelings and relationships with others. Whatever have been the results of the years you have spent in the raising, nurturing, and loving of this child will not be erased away by this search. As we have said, every one has plenty of love to give and the extent to which new affection arises for others as a result of this hunt will not cause the child's affection for you to be in any way diminished. Just as you have the capacity to give love in unlimited quantities, so too does your child.

Aside from your own feelings of fear and jealousy, you may truly fear for your child, for her emotional safety, and even of what might be physical results of any reunion. After all, you say, she will be stepping into another world that may prove threatening or even harmful. You have had concerns for all the years to now, and you will not stop worrying over your children now regardless of their age.

Still, this is but one more occasion when it is necessary for you to let them go. They must be allowed to venture again now and do so on their own if they so choose. This adventure, though far greater in magnitude of potential results, should be viewed as similar to when they went to school on the first day, rode the bus for the first time, rode a bike without training wheels, were issued a driver's license and then drove out of your sight and into their teenage world. A certain amount of preparation on the part of you and your child has gone into each "first," and you must realize that this is but one more such event. No matter your fears, whether real or imagined, you must once again send them on their way.

And there is a larger view of it all that may help you. Parents, whether adoptive or natural, have their children to raise for but a relatively short span of life, twenty years, more or less. You have had that interlude and have enjoyed being able to guide and participate in the lives of your children, but the day does arrive when it is time to stand back and encourage them to move on and once again drive out of sight. These are adult "children" now who are attempting a search. They are not youngsters learning to ride a bike or entering Kindergarten. At the end of the nurturing, it is the solemn duty of all of us to send a child forward into independence and the world. Your child now must be permitted to lead her own life, and she has no duty to gain your permission to do so.

As if the fears and traps were not enough, you may honestly feel that the social agency with which you dealt those years ago, as well as the law of adoption over which you had no control whatever, simply deceived you. At that time, those who had the interests and well-being both of you and of your soon-to-be child in their hands, strongly suggested—maybe even stated to you—that your child would neither have a desire nor be able to locate her birth parents. To this, there can be but a single response; who said what to whom is over and in the dim past; those words you heard and took as factual cannot be undone. If you were so advised, that simply was not what experience since the earliest days of adoption has revealed. Harsh as the advice again is, not only do you benefit not at all by rehashing those matters, but to do so is a dreadful waste of your time. Bluntly stated it is high time that you put those conversations and mistaken beliefs behind you.

The traps, fears, misinterpretations, and simple errors you have made over these years are and were honest, very human, and not unusual for those in your category of folks. So too, are any feelings you now may have about what should be done, and how your world would be better if only your child would change her mind about this search. You should have no regrets now unless, that is, you muddle on and wallow in those mistakes and misapprehensions. Again, and candidly put, forget equally about how you thought your world might have been and how now it seems it should be.

You are now called upon to replace any worn out old ideas through a realization that the past was as it was, and your qualities as a parent have long since been proven to yourself and to others. Expect your child to search, assist her if she so chooses, and then view the obstacles you find in your path as but one more set of difficulties, the likes of which you have solved many times in your raising and loving of this child. The Scriptures tell us, "This too shall pass." Not only will this period of your life pass, but also you may find that with the proper spirit, you will be able to receive many of the blessings meant for you and your life. Enough said, then about fears and trepidation.

The question now arises for virtually all adoptive parents: "Should I share my concerns about this search with my child and other members of the family who might be very much affected?" It is our advice that you discuss your concerns with your adopted child, not to dissuade her in her course, but rather to have her understand that the matter is difficult for you, just as it is for her. However, if you can not do so in a positive and encouraging manner, we feel that you should keep your thoughts to yourself until some future time when you are able to discuss it all in a way that is constructive and helpful to both of you.

With few exceptions, we feel that you should leave the decision to your child as to whether or not you will discuss the matter with others. The decision as to whom should be told of the intention and search plan is for her to make. The story that is yet to be written, after all, is hers to tell, not yours. Why? Because it may be difficult for her to discuss with anyone even her desire to know more about her birth parents, and it may be even more difficult to reveal her hope to find those people. Such feeling and her reluctance are every bit as valid as are your fears and concerns already discussed. So, unless and until she decides that her secret efforts should be revealed, it is her business and hers alone and as to that, her wishes should be held sacred.

All that said, in your very human need for a confidante, you might feel a deep desire to speak of the matter to select others. Just as she needs support, perhaps you need reassurances beyond what we have offered. If you and your child are unable to find strength each from the other, and you are unable to keep this "secret," you must solve the problem. We feel that the person you seek out is for you and you alone to determine.

Still and of the utmost importance, you must—repeat, must—be absolutely sure that the person in whom you will confide perfectly understands that by revealing the story to outsiders, irreparable harm may come to your relationships with the world and with your child. An untimely revelation of the story to others in the community well might even destroy the search itself. As someone suggested decades, maybe centuries ago, "One can not unring a bell!" Considering the high risk of dire consequences, we urge that you *tell no person* of the efforts to be made.

However, if you yet are unable to find solace or peace of mind concerning your child's plans to search, then it may be that you should seek outside help. That need gives rise to the obvious question: Whom?

Such help might come in the form of a visit to a support group or with your minister; time spent in prayer, a baring of your soul to your mate, brother, or sister, or perhaps, through the professional help of a psychologist, psychiatrist, or family counselor. But again, even those dialogues with outsiders MUST be efforts to reach an understanding and solution of your problems, and not merely a means by which to perpetuate, enforce, or vent your frustrations. Be also aware, as with other situations where outside help is sought, finding someone who has had similar experiences or has been trained to deal with matters of the emotions of adoption often helps more than seeking counsel of one who has no experience in such matters.

If after you have gained the thoughts of those friends or professionals, you still find yourself unable to emotionally accept this effort and offer assistance or meaningful encouragement, then it is your solemn duty to compassionately stand aside.

Of course, the best way is to share her journey, if you are at all able. She needs to solve this puzzle, complete this journey, and be about her life. This has taken much of her energy, thinking, and planning. Adoption has been and is now forever beyond her control. Others, including you decided her fate. Now, she seeks to gain knowledge and control of her life as an adopted person, which is as it should be.

WHAT FURTHER CAN YOU DO?

In those quiet moments when you worry over what, if any, role you should play in the search effort, remember the following. Though the perceptions of the law entertained by many are quite to the contrary, there is nothing illegal about what your child proposes to do (or has already done) by way of search. Virtually all of the materials and information she will seek out are public records and open to all, and those that are not simply will be made known to her and be unavailable.

Only the actual file created at the time of the adoption (and any additions to that file added in the years following) is closed. All else—virtually all other records—is open to anybody with a desire to search. Similarly, should you decide to participate, whether grandly or in but a small way, you too will in no way be skirting the law or be acting improperly in your efforts.

Before we suggest what you might do by way of assistance other than encouragement, it may be that the advice we have gleaned from other adoptive parents is of importance. One adoptive father interviewed undertook to actively participate in a search to the extent that his effort was greater than that even of his son. Though that son was less than thrilled with the results, neither the son nor the father now feels that they should regret their efforts. The matter was brought to a conclusion through a reunion of sorts, and the son's natural curiosity in no small measure was satisfied. Notice too, that through that reunion, the son might learn of his heritage and past before that parent. The lesson here, we think, is that assistance to the child will have some value, no matter the result.

Though standing quietly on the sidelines, another adoptive parent was able to encourage her husband and her son to proceed with a search for the son's birth parents. Our interview with her revealed that though the outcome had not been what she had hoped, she yet felt that a reunion at least might come about one day, since the searcher and the person being sought both now know of each other. She had felt that the search effort was part of his maturity and education, an integral part of the whole scenario of adoption, and it was not remarkable for him to go look.

Furthermore, all of these parents continue to enjoy a very close relationship with their children. It was not at all surprising that their search was not disruptive of their lives, and that their love and affection for each other were not diminished.

It is not the place of any third-party researcher or friend, to request, advise, or suggest that an adoptive parent assist in a proposed search for birth parents. Whether or not such help is to be sought is for the adoptee to decide.

As mentioned, at the outset you, the parent, may choose to but stand on the sidelines. That is fine, but, caution, if you do so choose, do not then pretend to be in approval, all the while and in subtle ways, permitting others to infer that you do not approve. Here, if ever, sabotage and subterfuge have no place. Such devious activities, however subtle, are but your attempts to create negative thoughts within either the child or outsiders. If you must have such thoughts, make every effort to subordinate those to the needs and desires of your child.

If you choose not to help, then tell the child and be done with the decision. Do not impose obligation for your child to make you feel better about the situation; he or she has no such duty.

Be honest with yourself and with your child. If there are matters of which you would prefer not to speak, forewarn the child that you will advise him or her when such moments arise. Both of you need such consideration in this emotionally charged undertaking.

Also, avoid using the search as an opportunity for manipulation, such as making it difficult for you and the child to advance any thoughts in the matter together. Should such behavior be a matter of course for you, then you may need to be a casual, though interested, observer and make no contribution beyond your recollections and such documentary materials that you may have or know of.

Presuming that your child has requested your help, know that the searcher MUST have a place to start. NO fact is unimportant, no matter how apparently meaningless it now may seem to be. Next, the search will revolve around the *wheres*—the locations—of every event involving the child. In fact, it is usually at those very places that the records that remain are to be found. Lastly, your memories, however sparse, are the most powerful resource at the disposal of the searcher, whether that person is your child or a professional.

To the best of your ability, recall any and every moment, place, relative, physician, lawyer, social worker, nurse, document, letter, note, and phone call that in any way involved this child or the adoption process by which she came to you. Permit your child to make notes and question you in-depth, as many times over as are productive.

It is hard to imagine an adoptive parent who does not at least know the place from which the child was given over. And, no matter what else you may have or know that *where* is probably the most important contribution that an adoptive parent can provide.

Be sure to search your files, old letters and papers or ANY document or writing that has to do with the event, and try to recall the very first person involved and the circumstances by which you learned of the adoptability of this child. That first contact may prove very significant in the actual search process.

Do your best to recall the last person to have brought the child to you and where that hand-over took place. If a lawyer was involved in the process, do your best to recall his name and where he practiced. Be sure to attempt to remember any friend or confidante who assisted you or had any interest whatever in your emotional struggles, as you may have revealed details to such people and yet not now remember those conversations.

So, share everything with the searcher, the only exceptions being those items, memories or records that might bring scorn, embarrassment, or ridicule to others. It may be that the circumstances and conditions surrounding the birth of the child will cause embarrassment for someone involved. If those recollections and records are not of importance in the search, then simply refrain from discussing such matters. However, here and always, your efforts must not be obstructive in any way.

With this writing, our goal is to help you be a part of a successful search. Whether choosing to be involved in a search or merely being thrust into one undertaken by someone else, all members of the adoption triad will be faced with challenges, some great, most small. We hope that as an adoptive parent, by reading this chapter, you have gained insights that will assist you with the difficulties that you will encounter.

While attempting to offer as much as possible by way of understanding, advice and assistance, we realize that not only are we unable to discuss every potential scenario, but you may not choose to rely upon our judgment, and that is your prerogative.

Though we believe our suggestions to be sound, utilize whatever techniques work best for you. Yours and other adopted children have known difficulties that are beyond your experience and attempts should be made by all members of the triad to at least be acquainted with those problems.

Advice to Adoptees

What sort of person ventures forth into the unknown, an unknown fraught with potential rejection, anger, and criticism? And did we mention failure? If you are planning a search, then you are such a person, an adventurer, sure enough. The trait commonly possessed by adventurers is a desire to know more, a will to challenge the elements and the odds, and the energy and strength of mind to prepare for and move against the challenges that may come.

This real-life adventure is not for the faint of heart. Yet, for adoptees such as Mary Elizabeth, you, and all others who seek reunion, there is a chance to share in a hero's drama. A drama complete with courage, deeds well done, a dragon slaying or two along the way, and the fellowship of others who have traveled the same route, as well as those who wish to share your journey.

For many, this journey begins at an early age. For Mary Elizabeth, though she sometimes pondered the matter of her adoption, she had felt no anger or resentment as a result of the past abandonment by her birth parents. Nor should you allow such feelings to disrupt your planned course. Just as she had long before realized, you cannot alter your past or the actions of others in those now gone days. Still, and as you may have, she often had an intense curiosity about the circumstances of her birth and adoption.

At those moments, and especially when young, her imagination and fantasies provided outlets and occasional entertainment for her. As a child, when her imagination ran wild, she thought perhaps that she was descended from royalty. Her family may have lived in a small and little known country and the pregnancy of her birth mother had met with the disapproval of the queen. Perhaps the princess had been unmarried and had become pregnant by some rogue of a man, of whom the queen did not approve. Thus it was, she guessed, that her princess mother had been sent away to give birth to Mary Elizabeth.

Or perhaps the queen's handsome son had dalliances quite unbecoming a prince and had impregnated some young tart. Of course, the queen had been foolish enough to believe that her prince son did not have the same urges as other males, and so she had been unwilling to deal with the consequences and had banished the errant pregnant girl from the kingdom. Unfortunately, a later marriage of the prince produced no heir to the throne and the queen desperately needed to find that illegitimate child of those years before. Though she could not realize it, such fantasies had served Mary Elizabeth well in her need for understanding why she was who she was, as well as lending a tone of humor to her thoughts of the subject.

Upon reaching adolescence, Mary Elizabeth had less time for daydreaming, but still yet thoughts of descent from royalty would reemerge now and then and amuse her. At such moments, she would again hope that she would be found, rejoin her royal family, and one day ascend the throne as queen. She was certain that she would be a good and merciful queen, and for sure, she could easily adapt to having a multitude of servants and wearing beautiful clothes. It also would be nice, she thought, if she were a queen of a tropical climate nation somewhere, since she so enjoyed warm weather.

It was during those years that she concluded that for whatever reasons those first parents simply did not want her or were unable to keep her. After all, she thought, she had witnessed many women share their excitement about the birth of a new baby, and she wondered why a baby would not be a welcome addition to any family, no matter the circumstances. More often, and as she neared adulthood, she viewed the matter ever more realistically, yet still sought to understand. She searched within herself for reasons that her birth parents had made the choice to leave her, a choice that had affected her so very much.

Such feelings can be very destructive of personality. Erroneous as such notions likely are, the feeling that one was rejected or not wanted by natural parents often gives rise to feelings of "not being good enough." Adoptees, having been given up, often take the view that the most important people of their lives rejected them. Indeed, Mary Elizabeth frequently entertained the idea that if those natural parents had not wanted her, how could she be acceptable to anyone else, and what could she do? Further, she wondered if having been given away once by those birth parents meant that they also would not want her to come back into their lives?

Facing the hurdles brought to her by such insecurity was but one of the challenges Mary Elizabeth would overcome. Thankfully for her, with maturity came the realization that the decisions of those unknown parents had very little to do with her and who she was and instead had resulted from circumstances over which those people very likely had little or no control.

As result of the comments over the years by her adoptive parents, she had come to take the view that nothing would be accomplished by discussing with them either her own adoption or adoption in general. Since asking questions also seemed disruptive for them at times, her secrets were kept and curiosity suppressed in favor of maintaining the status quo, however emotionally unhealthy that truly was. It was years before she came to the reality that, as was she, those who had raised her were but products of their own times, generation and environment.

That secretiveness upon which her adoptive family had insisted meant that in all conversation or exchanges of ideas her birth parents simply did not exist. They were excluded from her visions; gone, vanished, never to return again. Indeed, until the magic age of eighteen, Mary Elizabeth had been taught to believe that contemplating, seeing, or knowing of them was a taboo, legally, socially and in all other ways. Understandably so.

Finally, it was a common view of her day that to search or even to want to discuss those unknown people and adoption revealed, not efforts to understand but, rather, some deep emotional turmoil trying to claw its way to the surface of the adoptee's thoughts. That perception, she did NOT want. Still though, and following upon the heels of those thoughts and her curiosity, she realized that entering upon a search for her birth parents would require her to reveal her secrets; that, perhaps the most frightening of the prospects and but one more hurdle for her to overcome.

The sum total of all of those thoughts was that she assiduously avoided any discussions of any aspect of adoption, her own adoption, or of searches for birth parents. So secretive had she been that once she had revealed her intention to search, she came to realize how truly remarkable it was that in all of her years she had told so very few people even that she was adopted.

Thoughts of searching came sporadically to Mary Elizabeth as the years passed, those prompted by her marriage and the births of her children, and related to her desire to obtain health and genetic information. Still, her upbringing haunted her and persistently told her that a search was inconsistent with her upbringing and well might be met with some measure of social ostracism, regardless of how valuable the results of a search might be to her. Again, the influences of society were at play.

Mary Elizabeth struggled with other thoughts, some of which you may experience. In still another moment of thought she came to the stark realization that her parents had not chosen adoption over conception. They had tried for many years to conceive and carry a child of their own origins. That thought brought to her the conviction, right or wrong, that had they been able to do have a biological child; they would not have adopted her.

The totality of those seeming truths led to feelings that she was particularly indebted to those adoptive parents. After all, and as a neighbor of the Kurtzes once said, "You don't know where you could have ended up if your parents had not adopted you." As cruel as such words were Mary Elizabeth realized that she had come to believe and think such statements proper and correct. Those beliefs had caused her to live her life feeling more indebted to those who had rescued her from God-knows-what than she would have been had her birth parents kept her.

Another effect of having such ideas was that she had long felt that if she were the best daughter possible, and she accomplished much in her efforts to meet the needs of these adoptive parents, then this time, she would be kept. But still, as an adult and in contemplating a search, she had been able to come to know the folly of such thoughts. So too must you.

In addition, Mary Elizabeth been raised in an adoptive family where other members had a variety of physical and emotional problems, and so she had long ago fallen into a pattern of being supportive for them even to the point of sacrificing her own emotional stability from time to time. Though surely not intentionally, by reason of not knowing any differently she had allowed them to expect surrender—sacrifice really—by her in order that they "keep her."

She sometimes thought how mistaken it was that children often assume responsibility for many problems within the family that actually are outside their control and proper range of duties. Children, who have trouble even accepting responsibility for remembering to brush their teeth on a daily basis, come to feel responsible if there are major problems that occur in the home. Perhaps that is especially true of adopted children.

Even more than with her adoptive parents, Mary Elizabeth also came to realize, as you may, that she had taught and allowed others, even outsiders, to expect her to become involved in their problems. Still, she knew that those people were not at fault for so relying upon her since she had built those relationships and had been comfortable with that mode of life. To change that, her manner of treating others, would be difficult for her to accomplish and may be met by considerable resistance.

No matter her other thoughts and emotional difficulties, Mary Elizabeth loved her adoptive parents. While she did feel that no one could take the place of those parents or share in those years, for her and for others like her, a void had been created by those birth parents who had given her away.

Should she not be content with her parents and her life as it was? Did she really need to know where she came from?

Did she have any reasons for making these changes and bringing unknown effects to virtually all of her relationships, especially to her immediate family? Surely, a desire to have some new project was not any reason, she thought. She already had plenty to do. The presence in her mind of all of these difficult questions set the stage for even more emotional distress. Nevertheless, and no matter those myriad thoughts, with ever more conviction, she felt that searching, whether successful or otherwise, would help fill that void.

For many years she had remained busy with her young family, tasks, her marriage, and other interests, having decided there was no good reason for searching. For the time being, she had simply foreclosed such thoughts. And, really, wasn't she too busy to find time for what would surely be a major project in terms of time, energy, and finances? She had answered "yes" to that question.

Finally, though she was diligent in her other activities, she came to realize that her hesitations about searching were not due to others. She had to face the facts: she was afraid to search, afraid of rejection, afraid of failure, and intimidated by the world of secrets and places that she thought she could or should not go. It was much safer to stay where she was, procrastinating and avoiding failure. Yet, she also knew she was avoiding opportunities, as well.

Then the day arrived when she could no longer hide behind her distractions. She could no longer use her busy life as an excuse. She had trained as a social worker. She had learned that a certain amount of one's life and its challenges must be dedicated to solving the tasks at hand, rather than focusing on the obstacles to that completion. That training would serve her well.

Perhaps you, as did Mary Elizabeth, have begun to discard the myths and are no longer willing to pretend to have big secrets and quiet restraints. You have become strong enough to seek answers, however daunting that may be. Instead of looking for reasons to avoid a search, perhaps you now can redirect your focus, instead, to the tasks at hand.

Perhaps some of you do not have such struggles and the decision to proceed with a search is easy. More power to you.

Be about it, and in your hands is a guidebook, a road map to assist you. For others, you may very much need the material following.

EMOTIONAL PREPAREDNESS

"It does not do to leave a live dragon out of your calculations, if you live near him."[12]

The quest you must now consider includes a journey within. While you may face this alone, know that whatever new or different emotions may come to you, others have experienced the same or similar situations and have been made better by the challenges. There may be emotional bridges that you must cross, traditional paths from which you must deviate, and routes to choose and choices to make as to whether or not you will allow the dead ends that the system has erected to prevent you from completing the journey.

As with all voyages, making a wrong turn need not bring an end to the trip. When you do so err, and you likely will from time to time, you must go back and take an alternate route, some of which we will suggest as we move forward.

Tolkien, in *The Hobbit*,[13] tells a tale of dwarves who searched for a vast treasure guarded by an enormous, mysterious, and fearsome dragon. In the course of their search, while they often thought of the treasure, they made efforts to ignore the potential consequences of the dragon's presence. They focused, instead, upon the treasure that they believed was rightfully theirs. That thinking left them quite unprepared to deal with the beast when they did finally encounter him.

Your search is analogous to this story. Like you, the dwarves sought to reclaim something to which they felt they were entitled because the treasure had come through their ancestors. Your treasure—your heritage—equally belongs to

---

[12] J.R.R. Tolkien, *The Hobbit* (Houghton Mifflin Company, Boston, MA 1979), p. 229
[13] *Hobbit*, Ibid, generally.

you and for the same reasons. The difference is that the treasure you seek is a person and a family. That person represents and embodies that heritage, your link to the past, your very being, and the answers to myriad questions.

You must remain focused on the task ahead, just as did the dwarves. But, unlike them, you must remain always aware that there may well be dragons directly ahead. Again, in *Simple Abundance* Breathnach reminds us that "Our dragons are our fears...."[14] For our purposes here, it is the dragons in the course of your search that stand between you and the destination that you now will consider. The dragons you may encounter may come from within, as in your thoughts, or they may arise from those people in your circle who would deter your efforts for whatever their motives.

Remember this: as you begin the journey of search and consider your vision for the future, you must identify those feelings that yet remain from the past that might sabotage your success. You are the same human being you were when you were given away, however, to the extent that your thinking has not matured equally with your body, now is the time to bring such changes about.

In speaking of some of the dragons and the difficulties you may encounter we will not provide you with a rationale for fear of any sort. Just as the hero vanquished the dragon in *The Hobbit* because the thrush had informed him of the weak spot (the bare patch in the "waistcoat of fine diamonds"[15] of the dragon) we hope that through investigation and our efforts you will be prepared to confront and dispatch your dragons equally. In the story you will tell, you be the hero.

IDENTIFYING YOUR DRAGONS

We believe that most of the dragons lurking ahead in your path are illusions, just as were the monsters under your childhood bed. Still yet, while the fears such as of those monsters of your youth are now gone, we suspect there are other fears and concerns that are still very much a part of

---

[14] *Simple Abundance*, op. cit. P. "February 16"
[15] *Hobbit*, op cit., p238

you. Just as did the boogieman, those have roots in your childhood and the immature thinking of those early days.

We think that to accurately articulate the true nature of a problem or fear will bring most of the solution. That is, if you can precisely set forth exactly what problem is before you, you likely will have gone a long way toward solving it. So, it is time for you to write to yourself just what it is that you fear, hope to avoid, or that is standing as an obstacle to your search. Further, we think it will help if you do that at every point in your search when you do not know what to do next.

When you face problems having to do with your search, we suggest utilizing the ABCs of problem solving. Those are:

A.) Articulate the problem. Once you have precisely and fully stated the problem, there are two (2) additional steps to be taken, both of which again will assist you.

B.) Break that problem into parts, those that you believe you can solve now, and those that you likely cannot.

C.) Carefully consider the help from other sources that you may need with the remaining problems. After that exercise, move ahead with those with which you can cope, and seek help with all the rest.

Approaching the search problem is not dissimilar to the other tasks you face in daily life. Let us give you an example. Most of us are familiar to some extent with the task of house cleaning.

Perhaps the house is in disarray. The kitchen sink is full of dishes, the children and their friends have tracked dirt throughout the place, leaving clothes, shoes, and all else imaginable strewn about. You have identified the problem; the house is a mess. (It would be much easier to be queen, wouldn't it?)

Then too, on some days your housecleaning tasks are easy and are accomplished quickly. At other times, quite the opposite is the state of affairs. So too is it with searches for adopted children or for birth parents. Some are quickly concluded, while others bristle with difficulty—mostly dead ends and records not to be found—and will not be quickly accomplished.

Whether it is the house or a search, divide the tasks into smaller pieces, into manageable quantities. Those, you will attack one at a time. Again, as with the house where there may be no set order for cleaning, so too with the search. Notice that in both tasks, the next steps will be determined by the time available at that moment for that effort, finding the means by which to do that work, and the decision to do it.

As said, you may need help. Some of the effort simply may be beyond your capacity and experience. For those problem areas you must select others with knowledge or skills that you do not possess.

Early on, legal problems may arise for which you will need a lawyer (of which later). Such efforts as Internet or phone number searches may be required and a friend or one of the young people in your family might assist there. Then too, and without doubt, there will be tasks which only your spouse, a grown child, or such as a sister or brother will be able to accomplish.

The best of approaches to a particular problem may fail now and again, requiring you to remain flexible. If you are spending hours on the Internet or in some other search effort without results that justify the time being spent (and that is likely), reread the suggestions in this book, abandon that effort for the time being, and try another approach. Discard any ideas that are not producing results; you have no time to waste.

In assisting Mary Elizabeth search for her birth mother, Owen learned upon arrival at the hospital in which she was born that they routinely destroyed all records forty years after the creation of those records. Owen arrived forty-one years after her birth, and so was called upon to at once adapt to that new circumstance. Similarly, if in the course of cleaning your house, you find a leaky faucet, all is not lost. Though the housecleaning must be interrupted, the pipe must be repaired or a plumber called, and a new tack must be taken until that problem is solved. So, be versatile in both thought and action, and keep your vision of the entire effort before you.

As with your intention to end up with a clean house, the vision of your successful search is that result for which you strive and hope to reach as the outcome. That motivation and the strength that motivation provides will move you forward, just as it first brought you to the search effort.

Remember, your vision of the desired outcome of your efforts are unique to you and are not identical with those of any other adoptees. Your birth mother falls in the same category; her vision when and if she contemplates a search, is surely different from yours and is unique to her. It is not important if your hopes are to affect a reunion, to locate your historical heritage, to satisfy your curiosity, to gain medical information, or all of the above. It is only important that you carry that view of the desired future with you as you work at the tasks ahead.

Just as with the housekeeping metaphor, you want your result to be consistent with your vision as to how your house should look, much the same as you must remain focused on your vision of the future while you are searching. So long as your methods are consistent with and appropriate to your goals, you will be carried along in the right direction.

Remember you must be willing to make careful and calculated decisions regarding the resolution of your problems and be willing to adjust to changes that may reach to your deepest and most secret thoughts and emotions. You may experience painful growth, but growth nonetheless, even though you had not expected to do so. So, be willing to adjust your thinking—your mindset—as to the future and your directions to that place, perhaps even drastically and most disarming.

DEVELOPING A MINDSET

You will find that those problems having to do with a search may be divided in still another way. As noted, there will be dragons resulting from obstacles which have no existence or reality outside of your thoughts and that are or have been created as a result of fear, intimidation, or a lack of knowledge. Yet there also will be problems that have reality outside of you. Though you will have a measure of control over your emotional problems—the imaginary dragons—yet as to those others, you may have little or no control.

By overcoming each problem it will become easier to tackle the next, and also to more clearly focus on the remaining tasks. Then too, by moving ahead you will achieve personal growth and you not only will become more and more the heroine of the story, but you also will gain great satisfaction for having met and overcome the hurdles of the task.

In considering and thereby adjusting your mindset to meeting the dragons, we suspect that fear of the possibility of rejection will be the most common and recurring emotion. If that is a fear, now is the hour to consider the role such feelings may play in your search and life. While for some rejection may not be an obstacle, for others, that fear may be daunting enough even to prevent their search lest they be rejected once again.

Thoughts of rejection are familiar to many, if not most adoptees. You have concluded that since your own biological parents walked away from you when you were but a helpless infant, it is undeniable that they did not want you. In short, you feel that they, or someone acting on their behalf, made the decision to give you away to someone else to raise. That decision may have resulted in benefits for you, but it also may have served to bring to you a lifetime of feeling that somehow you were undesirable or not worthy of the affections of those who should have loved you.

Your perception that a birth parent or parents, having refused to give their love and affection and provide your upbringing brings the fear that upon a reunion, those same people might so react again. After all, those parents had rid themselves of you before, or so the thought goes. The prospect that you may be turned away yet again may be a most disarming thought for you.

In the case of Mary Elizabeth, she had developed ways of dealing with such fears. She avoided some of the risks of life in general, and specifically she hesitated to begin a search for as long as she could live with her procrastination and denial.

Even as a little girl her thoughts would more than occasionally drift to that other set of parents, the unknown ones, and those biological ones, those with no faces yet. As she gave thought to those strangers, she often wondered why they had not searched for her. Or had they? And if they had never searched, was that not powerful evidence that they yet continued to reject her, who she was, and even her very existence? On the other hand, she also realized that if they had searched and failed, she would not know of their efforts. Tedious, confusing and difficult thoughts even for an adult, much more so for a growing child.

As you also might feel, further fortifying Mary Elizabeth's hesitation was the concern that any search effort might bring rejection from her adoptive parents also. That possibility brought the fear that by realizing her desire to locate those original parents, she might end up with no parent at all. The potential of such a double loss, she feared to the depths of her soul.

CONQUERING THE FEAR OF REJECTION

However you view either matter, we say welcome to the world as it truly is, the world of your feelings. Whether or not you already have done so, it is the time again to stand back and view yourself as you truly are. It is here and now that you must move beyond any and all thoughts of rejection by everybody, those of the past and any who might loom in the future. And, you must do so no matter the extent of those fears. You must refuse to allow any such thoughts to interfere with your search plans. You simply must stop wasting time, thought and energy on both the past and the what-ifs of the future. Now is the time to focus only on the task before you.

In your hesitancy to move ahead, remember that the only alternative to searching is for you to maintain the status quo, continuing with the wishes and hopes of your childhood, and finding it easier not to try than to fail. If you choose to surrender to those thoughts or to any other dragons lurking in the path ahead, then do so, yet understand that you will have deprived yourself of what might have been a future of enrichment, delightful revelations, and many happy moments.

In your efforts to move beyond the thoughts of rejection, examine for a moment the question, "Why did the birth parents not come looking for Mary Elizabeth," or yours for you? Even if they have not done so, you must not assume that those parents remain as unchanged and frightened as they were at your conception and adoption. Just as other of their actions in no way reflect their present thoughts, so too must it be said that their past actions concerning you in no way may be taken to reveal the attitudes they now maintain. Their failure to seek you out may not be evidence of anything except that they have not yet found you.

How so, you ask. There are many other reasons why your parents have not appeared at your door, not the least of which is that they simply may not have known how, just as you do not yet. Then too, they may not have had the means or the time to dedicate to the task, what with the demands of their own family and the problems of life. Even more, for all you now know, one of your parents may be ill or disabled, or a parent's spouse may have forbade such a search or reunion. And, of course, those parents may have died. Notice that if any of those relationships or problems exist, at this very moment your parent or parents, though they might not be instantly overjoyed at your contact for whatever reasons, might very well be receptive to your call, to a reunion, and to a future relationship.

Remember too, as an adult now you must consider that still other reasons may have driven that parent to a choice to not search for you. Thus, you must, at least until it is proven otherwise, give that parent the benefit of the doubt that the actions of either were appropriate and also in your own best interest, given the totality of the circumstances of that day and time. Consider that, the word "rejection" may have been completely foreign to your birth parent or parents, no matter how it may appear to you now.

So, thoughts may exist only in your own mind and have no basis in reality for anyone other than you. It may even be that any past thought of rejection by those involved arose from the society into which you were born or from the system itself, which discouraged any further contact. Given that possibility, and since the views of society have undergone broad changes even within your lifetime; you must infer nothing from the actions or inaction of years long gone.

Even more than that, the notion that a birth parent will once again turn you away is not borne out by our numerous interviews and experiences. Our discussions with birth parents and adoptees alike suggest that at least at the outset there is a substantial measure of hope and pleasure in almost all reunions.

Still yet, suppose there is rejection? Painful and dashing of your hopes as that may temporarily be, all is not lost. Through merely identifying the parent, and nothing more, you will have increased your knowledge of your family sufficient to permit you to visit and enjoy the great panorama of our common history and of your place in it. Opened to you will be all of the records that are revealing of those parents, their lives, the lives of their immediate and extended families, their (and your) ancestors, and all of the many records concerning the daily and past lives of all of those people whose blood flows in your veins at this moment.

Even more than those possibilities, thereafter it will be a simple task to learn the identities of your brothers and sisters, if any, and whatever military service any of your new family may have contributed to our nation. So, whether or not you are rejected, either little by little or out of hand, you will be immensely benefited by your search results. Perhaps of the greatest importance to you, there will have been lifted from your shoulders the huge burden of questions and unknowns that have haunted you through the years.

So, we yet feel that you must presume that you will have an enjoyable experience or at least be received. Away then, with fears of rejection.

SEARCHING IN PUBLIC RECORDS

The second most common obstacle has to do with taking the first steps, and we are not referring to obstacles or roadblocks to be found in the search to be made. We mean mustering up the courage to step out into that adventure, exactly how to begin, and how to make available the time and money that will be required of you.

By reading this material and exploring other publications that might be available, you have already made the first moves along your road. This roadmap and guidebook will take you to the end of the search. Next, you should investigate local support groups and ask for publications and periodicals that your library well may have on the shelves. The Internet may serve you well, and use of that tool is described in the chapters following entitled, "Needles in Haystacks" and "More Detective Work."

In addition to your fears of the results, whatever those may be, you may experience unwarranted, albeit real, anxiety, upon seeking out and requesting information to which you long have believed you are not entitled. With those concerns comes the belief—again ill founded—that you will encounter prohibitions when requesting information and be embarrassed in the course of denials.

No matter from what source or when you have been told that searches for birth parents or for children once given over to adoption are not permitted, you must put such false information from your mind. That simply is not true.

You are entirely within your rights to search all public records no matter where those may be stored, the only exceptions being those few files which some states have declared "closed." Though there are some states in which no adoption files are closed, and the majority of other states permit access to those files in the form of registry systems of which we will speak later, all other public records are available for your inspection.

Even as to the closed files, all states provide devices by which either the court or the social workers may grant you access to a file, as we will discuss in those chapters having to do with the mechanics of a search.

Significantly, in a few states there are no prohibitions whatever to searching and no "closed files." At this writing, those states are Alaska, Colorado, Georgia, and Utah. Other states soon may see fit to join the ranks of those that now maintain open files, especially Washington and Tennessee. In that context, realize that the law is a fluid system and is ever changing, albeit slowly, and at this date there seems to be a trend toward "open" adoption files.

Though you are legally free to search, as you will, over the years you may have been led to believe that somehow what you are about to do is socially unacceptable. That idea also has no basis in law or good manners, and likely arises from the fact that the system itself, more so in years past, has insisted that complete secrecy should be maintained forever by all involved. This idea that somehow your search is a social "no-no" may have been appropriate once, but it surely is not and should not be a guiding principal for the twenty-first century.

Caveat: There may be exceptions to our insistence that there are no legal or social restraints in your path. Ethics, perhaps here better-called "consideration for others," might come into play in those situations where your actions, intentional or not, might bring harm to others. So, be careful that those who stand innocently at the sidelines do not suffer from your actions. If that seems a likely result, make every effort to protect that person to the greatest extent that is consistent with your own need to move ahead with the investigation of your past.

Again to the issue of records and authority figures, we feel that you may experience a measure of timidity upon approaching such people, making telephone calls, or asking for help at the library. You must assume the attitude, or mindset, that there is nothing wrong, presumptuous, or rude in asking questions or seeking out information so long as it is done politely and with care.

The prospect of encountering rude or surly clerks in offices of public authority with whom you must deal, though not common, is real. Though some governments, agencies, courts and courthouse offices, clerks offices, newspaper archives, libraries and private parties sometimes have such inconsiderate and unhelpful employees, the best you can do is be polite, quiet, gently insistent, and businesslike. It was our experience, however, that most always, those able to help were willing to do so.

Of all the possibilities of failure that may lie ahead, we think that the only complete failure would be if the trail were to end without your having learned of the name of any birth parent, relative or contact. Still, even then and disappointing as such results would be, knowing that you had the courage and perseverance to follow your chosen path will provide for you much satisfaction and will put to rest the question of whether or not you could find them if you only tried.

In those rare instances, the searcher is rewarded in knowing that he or she has chosen to no longer sit, wondering what the results might have been. Instead, such a searcher has been willing to risk defeat by the dragons and for that willingness surely is deserving of congratulation. The alternative to embracing the challenge of search is to set aside the search, allowing your fears to defeat you.

Assuming again a successful search, an additional common fear that may be an obstacle is the thought that your birth parents or their station in life will not be as you anticipated or hoped they might be. Similar to those of rejection, such thoughts may be totally without merit. Remember that your control of the character of those strangers you find is about equal to your control over the appearance of the next child born to you; that is, none. Accordingly, you must put those concerns and products of imagination aside. Since your present thoughts change no feature or fact of those yet unknown people, to dwell on the character and station of that family you may find is a total waste of time.

Nevertheless, you must be careful of those thoughts, since such may be factors that are preventing you from moving on. In hiding your fears of results, you may have created another imaginary list of reasons why you are not ready or why it is not the appropriate time to enter into your search. So, be mindful of that list of apprehensions, know that you have all the elements, tools, and desire available to you, and you must not shrink back from the work ahead.

One final thought about the time required for your effort, particularly if you are telling yourself that you will make the effort, but that it cannot be right now because you simply are too busy. In fact, that may be the truth of the matter. As to that, however, you must be certain that you are not delaying by reason of the dragons. Be honest, arming yourself against such procrastination, rather than labeling poor excuses as good reasons. You must ascertain what if anything is providing you reason enough to keep you from progressing, and then defeat that dragon.

Imagine yourself some years from now living in a nursing home. You are sitting with several others or perhaps a friend discussing remarkable events of your lives. Will you be telling those friends, "Did I speak of the time that I considered looking for my birth parents, yet decided not to go ahead with a search?" Will you be happy then that you sat by as the years rolled on and failed to undertake that journey? Will that failure for whatever reason you may have had then be excusable? To these questions, we think the answer is "No."

On the other hand, the conversation could have gone something like this. "Say, Ethel, have I told you the story of when I searched for my birth parents?" Maybe you had told her, and in fact you thought you had many times but you could not remember (and Ethel did not remember either). She said "Why no, Myrtle, I did not know you were adopted." So you told her the exciting story in its entirety because it was a tale worth telling over and over.

Throughout the tale, Ethel replied with all of the appropriate Oohs and Ahs. And then with a smile you said, "Well, so much for finding out that I was heir to the throne, but still I sure did meet some fascinating people, a lot of ancestors, and I had a heck of a good time." No matter the outcome of your adventure, the story of your efforts will be worth the telling for years to come. And it is a good thing, because Ethel's stories were not nearly as exciting.

The point of it all is not that you will have stories to tell. It is about having undertaken frightening adventures of which you justly may be proud. It will be about stepping forward and confronting dragons, of going where not even you thought you could or should go, and of charting a course and moving forward, despite frequent trepidation and fears.

So what about being busy? Even if your daily schedule allows you but precious little time, you yet can make efforts such as you are doing by reading this, by calling support groups and reading articles, and by searching the Internet. Some small effort can be initiated in the matter of your search no matter how busy you are. As to search efforts beyond those, we think the only legitimate reason for hesitation is if you in fact do not have the financial resources to do anything further.

But even then, spend what you can, but because of your budget be careful. Do not pay anyone anything until you know just what services you will gain for your money, and that includes services offered on the Internet. Do not join lists that cost money. The same results almost surely can be obtained through the myriad free sources available to all members of the triad. We will speak further of such matters in the chapters following.

If any anger yet now remains from your life as an adoptee and is preventing your search, remember that such is in no way relevant, and now is the time to be rid of it, whether or not it has basis in truth. Anger serves no master and surely will not serve you in any way.

If anger yet remains, it likely has its roots in your desire that someone answer for your fears and disappointments. Still, while anger and blame may be a part of the equation for you, those must not prevent you from reacting favorably to the changes that have and will come to into your life. As with all other problems, carefully articulate the thoughts and how those affect you, and then find solutions. As to that, we have said enough, and you must dispel such thoughts now.

So, no matter how important or how insignificant, all fears that have become roadblocks must be expelled from your mind. To aid you, as mentioned earlier, we suggest that you should investigate and perhaps join a support group. Those often can be found even in cities of moderate size, are free, and since the leaders, members, and sponsors of such groups are familiar with adoption and the attendant problems, you likely will benefit greatly from their knowledge, support, and encouragement.

Should you feel you need further assistance, if you can afford to do so, see your family doctor and ask him for suggestions as to a therapist who might be experienced in both such emotional leftovers and adoption issues. Either will be time and money well spent.

Over all, and while developing an approach and a revitalized outlook, be always aware that your perceptions color your reality. So, stand back now and then, and view your situation and yourself objectively, as though through the eyes of an outsider as it were. Attempt to determine whether or not your view of yourself and of the situation is accurate. Remember, your perceptions may actually create problems that otherwise do not exist.

After undertaking to view yourself, as would an indifferent stranger, if you yet are uncomfortable with how your efforts are proceeding, step out of the activity and thoughts for a couple days or a week. Take a break. Rather than continue to focus on the problems at hand, consider and list the results you hope to achieve and the minimum findings that you might view as success.

Then, go back to it. Again, focus on the goals you have set and resume the problem solving. (Remember the ABCs of Problem Solving.) With the end always in mind and a fresh view of what you will accept as rewards, you may find that the techniques you next employ will differ from the methods you previously used. Such reevaluations may be necessary several times in the course of your efforts. So be it. Those mental exercises will help as you resume the efforts.

Just as your birth parent must, you should take up your paint brush of imagination, utilizing your new attitudes, and much constructive thinking, and undertake the task of changing the appearance—the landscape, if you will—of your life. Minimize the dragons, wherever those may appear in that panorama, hoping one day to color those out and gone.

This mental exercise and effort may take time. No matter what features that landscape may now reveal, this is the time to make the most of your opportunity to identify and paint away the obstacles that are interfering with your future. You need freedom, wings to fly to find your roots. Draw those in also.

INVOLVING OTHERS

As discussed, it may be concern for the sensitivities of your adoptive parents that is holding you back. That is true of many, we have learned. Or, maybe you are overly concerned about how other people will view your search efforts. Perhaps the most significant of your reasons is the fear that you will be called upon to reveal your long kept secrets. Those who may come to know of those anxieties may not understand even after you reveal your adoption, the attendant emotional difficulties, and your plans to search. Then, particularly if your revelations are followed by failure, you may feel that even more you will be the subject to criticism and that perhaps you should not have searched in the first place.

So, all that said, you now must decide how much the opinions of others should concern you, and that may be a difficult task for you. We all hope to be viewed favorably by everyone in our circle, but yours is a more difficult question; namely, will the strong opinions that a search might invoke so affect you as to prevent your moving on? If the answer is yes, you must grapple with that problem and win it over.

We think the reasons for involving anyone else turns almost entirely on your own need to share your thoughts and emotions. So then, to whom must you speak of your search plans and in what depth? The choice as to whom is entirely yours. Whoever you tell should be someone who encourages you and will lift you emotionally higher. Other than with the closest members of your immediate family you have no duties, ethical or otherwise to do so.

You will or should share your intentions with your mate and immediate family. Ideally, and by so doing, you will benefit from them by way of assistance and emotional support during the search effort. Then too, even if you do not gain total approval from your mate or family, you yet must proceed with your efforts. Unless to search will bring outright destruction of your family unit, their objections are not a sufficient basis for abandoning your plans. Still though, while moving ahead you should make all efforts to put your family at ease and accommodate their needs, as you satisfy your own. You and those members all have a duty to understand that those new relationships need not be foregone or even delayed for the benefit of pre-existing ones.

There may be problems within your family that will arise and remain with you throughout the course of your efforts, and yet have nothing to do with the search itself. Thus, if changes need to be made within your marriage that do not relate to your search, now may not be the time to undertake to make those alterations.

What might those be? Because of time constraints, your mate or your children may become jealous or feel unloved because of the hours that you will be called upon to dedicate to your search work. An adjustment to the new routine may be all that is required to calm that unrest. You of all people involved best know your family, so make such schedule changes as are necessary to bring contentment to those people, and as the weeks and months pass be sure regularly to share your successes (and failures).

Be careful too that you do not allow the search efforts to become reasons for other problems that are not truly related. Beware of abandoning the search because of problems that arise concurrently, yet are not traceable to the effort. Keep separate issues separate.

As mentioned briefly, if your children are old enough to understand you should include them in your discussions and plans. Still though, while the mechanics of the search are something that can be shared with your children when and if they are interested, not all of the emotional hurdles that you encounter need to be discussed. When they ask, share some of the challenges as long as those will not become a burden for them. If a child is not benefited in life by knowing of your internal difficulties, why tell them? So use good judgment when it comes to relating the total facts to the young. This is your journey, and they will likely not be affected as much as you will be.

There may be others within your close circle for whom you have such esteem or regard that they too should be included in your confidences. As to this group, if you feel you should share your intentions, then tell only those who absolutely must know. It is our advice that as others are taken into your confidences, you ask them to maintain the utmost secrecy in the matter. Why? Because for all you know, your birth mother or father may live just down the street, or may be a member of your own church or bowling league. He and she likely are somewhere, remember? That being the case, you will want to be the one to do the revelations, not someone who has little or no understanding of the matter.

Quite distinct from the decision as to those confidantes, the problems inherent in revealing your intentions and efforts to your adoptive parents may have a much greater impact in their life, and yours as well. Nevertheless, you may view that family as being among those in whom you should confide. However, it may be that you feel they need not know now. So, give careful thought to the desirability of telling them, particularly as to when you should do so. Whatever other relationships a child may have, affection and regard for those human beings who raised, nurtured, and taught to you the lessons of life have to be given serious thought.

There are as many different factors in this decision as there are adoptive parents and children. If you are comfortable in entering upon that discussion, then do so. If not, then put it off. The choice is entirely yours, and few are those who can help you make that decision.

It may be that you will want to tell your adoptive parents because they have valuable information, which you believe will aid you in your search. Still though, if that is the only reason for confiding in them, give serious thought to attempt to do without that information. What they know often is available elsewhere, and if revealing your purpose now might be disruptive, perhaps the extra time spent will have been the better choice. In view of those options, consider the age and mental health and well-being of those parents, and draw upon the totality of your experiences with them in deciding when to reveal your plans. Though you will have little control, you should be able to predict their reactions to some extent.

When you do tell them, you must assure them gently, compassionately, and with understanding that this will not diminish their position in your life, and that you do and will continue to love them as you have. All the while, keep them rooted in reality. Dispel whatever inaccurate or inappropriate thoughts they may reveal. Offer to help in answering any questions they may pose. We believe there will be but few questions that will bring to you great discomfort, and if such are posed you have every right to delay those answers; you are not there to be criticized or embarrassed. Do not feel apologetic; you have done nothing wrong.

Offer the possibility even of an increased mutual affection because they have showed willingness to support you in your needs. On the heels of that thought, we firmly believe that you should make a sincere effort to explain your reasons and assuage the fears that somehow they have lost something. We think that they have a responsibility to understand, just as you have a responsibility to reveal that which they want to know.

Failing an acceptance of your explanation and reasons, and while deferring to your parents and asking for their assistance, as an adult you must realize that you have equal control and determination with that parent in all matters of your adoption and search.   No matter your measure of deference in all other affairs of life, assume that equality, and gently insist that you be recognized as an adult and their equal in this matter, even if not otherwise. In short, adoption affected your life every bit as much as it did theirs.

If you have not felt constrained to tell them sooner, once you find your birth mother, you should realize that you have an obligation to address the whole subject with those parents and to include them in your discoveries. It may be that you will feel the need to become comfortable with your relationship with that new mother (or father) before you share that news with your adoptive parents. Again, so be it.

Moreover, in the unlikely event that you come away from the initial contacts with your birth parent or parents disappointed and unhappy, you may need even more time to deal with the issues before telling your adoptive parents of the search and results. Again, it is your problem, will have effects over the rest of your lifetime, so do that with which you are comfortable first, and if necessary leave the tale telling till another time.

However, if you do delay revealing the results of your research, let that delay be short. Why? Because, no matter your reasons, if you wait, say ten years or some other extended period, then your hesitancy may be viewed by your loved ones as deception.   Consider also the problems that might arise from telling your children, but not your adoptive parents.   By so doing, you will have imposed upon those children a duty of keeping secrets, even from their grandparents. So, the long and short of it is that you should soon reveal to your adoptive parents, if not the entire story, at least that portion that will bring them to date in your search. As always, in matters of adoption, we feel that only the truth can result in peace in your life.

Since keeping a secret prompted the need for Mary Elizabeth's adoption in the first place, she saw the opportunity to prevent yet another secret from wedging its way into her life. She realized that there was the possibility that the reactions of others may not be favorable and forged ahead despite that. Just as it was with Mary Elizabeth, the decision is yours to make when the opportunity presents itself.

It is our hope that you will decide to move ahead. It is your privilege and prerogative to do that which you are planning. So, while you should be ever conscious of the effects your search and its results may have on your world, still yet you must remain focused on your path and follow it. Follow it no matter the words of others, especially of those who know next to nothing of your past. Said more powerfully perhaps, a person who has not been an adoptee and yet chooses to be critical of one for searching is similar to that person who undertakes to describe a trip home from Chicago when he or she has never been there.

As in all of life during your search and whatever the products of that effort, you have an obligation to be forthright, candid and honest to the extent that you can do so without bringing serious harm to innocent bystanders. Those who would continue their relationship with you have a correlative duty to attempt to understand, continue in their love of you, and cope with your honesty no matter its effect upon them.

Remember: your desire to go find those missing parents is not indicative of shortcomings of your personality, and your search probably has very little to do with your other relationships. A roll of the dice placed you in the family with whom you were raised, placed you with people of whom you were not a biological part. And such brought about the desire to set about this journey.

Moreover, in addition to the problems you may encounter, in all matters you have every right to claim control and responsibility over your life and your future and you must prepare to do so. In the future and upon reunion, you have no reasons to feel out of sync with the world of people with blood ties to others that you have not before enjoyed.

CONCLUSION

We have here attempted to equip you with the tools by which you should approach this search and subsequent results, whatever those might be. Once again, back to *The Hobbit* and as one of the dwarves said, "...I still think that when we have won it will be time enough to think about what to do about it."[16] In the final analysis, the Dwarves failed to consider the actual acquisition of the treasure, how to carry it, and how they would divide their riches. We hope we here have provided answers to some of those questions you might have upon the discovery of your treasure.

As Bilbo Baggins, a dwarf of *The Hobbit* said, "...he felt the adventure was, properly speaking, over with the death of the dragon...in which he was mistaken...."[17] You too will find further adventure yet ahead of you. You have chosen a better approach than did the dwarves, one that prepares you to meet any challenge that may come upon you. You have the weapons needed to slay the dragons. Unlike the characters in *The Hobbit*, you should by now have found that mindset needed to carry you through and then beyond where you think the end will be found. You can win those battles because you have donned the armor of emotional preparedness.

The journey within never ends and you will be called upon to face your fears at many turns along the way in this journey as in others. While doing so, you must maintain the desire to persevere, all the while developing the attitude that you will succeed. When your thoughts lead you to consider the potential for hurtful results, remind yourself that you

---

[16] *Hobbit*, op cit., pp242-243
[17] *Hobbit*, Ibid., p. 271

now are equipped to cope. So, prepare for the unexpected and that will equip you for a life different than it has ever been.

The treasure is not yet yours, however. Are you ready for the rest of the journey?

Needles in Haystacks

"...It is the unknown with all its disappointments and
surprises that is the most enriching."
-Anne Morrow Lindbergh

Whether she cared to confront the fact or not, Mary Elizabeth was on the brink of venturing into the unknown. She had not known where to begin, since she had very little information that would lead her to her parents or to anyone who might know of them. "Looking for a needle in a haystack" was the expression that often came to her mind. More than that, though she could not predict the future, she thought that she faced the prospect of seeking out information from her file and otherwise in one of the most restrictive states of the Union.

She knew only what she had been told by Mrs. Kurtz as to where and when she was born and approximately how much she weighed. She had very little information with which to begin a search for a missing person, indeed. She suspected that her adoption file in North Carolina contained names and places that would help her with a search and perhaps even provide answers, but that file had been permanently sealed, or so she had been told.

As have many adoptees, she simply had no answers and did not know where to commence to find those or even if she should begin. Mary Elizabeth found herself at square one with an important task to accomplish and no knowledge of how to do so, should she develop the resolve. Finding a starting point would prove to be one of the easy parts of her efforts.

A DIFFERENT FUTURE, MAYBE

At that time, she could not have known the changes the future would usher into her life. And maybe that was for the best. Oftentimes, if a task ahead of us is a difficult one, thoughts of facing the unknown bring indecisiveness to the point of dread. By yielding to those fears, procrastination, fear, and ultimately, a refusal to move forward are likely to follow. Mary Elizabeth found herself caught in limbo, as she contemplated the future and whether or not to consider the future to be an enemy or as a mystery to be dreaded. The future is ripe with possibilities, opportunities, and challenges for those who wish to embrace it. Sometimes the future brings such gifts even to those who hesitate.

So, Mary Elizabeth would take advantage of the opportunity to venture beyond her life as it was and into an unknown world of people and places of her imagination. A window of opportunity was open for her and she needed only to decide whether to venture out and then beyond. Though quite unprepared for the emotional challenges she would undergo, in retrospect, she realized that, little by little, she had undergone and coped with the changes within her life and perspective, and how incredibly enriching those truly had been.

FEARS AND MISCONCEPTIONS FROM THE PAST

Further, as you may do at this beginning point in your search, Mary Elizabeth had clung to and perpetuated many of the adoption myths that she had learned as a child. Still though, as she looked for a starting place in her search, the courage to embrace the emotional transformation that naturally comes with such efforts grew within her. She assessed the mental and emotional inventory required to proceed, then did so. So too must you.

Many of her fears and concerns had been passed on to Mary Elizabeth during the course of her upbringing. Fear of strangers, of the unknown, and of taking risks, combined with a lack of comfort regarding her adoptive status, all made taking a leap of faith very difficult for her. "Better safe than sorry" had been her approach to life. Those fears and thoughts were but a part of the challenge.

There was also the concern for her parents. Mrs. Kurtz had told Mary Elizabeth that she would understand if one day Mary wanted to find the woman who had not kept her. Still, Mary Elizabeth suspected that those words had been bravado; mere words to hide fears of the unknown and of the possibility that she might be replaced as a mother sometime in the future. And her intuition would serve her well.

Through her younger years Mary Elizabeth had gone and would continue to go to extremes to protect her parents from being upset or hurt. Nevertheless, she took the view that, even though Mr. Kurtz had died years before, waiting for Mrs. Kurtz to die before a search was commenced was not a good idea. After all, her birth parents also might be dead, were such delay allowed. Mary Elizabeth therefore reasoned that she would need to protect Mrs. Kurtz from the perhaps painful knowledge of a search.

Whether or not she was ready, Mary Elizabeth thought that her ability to risk painful growth was about to be tested. In the course of having children of her own she realized, however, that all children should be nurtured, loved, and encouraged into becoming separate beings, not extensions of her and their father. She believed that as children grow to adulthood they must become ever more responsible for their own choices and that at adulthood, they must be prepared to assume independence even if it meant taking calculated risks.

Mary Elizabeth was about to mature quickly, making difficult decisions as she did so. She decided early on, and rightly so, that the approval of Mrs. Kurtz was not a prerequisite to a search. She had not chosen to be born, to be adopted, nor had she decided who was to raise her. She could choose, however, to stop living in her world of dreams about finding her birth parents and turn her dreams into reality. Her focus for the moment had to be on the task at hand.

As it will for you, searching has provided many with the opportunity to achieve a higher level of understanding. They have merely to embrace the desire to be receptive to whatever

gifts life has to offer.   Mary Elizabeth confided only in a few
people about her desire to do so and felt that the support
from her immediate family would go a long way in supplying
that measure of confidence and justification needed.   Though
she could only later understand, you may benefit from
knowing in advance that she found that the advantages of
searching far outweighed any of the risks, not only for her,
but also for all involved.

THE LAW, FIRST

Whether Mary Elizabeth or any other member of an
adoption triangle, before one can effectively search, some
knowledge of the applicable statutes and rules must be
achieved.   So, the question becomes "What law affects a
searcher?"

The answer is that the law of the place of birth and
adoption of the child quite usually controls.   However, it also
is important to notice that if the state of birth of the adopted
child was different from the state in which the adoption took
place, all members of that triad will be involved with the laws
of both states, and those laws may differ.

Not only does the law vary from state to state, but also the
rules, procedures, and administrations having to do with the
operation of those legal provisions vary, as well.   While
legislators and legal draftsmen and women have pursued a
"Uniform Adoption Act" for many years, there is yet no wide
acceptance of that proposed universal legislation.   It follows
that it well may be that the law and practices where you as
an adoptee, birth parent, or adopted parent now live are quite
different from those in the state or states in which you were
born and given over to the system by your parent or parents.

Accordingly, before you undertake any search effort, you
will do well to familiarize yourself with the rules that
probably will apply to you and your efforts.   So, contact that
county in which you were both born and in which you were
adopted (if those are not the same), that county in which you
became an adoptive parent, or that in which you gave up
your child.   This is easy to do, since all have telephone
listings, and in ever-increasing numbers, our counties have

websites that list county departments of government and courthouse main numbers. As is apparent already, always keep in mind that MUCH of your search can be done by telephone and Internet from your home.

If your Internet search fails to lead you to an office dedicated to adoption matters, or you are not a computer user, simply telephone that county courthouse main number ("operator"), and ask that person to connect you to the offices of the "clerk of courts" or of the "county clerk." When you reach either of those offices, request the name and number of that specific county office where you may inquire as to their laws and regulations concerning adoptions. We suggest that you ask for nothing more in this first call, since you do not yet really know what information or assistance you will need, and there is no good reason to tip your hand.

Be aware that someone at one of those numbers may refer you to some office at the state capitol. If that occurs, before you hang up, politely ask again for some LOCAL county office that might help you with "basic information" having to do with adoption records. Even if, in that state, all adoption questions and problems subsequent to the actual adoption proceedings are resolved at the state level rather than within that county government, there will be somebody in that courthouse who can and will help you with your basic and preliminary questions.

By the way, since it is likely that you will make such calls to courthouses more than once, you should try to make a telephone friend/acquaintance there. By so doing, future contacts may be a bit easier.

Incidentally, those state departments are variously titled. For examples, the California "Department of Social Services," the Colorado (and Ohio) "Departments of Health," the Missouri "Division of Family Services," and the West Virginia and Virginia "Department of Health and Human Services," are the names of but a few. So, whenever the department title being related to you is confusing, do not hesitate to ask again, and then note the precise name of that department that has to do with adoptions.

When you make contact with that office, whatever it may be called in your state, whether that contact is in person, through the Internet, or by telephone, your first question should be "Are your adoption files open or closed?" Since there presently are but four states with "open files" (Alabama, Alaska, Kansas and Oregon), quite usually that answer will be "Ours are closed."

There is another warning: Do not say anything to anybody in any public office about granting you access because files and information are "public record" or that you should be entitled to data because of the "Freedom of Information Act." Those legal terms have to do with law that is highly complex and difficult to understand, and almost never apply to searches such as yours. In short, forget those legal terms; those serve only to antagonize folks.

You then also might ask for instructions as to how you can gain a copy of the "State code" provisions that have to do with adoption. These legal rules may or may not be readable for you, but such surely will save time and effort for any attorney who might later become involved in your behalf, especially if your state of residence and that of the adoption are different.

PRIVATE OR PUBLIC ADOPTIONS

Adoptions fall into two main categories. Since the completeness of the information to be expected and found in the separate files of those two groups likely will vary substantially, it is important that you be aware of those categories.

A "private adoption" is one arranged by the parties and is quite usually brought to a conclusion by lawyers. There likely will be one or more attorneys for the adopting parents, and one or more for the birth mother and father, and if any agency is involved, that organization also may have a lawyer.

The potentially conflicting interests found in adoptions, especially private ones, require that you be aware that the interests and care taken in dealing with all the members of an adoption triad, and particularly of the child, may—MAY—have been other than the primary objective of the lawyers involved. If those folks who wished to adopt were in a hurry, or the birth mother was anxious to be about her life, either party may have been willing to move ahead with less than a thorough investigation. If that was the case, their lawyer may have been instructed to move more quickly and thus may have been somewhat less thorough.

Accordingly, should you gain access to the files, the records of "private" adoptions may be a bit less complete than you anticipated. Nevertheless, thousands of adoptions have been negotiated in private and the vast majority has been more than satisfactory.

On the other hand, a "public adoption" is one in which the state, in the form of a social or child welfare department, has taken charge of and has long-term jurisdiction over and responsibility for the child and for the adoption processes. That department or agency of the state sees to the necessary investigations of the parents-to-be, of the child, and of the mother of that child to be adopted, usually makes a rather complete report, and stands ready to advise the court handling the matter, should that information be required.

By reason of the involvement of the state government, public adoptions require a greater measure of control, and because our courts are always crowded, such proceedings take longer to conclude. Still though, the time spent may have been worthwhile, since trained and experienced social workers or (and) investigating officers of the judges quite usually were (and yet are) responsible for the well being of the child and also often come to know well the other persons within the adoption triangle. That extended effort may have contributed much, not only to the success of the placement but also in the completeness of the records that remain.

In this context, notice that for many years Catholic Charities, though not government controlled by any means, among its many other good works has acted in a most responsible manner and has overseen tens of thousands of placements of children with great care and regard for everyone involved. There are other similar private organizations that have and continue to act with high levels of responsibility, the names of which may be gained from the Internet, of which, later. Once more, the greater the care taken in the initial adoption procedure, the more information you may expect to learn from any of the files you may locate.

REGISTRIES

Tedious as such discussions may be, you also should have some basic familiarity with such as "closed" and "open" files, "registries," "intermediaries," courts, and the terms used within those systems. So, bear with us, and shortly we will return to Mary Elizabeth, her birth and adoptive parents, and their search plans and efforts.

Those states in which the legislatures and courts have ordered the "sealing" of public adoption files have come directly into conflict with those of our citizens who believe that such information should be freely available. Indeed, over the years, organizations and groups by the dozens have clamored for access to such records. To answer those demands through compromise, the social workers and the legislators have devised "Registries."

Through practice and experience, Registries have proven to be quite effective; though the most vocal of those who would open "closed" files remain unhappy with these devices. The term Registry simply means that a state with closed files has provided mechanisms by which adoptees, birth parents, and other interested parties may voluntarily enter their names on public lists. By so doing, those registered people reveal to all others that they are searching or are willing to be contacted.

Such registries are designated either as "passive registries" or as "active registries." The passive registries are also called "mutual consent" or "volunteer" registries. This category permits both parties (birth parent and adopted child) to register. When both have done so and a match occurs within the records, an administrator or court officer seeks to negotiate a contact or exchange of information between the parties.

The other and rather successful category is that of "active registries." Those require that only one member of the triad be registered.

Following that "active" registration, a representative, or appointee of the court or social agency examines the "closed file" for some identification of the person sought. That investigator then undertakes to locate the unregistered triad member. Once (and if) that person is found, the officer then makes contact and determines the desire or lack of the same of that person to be placed in contact with the registered party. Significantly, if the sought-after person chooses not to be contacted and to deny access to the file, the matter is closed.

As of now (2003), the states with "passive" registries are Arkansas, California, Colorado, Florida, Georgia, Hawaii, Idaho, Illinois, Louisiana, Maine, Maryland, Massachusetts, Michigan, Missouri, Nevada, New York, North Dakota, Ohio, Oklahoma, Pennsylvania, Rhode Island, South Carolina, South Dakota, Texas, Utah, Vermont, West Virginia and Wisconsin. Those with "active" registries are Indiana, Kentucky, Minnesota, New Jersey, and Oregon.

So, how does a person register? The process is not complicated, even though you will find slightly differing rules in the several states. There are four types of these registrations.

Those four are almost universally known as a "confidential intermediaries" system, an "affidavit" (or "consent") system, a "veto" system (or "proactive veto" system), and a "search and consent" system. The state in which you are involved will have pamphlets and people to assist you in understanding, once you have made contact with that office. Still though, although those folks will assist you, you will be well served to have the following minimal familiarity with each of the terms.

"Confidential intermediaries" are state government appointees (or sometimes volunteers) who have access to the closed files. Upon request and the payment of the usually quite reasonable fee, those people seek out the missing triad member, determine whether or not that person desires to be contacted, and then inform the searcher of the result of that inquiry. If that person contacted desires to be identified to the searcher, the appointed person assists in arranging a meeting by telephone, letter, or otherwise.

Under the "Affidavit" (or *Consent*) system", any member of the triad (including you, of course) may file with that state an affidavit (a sworn statement, a "release") stating that he or she consents to the release of his or her confidential information under certain conditions. This filing quite often goes hand-in-hand with the "Search and Consent" mechanism (mentioned below), since virtually all who would pay for a search also would be willing to be found or at least to release some information.

That "Search and Consent" system, as the name suggests, permits public and private agencies to do the search for you. Usually for a fee and expenses, those searchers examine the closed file in order to identify the party to be found. They then undertake to make contact with that person, and determine whether or not he or she wishes to release the identifying information that is in the file. If so, then the court steps in and decides whether or not that information should be disclosed to the searcher. Notice that if the person sought has filed the sworn statement ("affidavit") of permission mentioned above, the court is no longer needed to gain that permission; it is of record in the form of that affidavit.

Finally, there is the "Veto system." Here, any member of the triad may file a sworn statement of record stating that he or she does NOT wish to be contacted by or permit information to be released to anybody. Importantly, where this method of registry is available, the person filing the veto, even though not wishing to be contacted, nevertheless may be willing to provide that the birth certificate of the adoptee (and sometimes other specific information) be released to the adoptee or to adoptive parents.

It is important that you remember that these methods and devices are designed to assist you in working within the system, and to do so without the usually expensive legal services that might be otherwise involved.

Do not forget that even if these methods are met with a refusal to be contacted or the person sought has not been located by the agency, though you then may come away from there knowing nothing, there are yet many ways by which you may continue your search. As to those, we will speak shortly and at length.

As we have stated, the system, rules, and devices having to do with public adoptions are not perfect. Nevertheless, in light of the differences in opinions and how unwieldy government can be in dealing with tedious social problems such as adoption, the system is the best devised to date. Whatever the shortcomings of these methods, we very much suggest that you join these registries while your other search efforts are underway. Enough then, for the moment, of laws and regulations.

AVAILABLE SEARCH BOOKS

There is a number of books available having as a subject "how-to" find birth parents and children previously adopted out of the system (see the Bibliography). A few do a more than passable job of explaining the efforts most needed and best employed for locating such people.

That said, most readers are not accustomed to interpreting statutes, working with public and courts' records, nor are they lawyers or social workers accustomed to dealing with those professions. So it is we have undertaken here to assist those who find such materials confusing or difficult.

INTERNET SERVICES AND LISTS

As said, you should first join any registries provided by your state, and then, as Mary Elizabeth did, we recommend that you also use the Internet. You will be served well if your name, purpose, and basic information appear in several of the numerous reunion sites there available, limited in audience as those yet may be. A "search" of the net for the words "adoption reunions," "reunion registry" and "adoption registry" will yield many such avenues and sites by which to inform other Internet searchers of your presence and those whom you seek.

There too will be newsletters providing updates in matters such as changes in the law and new indexes and lists that have become available there or on line. At this writing, for a well-written, and helpful source, serving all members of the triad we might suggest, http://adoption.about.com/. Once you reach that site, you will find many other helpful aids, sources, and lists.

It is our recommendation that for now you purchase none of the services or reading materials, and that you pay for no listings in registries advertised on the Internet or otherwise until you have thoroughly examined the many free sources available, especially those for your state or section of the country. While professionals and lists abound who will and are often able to assist you in one way or another, the price may be high and the services offered perhaps unnecessary.

So, wait until you have come to understand exactly what help you need before paying for the efforts or services of others. There are many avenues to good advice, and since you will be able to do much of the work yourself in your spare time, you may find that you need none of those costly "aids."

No matter whether the adoption in which you were involved was public or private, you surely also must "search" the Internet under the name of the county where that proceeding took place. The "net" provides newspapers, physicians, lawyers, and social agencies of the counties and states of the United States. Make notes of or print out the names, telephone numbers, and addresses of all organizations that might even remotely be of help in the coming months. Also, be sure to check the yellow pages for that city, county, or state under "adoptions" and "adoption services" for entries that may prove helpful.

You should also then spend the time needed to gather such other addresses (including e-mail addresses) and telephone numbers for such as the county or private social services, the hospitals, the Bar and Medical associations, and the office of vital statistics (if that office exists in that county). While searching those telephone directories, also check for libraries and genealogical associations, any, or all of which you may well need in your efforts.

Your purposes in now acquiring such addresses, telephone numbers, Internet addresses and details are not only so you will have such data when you or your searcher need it, but also to save you time later when you are hot on the trail of your person. Time and travel are very expensive, and the more hours and sources you are able to provide from home for yourself and for those others who may assist, such as investigators, lawyers and genealogists, the greater will be your savings.

Caveat: remember, the Internet is but one more tool, and most answers are not yet to be found there. While it is true that every day there are more people and organizations accessible through that medium, many folks and groups that well may be important to you are not yet present there. Accordingly, failure with that source, voluminous as it already is, means almost nothing to you. Enough for now, of search aids you may need to seek out.

AN EMERGING PLAN

As so often, we are best able to discuss methods for searching by revisiting the characters in our story. We have watched Mary Elizabeth grow up, marry, have a family of her own, and struggle to cope with her fears, and her hesitation regarding and consideration of a prospective search.

In Mary Elizabeth's mind, another thought is forming as she questions why she had been placed in the situation in which she found herself. In an effort to understand, she begins to wonder how her search experience could be used for the purpose of serving others in similar situations.

Regardless of such thoughts, at age 40, she is planning that search for her birth mother. Moreover, should that effort succeed, she hopes then to seek out her natural father. In following her efforts, we will simultaneously speak of methods that her mother, Barbara, (or her unknown father) might employ, were she to search for Mary Elizabeth and in doing so encounter the same or similar problems.

At those points in the story where any of the methods used did or might have failed, we will add facts and additional methods and records that have been successful in similar search problems of others. Notice too that the methods suggested apply equally to public and private adoptions, unless we note otherwise.

Over their years together and in deference to Mary Elizabeth, her husband, Mike, had helped her maintain near total silence about her adoptive status. As do many adoptees, she had perceived that silence to be very important. For those reasons, it was rather remarkable that one day when Owen, a genealogist, was at his office, Mike mentioned that Mary Elizabeth had been adopted. Following that short exchange and those that followed, and despite her fears of failure and the demands of her busy life, something of a search plan began to arise from their conversations.

Owen had assured Mary Elizabeth and Mike that, while it would be tedious at times, she likely would be able to do such a search with but little outside help. She decided to proceed as time permitted, and Owen was happy to assist her where needed in both planning and moving ahead with the effort.

As it should have been, and in keeping with her long reluctance to speak of her life as an adopted woman, coupled with Owen's suggestion that a premature revelation of her efforts might cause problems with the search, it was agreed that the utmost secrecy would continue by everyone involved. They realized that for all anyone could really know, the birth mother, father, or someone who knew those people might live across town, or even perhaps a block away.

Notice that it would have been the same if Owen, instead, had been advising her birth mother, Barbara, in a search for Mary Elizabeth. As with all of our personal business, and particularly with a search such as these, we should tell no one who does not truly need to know.

EXPECTATION OF SUCCESS

As do most, at the outset Mary Elizabeth had but little expectation of success in locating either or both of her parents. By reason of that concern over failure, and as a safeguard for her emotions should the trail reach a dead end, she maintained a guarded approach to the search and rationalized that at the least she might glean genetic information, or health history, and perhaps both.

Because of her concerns that disappointment might result, she indulged herself in the more comfortable thoughts and distractions at hand. Such were the care of her children, her work, her duties at home and to Mike, and her community activities. By so doing, she hoped to remain occupied and distracted from whatever adversity might come her way.

Mary Elizabeth felt that it was safer to continue her life as it was rather than to risk the achievement of the life that might have been.   Lack of confidence and fear of the unknown often prevent us from reaching higher and asking for more in our lives.   Yet, if we believe that seeking and being willing to receive the gifts that will come to us are all that is required, we will be quite able to be rid of fear, cease the worry over what others think, and shed our hesitancy to believe that we are entitled to what we receive.

As the months passed her confidence grew, reinforced by reason of Owen's often-expressed view that one day she, as do most patient searchers, would learn those identities, even if those discoveries might be years in the future.   Those assurances coupled with the support of family and friends fortified her, since her thoughts that a search might fail, or that she might be even more disappointed by the results, had long kept her from making the commitment even to commence the effort.

There was yet another concern.   What if Mrs. Kurtz withdrew her affection after learning of the pending search, and then that effort failed, would Mary Elizabeth be left motherless? And could she handle that? She thought she could, even though, tragically, for some adoptees that fear is not unfounded.

Many, if not most, adoptees and birth parents have similar nagging reservations, and so it was that the planning only sputtered along for six months or so.   Still though, the following winter Mary Elizabeth decided that come what might, her need to search would be satisfied and not be further delayed. She found the spirit and strength needed to begin to face certain fears. Is it not so often true that by confronting the demons within us we learn to be unafraid?

WHO IS OUT THERE?

Again, as most searchers do, she came to be ever more aware that there were no means by which to anticipate whom or of what character might be those people who she would uncover. She was reminded, again, of the words "It does not do to leave a live dragon out of your calculations if you live near one." Whether or not she would encounter dragons, she could not know, but if such were about, she would steel herself to do her best to deal with them. When you reach the Reunion chapter, you will gain a glimpse of the secret found by Mary Elizabeth, the chinks in the armor of the dragon.

Still one more consideration weighed heavily on Mary Elizabeth, as it does with many searchers. No matter even if it was required that the effort be abandoned because of the dragons or by reasons of disheartening discoveries, she could do no less than to protect her children in every way from whom or whatever might be out there.

FIRST STEPS

So, the search would commence, but what should she do first? She and Owen could have no notion whether or not Barbara or any other persons who had known of Mary Elizabeth's birth had access to the Internet. Still though, as you will, he had entered Mary Elizabeth's name and a few other facts about when and where she had been born and adopted on several Internet search lists. He would have entered that data in a state registry, however North Carolina has not seen fit to so provide.

Next, and as all searchers must, she undertook to learn and make notes concerning every bit of pertinent information available, no matter how small or seemingly insignificant and unimportant. She calculated rightly that any or all of such facts, even the most casual and no matter from whom or where those might come, could prove to be helpful or even critically important as the search effort moved forward.

Notice here that adoptive parents and birth parents alike quite usually will have within their individual memories many, if not most, of the facts surrounding the original adoption proceedings. After all, those people were present and directly involved with those proceedings. Not so, the adopted young child, of course, who likely will have none of those same bits of information except such as might have been told to either as she or he grew to an age of understanding.   Remember too that the birth father very often had none of this information.

With the reminder that before a search may begin birth parents also must gather together any and all memories they and all others involved can now recall, we will continue with the search efforts by Mary Elizabeth. So, what now?

THE *WHERES* OF IT ALL

Though it seems so obvious as to not be worthy of mention, the fact is that many searchers fail to constantly remind themselves that the key to success is to learn where everybody involved was located on every important date. Since one can hardly search the whole world, a locale is required at the very least.   As in ordinary genealogical searches, where residences and whereabouts of ancestors during significant periods of time are critical, so too are those wheres indispensable to your efforts.

Remind yourself, also, that in investigations such as that you propose, until you have learned the names of the persons sought, you have nothing except the wheres by which to focus and direct any search efforts.   And so it was with Barbara and Mary Elizabeth, who, remember, not only had no idea of the whereabouts of the other or even whether or not each was alive, but also they had no name with which to begin.   The common denominator for both of them was the location—the where—of the birth of Mary Elizabeth.

It is of the utmost importance that you bear in mind that whenever we here recommend, or you otherwise are called upon to search county records, you should first go to the Internet. There, search for whichever state you are studying, and at that state website observe (and note in your file) what records are available for viewing on-line; all states have such web sites, some complete, some not at all so. No matter what records you find there, you must also search the significant counties within that state for the same materials that are of interest to you within that state.

The materials most valuable to you that might be found within those websites of states and counties are "vital records," "vital statistics," "marriage records," "birth records," "death records," cemetery records" and "court records." So, first use your computer whenever it is suggested that state and county sources may be helpful. If you do not have a computer, ask a friend to help you with that source.

Later, after you have gained a name for the child or either of the birth parents, the *wheres* you have gathered and noted will be even more valuable. With a name and a place, you can learn of such as baptism and other church activities, census records, military service, marriages, divorces, criminal, school and tax records, lands owned and mortgaged, drivers' and professional licenses, business efforts undertaken, voter registrations, and unions or societies joined. If need be, and as mentioned, you may be called upon to search as to where and when the person whom you seek may have died. As we move through the search with Mary Elizabeth, we will consider those categories of records in more detail.

So, as to every person even remotely related or in any way involved with the person for whom you search, you must learn as much as possible about where each was located or lived at all important dates, particularly the dates of the birth, the adoption, and the court proceedings and decrees. Once again, *WHERE, WHERE, WHERE* is what a search is all about!

MEMORIES OF ADOPTIVE PARENTS

If you are an adoptee and feel that your adoptive parents are not your confidantes, then you must decide whether or not to seek the information they may have. While we also will later speak of those relationships where an adoptee feels that he or she is not able to so confide, for now we will presume that you will find that discussion appropriate.

Though it would not be at all unusual if Mr. or Mrs. Kurtz thought that they remembered nothing that would be of assistance to Owen and Mary Elizabeth, an in-depth interview of those adopted parents might reveal quite otherwise. If their individual memories are piqued a bit, either or both may remember where and in what hospital or home Mary Elizabeth was born, perhaps the names of one or more of the social workers involved, and the name and location of the social agency that investigated them and their home.

Those parents also may recall the names of doctors, nurses, lawyers, judges and other officers of the court who were involved in one way or another. Then too, each may know and, during the interview, may recall bits of information that the other adopted parent has long forgotten. Any such tiny bit of evidence or name might be that one source that one day will spell the difference between success and failure, so make very careful notes.

In earlier years, when Mary Elizabeth had asked the Kurtzes for details surrounding her birth, they had told her that they had absolutely no information. At this particular point in time, Mary Elizabeth felt that nothing could be served by discussing the search with Mrs. Kurtz and in fact, there may be much to lose. Mary Elizabeth further thought that encouragement rather than dissuasion was what she needed from others at this time. Since she also felt that Mrs. Kurtz might be hurt by the revelation, she chose to delay it.

CONTACTS WITH LAWYERS

So too, a birth parent who is now searching for a child often will recall the names of many of those same participants. Further, because of the gravity of the situation to her particularly, her recollections of those people and facts might be the most vivid of all. Also of the greatest importance is the fact that if the adoption was "private," for his own protection and as a matter of good business, any lawyer involved probably preserved a file, perhaps for many years, and maybe even to now. Notice too that even if the file was long ago relegated to the trash bin, if he is yet alive that lawyer well may remember something of the case and of some of the parties involved.

You need to bear in mind that in private adoptions, unless you were the original client (or are his or her sole heir) you have NO rights whatever—NONE—to read or copy any of the contents of that file. Such work products of attorneys are not "public record" and are confidential as between those lawyers and their clients.

Accordingly, unless the attorney has the permission of the original client, he or she very likely will feel ethically bound to maintain the confidentiality of that file. Still though, if that original client is dead or has long ago disappeared, and if you are the adopted child, or perhaps even the birth mother, many lawyers will relent to some extent and assist you as their conscience and ethics permit.

We think that you should call ahead and seek to visit personally with any lawyer who was involved; to attempt to gain what you need by telephone conversations is almost never successful. If you do visit the attorney, be courteous and ask him politely for whatever help he feels professionally free to provide. Should he be dead, it may well be that the attorneys who assumed his practice retained his old files, so be sure to ask for their help, as well.

We know of very few lawyers who have refused to help to some extent. We also suggest that before commencing your conversation with the lawyer, you should inquire as to charges, if any, for the time he or she might spend with you. You need no financial surprises.

Significantly, if the adoption resulted in a decree from a court—and most did—Mrs. Kurtz almost surely kept and yet has a copy of that paperwork. In fact, she had long before given Mary Elizabeth a copy of the Interlocutory (preliminary) and Final Decrees and also the amended birth certificate issued by the court. The decrees contained her date of birth, the date she was given over to the Kurtzes, the full names of Mr. and Mrs. Kurtz, the court handling the matter, and, of course, the name the Kurtzes gave Mary Elizabeth.

Notice that if the adoption was "public" Barbara, as the birth mother, likely did not see, participate in, or have details of the proceedings in which the Kurtz family was identified, nor could she know the new name assigned to her baby. Through that built-in confidentiality, Barbara's knowledge of the adoptive parents was as incomplete as was the knowledge of Mary Elizabeth concerning Barbara.

Mr. and Mrs. Kurtz might even recall matters of importance concerning the actual proceedings, especially if there were social workers or witnesses in attendance who they only then met or did not expect to be present. Remember too, that if the adoption was privately arranged, there almost certainly was a contract—an agreement—signed by both the adopted parents and the birth mother, or by both parents.

Then too, and importantly for your search, in almost all jurisdictions that document was approved by a court and (or) recognized by a formal "decree." Whether by contract or decree or both, such documents quite very often were placed of record in the offices of the "Clerk," "Recorder," or "Registrar" (sometimes also called "Register") for that county. When you later go to that courthouse, simply ask for the office where people "...record their adoption decrees." They will know what you mean and will point you to that office. Remember, however, that while such recorded documents do not identify the birth parents or the name the adoptive parents assigned to Mary Elizabeth, there will be clues there that will lead you to other sources.

Finally, just as a natural mother remembers the birth of the child and many events surrounding that birth (and, probably of her conception, as well), Mrs. or Mr. Kurtz also almost certainly would have some details of great importance concerning the birth. Significantly, if the adoption was private, Mr. and Mrs. Kurtz almost surely will have some recollection of the birth mother, if—IF—they met her. Then too, Mrs. Kurtz probably remembers the color of Mary Elizabeth's hair and eyes, birthmarks, and her exact weight and height on the date she was surrendered to the Kurtzes by the birth parent or parents or by the agency from which Mary Elizabeth came.

These memories and notes are most important since, based upon such small details, a searcher might well be able to distinguish between a written record of this child and that of another child with nearly identical features. So, as always, make careful and complete notes for later use.

So, through the examination of the preliminary and final decrees from the adoption, Mary Elizabeth had verified some important *wheres*. She likely knew the city, county, and state in which she had been born, and from which county a judge had ruled in the matter, those places being among the most needed if she was to move ahead.

Notice that had the searcher been Barbara instead of Mary Elizabeth, she would use the very same facts. Barbara would gain her information through the offices of the clerk, registrar, or recorder where the decree or contract was recorded. Incidentally, there are almost NO secret or confidential records in the offices of county recorders and clerks. Thus, any of the parties may go into those offices and for small fees gain copies of almost any materials recorded there.

Once those *wheres* of the birth and adoption proceedings are noted Mary Elizabeth (or Owen) might then need to move again to the telephone, the Internet or to their desk to write letters. They would seek to learn any details stored in memories of those other participants, if any, who were discovered in the recorded documents. A birth parent doing a search would seek to recall and locate those very same details.

NON-IDENTIFYING INFORMATION

While working to gather the data that is available from all the people in any way involved, it is equally important that searchers (whether birth parents, adopted children, or adoptive parents) gain a copy of those facts known generally as the "non-identifying" information. That material is universally available from the states or from counties within the states in which a public adoption took place. So, what is this all about?

When any agency of government becomes involved in an adoption by way of social services, through actions of the courts, or otherwise, a file is created. That file contains information thought important and legally significant concerning the birth and the parents (both birth- and adoptive-) and having to do with the adoption procedure itself. That file also contains what, if any, further information may have grown out of any post-adoption activities.

Just as were the Registries created by many of the states, another compromise between the interests of those who would close all files and those who would open the same permits certain information to be abstracted from those files and made available to those interested. That information is then called the "non-identifying" information of which we speak.

Notice that the non-identifying information will not include names, addresses, relatives, witnesses, or any other facts by which you can identify birth parents, adoptive parents, or the name or whereabouts of the child. Scant as it may be, having what little data is available to you from that source is critical, just as are the recollections and documentation held by the parents and any further information you might gain through the Internet or the state registries. Directly, we will discuss what is to be found there.

So, to review, though she has yet to receive what non-identifying information may be open to her, Mary Elizabeth has some information from her adoptive parents, their memories, and their paperwork. Similarly, if the searcher were the birth mother, Barbara (searching for Mary Elizabeth), she would have the same information, those details also arising from her memory and likely will have the decree or order that may have been placed of record in the county of the adoption.

Thus, all would (or could) have nearly the same facts at this point in time. Notice, however, and significantly, none would yet have names, addresses, telephone numbers, social security numbers, or any further information that would lead directly to the other parties in the triad. So, what next?

The information and the memories of both sets of parents, and of Mary Elizabeth from what she had been told over the years, all would reveal that she had been born on a certain date in a certain place. Let us imagine that Mary Elizabeth was born on December 1, 1958, at Asheville, Buncombe County, and North Carolina. Thereby, that city now becomes the next important *where* for the search for her birth mother.

As a brief aside for a moment, notice that the governments of some cities and counties have merged in recent years. Such mergers are common, and a few examples will suffice.

Such are Nashville/Davidson County in the late 1960s, Miami/Dade County, even earlier, Elizabeth City County/Hampton in 1952, and Nansemond County/City of Nansemond in 1972, which entity then merged with the City of Suffolk in 1974.

Thus, if you learn that you were born in Princess Anne County, VA in 1960, you must now search the records of the City of Virginia Beach to find yourself. So, if you know the city and not the county of birth, or vice versa, check an atlas and learn the name of applicable county as it is known now. Or, simply call the courthouse of the principal city in the area and ask the clerk's office when and what "cities and counties" were merged, if any.

Before we leave the matter of county governments, it is important that you recognize two other details about those political subdivisions. First, almost without exception all adoption and court records that you may need will be housed in the records offices of either the counties or the states, and not within the records of cities. As mentioned, the exceptions are cities and counties in which the governments have been merged.

The other factor that might be encountered is that during the years since the adopted child was born, some courthouses have been burned or flooded, and the records lost. As we said, since the originals or copies of most adoption records were forwarded to the state, if the records with which you are involved were burned or otherwise destroyed, simply ask at the local courthouses which of such materials were forwarded before the destruction and to what state office. Having gained that information, go to that office and again take up your search. No matter what you do or do not find there, move ahead with the other sources discussed here. You must not use any local loss of records as an excuse or reason to end your search.

Back to Mary Elizabeth. Her county—Buncombe—is the *where* of the moment for the search by Owen and her. It was in that place that she first drew breath, and so it is there that some record (though perhaps well hidden) of her presence and that of her mother may be found. It follows, of course, that if that county is where the birth and (or) the adoption took place, that courthouse, its records, and the lawyers practicing there likely also will be prime targets of a portion of your investigative work.

BIRTHS

As we have seen, regulations and practices concerning adoptions vary widely across the United States and the same services and offices may be called by different names in different states. Moreover, once again, most of our states require that adoption files and records of judges' activities relating to those files be forwarded to a state division of social services or department of vital statistics. Rather than have a duplication of records, a county may choose not to keep copies of such records that have been forwarded to the state. So, you must come to know what rules apply in your *where* county.

Just as you did in the first phone call when you sought basic information, again call a main number at that courthouse and ask to speak to that office where you can learn of the handling of adoption records in THAT courthouse or county. They will connect you with someone.

Always bear in mind that courthouse people are busy with county business and have little time for non-county business. So, VERY briefly state that you are seeking to locate a person who was adopted or (if you are the mother) a person who gave birth to a child there in a certain year. Without giving your adoption status, continue by asking if such birth and adoption records are maintained in that county or have such been sent to the state. They will tell you.

Then, ask that clerk for a form or for an address to which you may write to gain the "non-identifying adoption information." If you say it in that way, they will know what you mean and will give you that information. They may also supply forms and explanations on their website, so you also should inquire of that clerk about that possibility.

Notice, however, that while non-identifying information will assist the adoptee or any adoptive parents in their search efforts, which data would be of almost no help to the birth mother. Unless that mother simply needs to review the facts in order to refresh her memory, it would be information that she had personally participated in, known, and witnessed.

Be aware, however, that a birth father seeking his natural child would be in a quite different position. He likely would know approximately when the child was born, and surely would know the name of the mother, yet if he did not know where she had gone to have the child, he would be at a dead end, at least temporarily.

If you learn that the file and information you need is yet kept in that county, ask what steps must be taken for you to gain copies or access to the information. If, instead, you learn that the file you need is at the state capitol, as in North Carolina where Mary Elizabeth was born, again ask if there is a state form or a website by which you may request copies from that office.

Throughout all of your search efforts, it is our suggestion that you reveal to no one what your purpose is for calling or requesting information, and that you say nothing about being a birth parent or an adopted child. Unfortunate as it is, the words "I was adopted" or "I gave up a child" seem to wave a red flag at some records keepers. The reason is that there are those, even yet, who feel that you have no business seeking to locate other people involved in or to probe even in your own adoption files, and that they should not help you, even though they may be permitted by law to do so.

So, should a clerk ask for your reasons for needing to examine such files, be prepared to tell them that you are doing research of your family "genealogy." That is exactly what you are doing; seeking family history, and that answer is truthful and often will suffice. We do not suggest that you be untruthful with anyone ever, however we do suggest that to the extent possible, short of that, you say no more than is absolutely necessary. In short, concerning your purposes and status, remain quiet with everybody.

There is an additional reason for maintaining secrecy. Though the files may be closed, there are other legitimate avenues into records that you should not now divulge or discuss with anyone.

WHAT IS, IS

So, all else aside, whether the laws in effect for your state provide for "closed" files, "open" files, registries, intermediaries, or some variation on those themes, whichever system it is, it is! If the files indeed are closed, do not—repeat, do not—debate the questions of "open" versus "closed" with anyone, especially in courthouses. Those clerks and officials did not make the laws or the rules, can not change or vary any of those, and may have strong beliefs in the matter, which convictions well may differ from your own.

So, thank that courthouse person you called for information, and then hang up. To voice objection to their advice or comments may serve only to cause that official to consider you as an annoyance, which you surely do not need when you go back to that courthouse (and you probably will). So what next?

Back to Mary Elizabeth and Barbara. Although North Carolina is one of the states that has closed files and also forwards all completed files from counties to the state offices in Raleigh, rather than leave those in the charge of the counties, all was not lost. It was then time to make the request of the state for the non-identifying information, which Mary Elizabeth did immediately after learning that the files concerning her adoption were not at the county level.

COURTESY IN GENERAL

As an aside, when Mary Elizabeth called the Buncombe County, North Carolina, courthouse the clerk with whom she talked volunteered that she—the clerk—would request the records from the state offices. She thought the matter might be taken more seriously than a request made by Mary Elizabeth. That gesture by the clerk was very much appreciated, and revealed to Mary Elizabeth that her own kindness and businesslike, courteous, and subdued approach in the contacts with officials had served her very well indeed.

So, the request was made, and Mary Elizabeth sent the small fee. A month or six weeks later, she received that non-identifying information. Though there were NO names, addresses, or photographs, for the first time ever, her natural mother and father were no longer mere fantasies. To her, they were becoming "real" people. There was enough information found on that document to allow Mary Elizabeth to begin to form a mental picture, a profile of sorts of her birth parents. How exciting it was that a single sheet of paper that had rested quietly in a file for all of her life could contain information that had eluded her for all of those years.

That message from the state confirmed that Mary Elizabeth had been born early in the morning on a cold Monday, December 1, 1958, and went on to reveal that she had weighed 8 lb., 3½ ounces. Further, that her mother (name not given, of course) had been in her mid-twenties, weighed 125 lbs., had blue eyes, blonde hair, was 5'8," and had not finished high school.

Her father, it was there stated, also had been in his mid-twenties and had completed high school. He was tall; it said—6'3½"—and had brown eyes. More than that, the short report revealed that the father also had dark brown curly hair, weighed 185 lbs., and his mother—Mary Elizabeth's grandmother—had died shortly after his birth. It also was stated that Barbara's parents were yet living when Mary Elizabeth was born. Finally, though there was no other medical information to be found, it stated that there had been no mental illness known in the families of either parent.

Since Mary Elizabeth also had brown eyes, that tiny scrap of information suggested that when looking in the mirror, she was seeing her FATHER'S brown eyes! Her imagination was set into dizzying motion by those few words about who they were, and those few specific characteristics provided some evidence, sparse as it was, of the physical appearance of the close ancestry of her and her own children. Mary Elizabeth then could begin to develop a sense of what these people were about, at least at the time of her birth. She was delighted to be rid of some of the features she had been required to draw from her imagination!

That meager information, so commonly known to most of us, made Mary Elizabeth feel like she had accomplished some kind of deceit, as though her grandmother had told her she could eat some chocolate cake after her mother had forbidden such a repast. It was a delicious feeling to have in her possession that which was previously forbidden and which had been denied her, even though those facts truly were hers, she felt; knowledge, albeit but slight, of someone to whom she was truly related. While most children grow up knowing that they have their mother's eyes or the smile or height of an aunt, or that their grandmothers were alive or dead when they were born, Mary Elizabeth had known nothing until that mail arrived. What a thrill!

The hunt was on in earnest now, and it was time for a research trip to Asheville by Owen. While he might have attempted to do what had to be done by telephone, e-mail, or mail, it was thought that the number of contacts he likely would be called upon to make simply could not be done adequately by other than face-to-face interviews.

THE NEXT *WHERES*

Owen's first stop in Asheville was the hospital in which Mary Elizabeth had been born. As he would do many times, he introduced himself to the receptionist as a family history buff who was tracing a baby born on December 1, 1958, whose name and whereabouts were now unknown. With the help of that person and a number of others on the hospital staff, he ended up in the hospital "Records and Archives" office.

To his great disappointment, and despite the cooperation and openness he gained from the staff there, Owen learned that the policy of that institution, as with many, was to destroy all records forty years after the last entry was placed in the file. Mary Elizabeth had been born forty–one years before his visit. He was one year too late!

At times such as this, you must not be discouraged. While you have no control over the limits placed upon you by your society, you are able to rid yourself of limitations you are tempted to place upon yourself.

That potential source having been exhausted by Owen, the next step was to seek out anyone else involved with that hospital that might have remembered that birth event. Forty years ago women often remained in the hospital as long as a week after having given birth, so friendships sometimes developed. Owen sought the personnel director and inquired of that fellow as to whether or not anyone was yet employed at the facility who had been there for more than 40 years. There were none.

It is generally the libraries that store and offer old newspapers for research, those usually in bound volumes and more recently on microfilm. So, Owen's next stop was at that local facility. He learned upon his arrival that in this city the newspaper office maintained its own more recent archives. Significantly, and as you must, Owen made sure there were no other newspapers in existence locally in late 1958 when Mary Elizabeth was born. Had there been, he would have visited all of those businesses.

So, to the newspaper office for a search through the "vital statistics" and "births" sections of the newspapers. He searched the papers for a few days before the birth seeking notices of admission to the hospital. Then too, he searched every issue for a few weeks following Mary Elizabeth's birth on December 1, hoping to find a notice of her birth.

Those newspapers revealed seven such happy events at that hospital on that same winter day, only two of which were girls. Neither of those provided further clues nor revealed a birth to a mother who did not also have a husband listed.

Parenthetically, a birth father seeking Mary Elizabeth would have equally benefited from what she was about to find. Such a father would have known the mother's name, and so would thereby have confirmed the birth of his child and at the same moment have a very important *where*. Still though, other than the names of other children born on that same day, a mother already knew all of the facts that might have been found in any newspaper.

That absence of any mention of any birth that might have been Mary Elizabeth caused Owen to suspect that illegitimate births, or those that for some other reason were to remain out of the public eye, had not been included in those lists. As it turned out, he was correct in that surmise and the same may apply in your search.

He took note of those other births, especially of the two little girl babies, and of their parents. Why? Because, had all else failed in his future efforts, Owen would need to go seek out each of those children and their parents, and exclude those families as having been parents of Mary Elizabeth. He also would hope that one or more of those parents might remember Barbara as a delivering mother those years before.

SOCIAL AND CHARITABLE AGENCIES

The next stop would have been the local Catholic Charities or Florence Crittenton Home, very well known and highly regarded national charitable institutions for unwed mothers and abused and homeless children. Though the paperwork that the Kurtzes possessed revealed no institution as having been the facility where Mary Elizabeth had been housed for any period of time, since he was in that community Owen decided to visit the director of those organizations. Although he thought that such a visit likely would be unproductive, just as you should he knew that he dare not neglect any potential source, lest he be called upon to return there again if all else failed.

As he suspected, the local Crittenton organization, as with Catholic Charities and most other organizations of high goals and reputation, simply does not discuss any of its past clients in any way, for any reason, with any person, except by order of a court. As it should be, he knew.

Quite unknown to Owen, shortly before his arrival, that same Florence Crittenton Home had received a letter from Barbara seeking information.

As an aside, though she could not have known of that request when it was made, Mary Elizabeth had sometimes thought that it would be much easier to be found than to search. She had entertained the idea that by playing a passive role, the problems she might encounter with Mrs. Kurtz would be fewer, just as would the hurdles in explaining to those other folks who knew her. Still though, she also was aware that such thoughts were but her efforts at avoidance of or confrontation with the unknown. What was more, Mary

Elizabeth knew that her mother just might not be out there looking at all. Finally, as an overriding principle, just as you must, she knew that she and she alone should and could choose her path of life for the future.

When Barbara told them of her past, her family had reacted favorably, and armed with that encouragement and that of her husband, Barbara had attempted to find her "little girl" whom she had given up those many years before. She had composed the letter to Crittenton requesting any information they would share with her. Though over the years she had attempted to forget that such a child ever was born, she had finally came to the stark realization that she simply was unable to so forget. That baby was to remain just beneath her consciousness for all of her days, it seemed, and the urge to make that contact was powerful.

She received a reply from them. Encouraged, she opened it. Contained inside was a copy of the initial paperwork that she had completed upon her arrival, but nothing more. Finally, the short letter enclosed explained to her that no further information was available and that the records had been destroyed. She had been so hopeful and, those hopes dashed, she had no knowledge of any other avenues open to her. She gave up the effort. How different the reunion might have been, had Barbara succeeded. But, she didn't.

Owen left the Crittenton facility, went to the courthouse, and there located the office where such records would have been filed. How? Again, by simply asking an employee in the clerk's office where such files might be found. He was directed to the "probate division" of the courthouse. His search there revealed no record of anyone having been adopted who was born anywhere near Mary Elizabeth's birth date. As you must, he checked for ten or so years following her birth, since there was the possibility that some legal action concerning Mary Elizabeth or either of her parents might appear of record long after the adoption.

He found no such events by or for any child born on or near Mary Elizabeth's birth date. Then too, though he had no names and could not be at all sure, the divorce and death records also revealed no events at times near the birth date that appeared pertinent to that birth or to any folks who might have been parents of Mary Elizabeth.

ADVERTISEMENTS

Having exhausted all local courthouse records that might have been helpful where nothing more than the birth date and hospital of an adopted girl child were known, Owen headed back to the newspaper to run an advertisement. Though the odds of that mother reading that column in that newspaper on the dates he would choose for publication were remote, small ads are not expensive, and the chance surely was worth taking.

Remember, many young women, during those years especially, went "out of town" to have illegitimate or unwanted children. Thus, there was no good reason for Owen to presume that Mary Elizabeth's mother had lived in that immediate area on the date of the birth or that there was anyone else nearby who would have known of her birth. Nevertheless, and as did he, we think an expenditure for such ads is worthwhile for all searchers.

Based on the advice of the classified advertising consultant at the paper, he decided upon an ad in the "Personals" column. Be careful, and unless you are experienced at advertising, we suggest that you take the advice of those who have knowledge of such matters. So, Owen's ad was short, precise, to the point, and was to run for six consecutive weeks in the Sunday edition, since that edition had the widest circulation of any.

It read,

"You had a baby girl on 12/1/1958 in Asheville. She now has children and needs her medical history. Please help. Thank you. Call collect (followed by the Owen's telephone number)."

It was important to the safety of Mary Elizabeth and her family that his phone number be given rather than hers, lest anyone reading the ad might bring harm to her for whatever reasons.

None of the local sources having been of any assistance to the search, it was time for Mary Elizabeth and Owen to await response, if any, from the ad. Three Sundays passed before any call came, and it was the only one. It was from a woman from Asheville who had once been employed in the hospital in which Mary Elizabeth had been born. Although that woman was too young to have known of Barbara's birth event, she was familiar with the local record keeping and was an amateur genealogist and, significantly, also an adoptee.

ORIGINAL BIRTH DOCUMENTS AND CERTIFICATES

The local lady revealed that Buncombe, the county of Mary Elizabeth's birth, was one of those many, nationwide, wherein the physician who delivered or attended a birth was (and yet is) required to complete and file a birth certificate for every birth. More than that, in this county those original certificates were stored in the local county office that records births and deaths. Those certificates were so filed, even though, as a matter of course, the court later issuing a decree of adoption would create a new and different certificate naming the adopting couple as the parents of the child.

She suggested that it was not uncommon for a copy of those original birth records to remain in the county, while the original was sent off to the state, even though the rules and regulations governing such did not usually provide for such retention of copies at the local level. Following that advice, Owen checked with the clerk in that office where birth and death records were housed.

He found those open to the public, as he expected and, as good fortune would have it, lo and behold, there, indexed under the dates of birth in that county, was a certificate for an unnamed little girl born to a woman named Barbara on that precise date. The likelihood of such filing and storage errors by courthouse employees, though not common, is not unheard of and is surely worthy of pursuing. For Mary Elizabeth, that oversight by a clerk 40 years earlier was pure good fortune.

Many counties in many states similarly file the original certificates within their own birth records, and still yet, send copies to the state, or vice versa. As with the names assigned other courthouse offices, notice that the name of the office of births and deaths records may vary in different states of the United States. So, simply ask anyone in the courthouse where you might find birth certificates, and when visiting that office, once again, do not in any way reveal your purpose.

If asked why you seek such data, as before, state that you are doing genealogy and would very much like to see the list of births for the month and year in which you are interested. Don't reveal the date of that month, unless you are required by the clerk to do so, and even then try not to state anything other than that you suspect one of the people missing in your genealogy was born in that county in that month and "near" that date.

Be aware, however, that were it Barbara searching for Mary Elizabeth instead of vice versa, she would learn nothing from that certificate that she did not already know. Conversely, a father searching for Mary Elizabeth would be much rewarded, since he would again have confirmation of the birth of his child.

Such records are gold mines, and many hours, quite likely even weeks, of research will be saved by learning what is to be there found. In the certificate for Mary Elizabeth was found the name of Mary Elizabeth's mother, Barbara. It also contained a reference to Barbara's birth in Newport News, Virginia, and, most important of all, it revealed that at the date of Mary Elizabeth's birth, Barbara had given as a residence address a street and number in Fayetteville, North Carolina.

What a pleasure-filled moment it was for Mary Elizabeth to learn the name of her birth mother. Barbara was such a simple name, yet her new knowledge of it had a profound effect upon Mary Elizabeth. While that name would prove to be an incredibly valuable tool for furthering the search, it also made Barbara "real" for Mary Elizabeth; she had hoped to know that name since her early childhood.

So it was, and to their great relief, Owen and Mary Elizabeth had a *where* of residence forty years earlier and the name, "Barbara Hunt Parker." Mary Elizabeth felt that she was no longer looking for the proverbial "needle in a haystack"; she was seeking a certain person! As such will be for you, they had gained so much more than before! But, would Barbara be alive now, these forty years later?

More Detective Work

Before we take our post at the sidelines, there to watch
Owen and Mary Elizabeth search as a result of the
information about Barbara found in the birth certificate, we
should consider the course their search would have taken if
that original certificate had NOT been uncovered.

They had learned only those few facts found in the non-
identifying information; namely, that Barbara had not
finished high school, the father had done so, both were "mid-
20s" and unmarried, there had been no mental illness
observed in their families, and he was 6' 3½." By inference,
they also knew that Mary Elizabeth likely was conceived in
early to mid-March of 1958, hence her parents, whoever they
were, were together in those days, even if for no longer.

USING THE COURTS

With but those facts as a basis, and while Mary Elizabeth
and Owen continue their search efforts through different
avenues, were you at that same barrier you next should
consider seeking a court order directing the opening of that
"closed" file.

As you give thought to that approach, remain aware that if
you prevail in your case and thereby gain access to that file,
you then will have quite nearly the same information that
you would have found in the original birth certificate.   So,
you need not proceed with a lawsuit if you have obtained a
copy of that birth certificate; what little more, if anything, you
might learn almost surely would not justify the costs in
money and time.

It is noteworthy that there are very few lawsuits filed
wherein an adoptee seeks the name of the birth father. The
reason is easily stated; if the birth mother knows and has

told no one, it is highly unlikely that any court would order her to divulge such information. Still though, if your medical concern has to do with a potential for grievous illness that might pass from a father to a child, and it might appear in the closed file, then seek the advice of an attorney and proceed as he advises.

Presuming you are ready to seek a lawyer, know that in most jurisdictions where the law has determined that files should be closed, those legislatures also have provided that files may be unsealed if—IF—a judge finds "just cause" ("ample cause" or "sufficient cause") so to rule. Thus it is that the hearings in such cases serve one purpose only; to give an adoptee (or birth parent, occasionally) an opportunity to appear and to convince that court that reasons exist that are weighty and of sufficient merit and immediacy to justify the unsealing of the file.

Beware.   Lawsuits are never easy; even though final decisions in such closed file cases are usually comparatively quick in coming. Quick, that is, when compared to the years that other litigation often requires.   Then too, the many dollars required for a lengthy search will be saved if you are successful, and if not, those other search methods and sources yet will remain open to you.

DO YOU NEED A LAWYER?

Since the law does NOT anywhere require that you do so, should you hire an attorney for such a case?   This is a tedious question, since if you do not hire one and then lose the case, a subsequent lawsuit filed by an attorney likely has little chance of success. Why? Because judges do not like answering the same question a second time and are prone to conform their decisions to that of prior judges. On the other hand, if you do employ a lawyer, the expense likely will be substantial.

So, we suggest you confer with your own family attorney, pay him for an hour of advice, and tell him that you are on a limited budget and would hope for his advice and thoughts as to your capability to handle the case yourself. He not only is acquainted with you, but also is acquainted with the local judges, their rules, attitudes, and their predisposition to be patient and helpful with persons appearing without an attorney. He also probably knows something of whether your judge will be sympathetic or unsympathetic.

Then too, since he has helped your family in the past, that lawyer almost surely will advise you to the best of his ability. So, we recommend that you follow his suggestions, whatever those may be. If the county in which you were born is not near where you and your attorney live, then ask him to refer you to a lawyer in that other county. Lawyers come in every category of practice, and yours will be able to assist you in gaining one in that other geographical area who has expertise in such matters. Then, once again, take the advice of that attorney to whom you have been referred.

Still though, there may be a middle course open to you. If your attorney feels that you can handle hearings and personal appearances in the matter in propria persona (sometimes called pro se, both meaning "for yourself"), then you might make an arrangement by which you pay for whatever of his time is required for the drafting of the initial filings. The format and the wording for such are very important and will state your claims in acceptable legal terms, after which you can make your own appearances at court, answer questions, and say what you need to say.

If your attorney finds that arrangement agreeable, have him move ahead with the drafting of your petition to the court (also called a "claim" or "complaint" in some states). Finally, ask him in what courthouse office that claim should be filed, and then proceed. This method should save you considerable money, since he will not be charging you for his valuable time out of his office and in the courtroom.

HEALTH AND HERITAGE IN THE EYE OF A COURT

Your stated reasons for asking that the court direct an opening of the file to you, most importantly, that you and your family very much need information concerning tendencies to diseases and debilities that might be inheritable - passed genetically from parent to child. Unlike when you were born, modern science now is able to make predictions with some accuracy as to such lurking tendencies, and many judges recognize those realities and understand your needs to know of such potential problems.

Our chapter "The Importance of Medical History to Adoption Families" speaks further to these needs of you and your family. Suffice it here to say that you will need to speak to the matter with your family physician, for the reason that a concise, complete, and well-written letter from him explaining your particular need to know will be most welcomed by the judge. Letters from two physicians would be better, and better still, three, providing that those physicians truly are acquainted with you.

There is another reason for your request to the court. As discussed earlier, we all have a rich heritage and an historical background of colorful ancestors, some brave, some not so, some successful, some who suffered abject failure, some who were long-lived and some whose lives were snuffed out before their time. Then too, a few rose to fame, and it would be fair to label some others as reprobates or "black sheep." Still, all will be interesting for you.

To their great loss, adoptees have been foreclosed from establishing their connections to any of such fascinating people and events, are excluded from patriotic organizations of descendants, and can and often have strong feelings of emotional emptiness and of desires to know.

That need to know of your history and heritage is a facet of intellect that most judges recognize. You will be well off to offer that need as an additional reason for asking that the file be opened. Caution, however, desire and curiosity standing alone, no matter how deep seated and abiding, are not legally sufficient to gain the court order you need. Still, when those important desires are added to your medical needs for an opening of the file, such may tip the scales of justice in your favor.

Though you should not rely on the presence of such an attitude in your judge, some judges have come from our recently more permissive society, and may take the view that in some measure you deserve to see your file, simply because you have a desire to know your parents. Whether or not you do find that openness in the judge presiding over your case, we know of very few who have refused permission under ALL circumstances.

Throughout your lawsuit and in all other matters of search, you must remember that judges do not make law, and, just as with the clerks and social workers, they have no power to change it; legislatures do that. Still, because the legislatures have so provided, judges do have the authority to rule that you have presented good and sufficient cause for the file to be opened, that you have presented those reasons in a clear and convincing fashion, and that you should be granted that privilege.

HEARINGS OF COURTS

Most hearings in such matters are held in the judges' chambers and are rather informal. You should be prepared to state your reasons clearly and to answer all questions honestly, candidly, and in a forthright fashion. It is critical for you to remember that in such hearings the burden is upon YOU and you alone, to convince the judge that your request is honest and sincere and that your reasons are powerful.

One more reminder; you should never, under any circumstances, argue, debate, or show disappointment at the words spoken by the judge or by any person present. They have their well-considered views, just as you do, and if you are going to lose this round of the legal fight, better to do so with a smile and a closed mouth, than with ill-feelings. In short, if you have a temper or are lacking in patience, by all means leave those character traits at home!

So, spend as many hours as it takes to prepare yourself to clearly state your reasons and arguments and do your best here, if ever. You may not get another chance to state your case, except through very expensive, time-consuming, and often unsuccessful appeals.

If you win, you have a measure of duty to keep what you learn as confidential as those facts were before your case was filed and heard. What you learn should be shared only with those who truly are your confidantes and really do have a reason to know. Why so?

In the mind of the judge, it was YOUR presentation of YOUR reasons that was sufficient to justify the opening of YOUR file; in considerable measure his ruling was personal to you.   There are those who, upon learning that you succeeded in gaining access to the file, might also seek that opening with reasons that are far less adequate and convincing. Worse still are those who, though you told them nothing more than that you had seen the file, would insist to the court that since you accomplished that unsealing, so too should they be permitted. Enough, then, of litigation.

DEAD-END?

You will remember that we considered the lawsuit possibilities because, up until then, Owen and Mary Elizabeth had failed in their efforts to uncover more than the non-identifying information from the state and county files. So, back to their predicament.

Having failed to convince a court of their need to open the file, they did not despair. There were yet avenues for search. Still though, you should expect that those other avenues will be tedious, time consuming, and will test your determination. Difficult, indeed, however many searchers have succeeded.

Through the non-identifying information, Owen and Mary Elizabeth found that her mother was twenty-five years old in December of 1958 and had not finished high school. From that information, it would seem that she was born very near the year 1933. It follows that she would have been in high school sometime during the years 1948 to 1951. So, as did they, when searching for such a mother, your next *where* will be the library and the high schools within a radius of about fifty miles of the birth. For what purpose?

Throughout the first six decades of the twentieth-century, because of the relative difficulty of traveling greater distances, young women of average or lower means needed to go no further than fifty or so miles from home to achieve the secrecy they felt necessary when faced with illegitimate birthing. Did they go further sometimes? Of course, however you must start your search efforts within some geographical area—some *WHERE*—so we suggest that distance within which to commence.

Then too, as we said, the father was likely in close proximity to the mother during the weeks before and shortly after the conception. So, to begin the search for either, visit all libraries in that radius. Children very often have the same or similar features as do their parents, and it is that fact upon which you will proceed. As stated, the non-identifying information revealed that at her birth, Mary Elizabeth's father was of approximately the same age as was the mother, about twenty-five, and that he was very tall, especially so for the period 1940-1970.

COMPARING FEATURES

Upon arriving at those libraries (or schools), you should examine the high school yearbooks for the years during which those two people may have gone to high school and graduated. If the libraries do not have those records, visit each high school within your search area. While in your search effort, the mother may have had no remarkable features. Still, as we will discuss again, by comparing pictures of yourself as a teen-ager with photos found in those yearbooks, you may find one or more young women of similar appearance or features.

What is more, you may find pictures of boys who will either remind you of your own features or whose stature might compare with yours, especially if you are particularly short or rather tall. So, here the non-specific information may be very helpful in what it reveals of either or both of your parents.

Since Mary Elizabeth's unknown father was 6'3"+ in height, Owen searched the high school annuals for any mention of basketball teams and there gained the names of the players. If the annuals reveal no such photos or names, then he will gather names of other male students who either were voted as the most congenial, most friendly, most like to succeed, etc., those people presumably having enjoyed a wider acquaintanceship in school. It is difficult to use the names of female classmates, since only by pure coincidence will those women have maintained their maiden names for many years after high school.

MAKING CONTACTS

In the steps to be followed, the searcher must be most cautious. Though contacts must be attempted, since there are no other means by which to advance the search, there is always a risk of revealing to the person you are seeking or to a friend or acquaintance of that person. So, caution is the watchword.

It may be that, despite your best intentions, you are simply unable or feel incompetent to attempt such cold contacts with total strangers. If that is how you truly view the matter, we can only suggest that it may be time for you to consult a professional searcher or private detective.

Having found such names, you must then undertake to locate those people through the local telephone directories, city directories, or by way of the sources available on the Internet. Almost surely, at least some of those people will have remained in that area.

Your purpose here is to inquire if any of those people remembers a particularly tall classmate. Some of those classmates will yet have a copy of the annual and may be able to refresh their memories by that means. Remember to mention to those folks that you are doing genealogical research and seeking medical records, and that you have nothing to do with any police effort or crime.

If you locate any classmate who does remember such a student, make all efforts to meet with that person. After some discussion, he or she may remember both that fellow and whom he dated. If that memory is revived, you should ask if that girlfriend finished high school. If that fact is not known, the next question will be, "What girls of your class did not finish high school?"

If that person remembers any that did not graduate, you will be off to search those out, precisely as you would any others whose names you know. We will discuss that search very shortly. Failing all of that, you must go back to the annuals for the two years before and after your first target year, check the names of the junior year girls and then see if those all appear as seniors the following year. If not, those who are missing will be your next search subjects. Having gained those names, you will return to the city directories in order to ascertain whether that family moved away or remained, even if at a different address in town.

If these search efforts all fail to supply you with contacts, you may have reached an impasse, at least for the time being. If you do locate a man or woman who has all the signs of being the parent you seek, there is but one course open to you and it is tedious at best.

Presume you are yet searching for the father. Call the number you have found, ask if he has time to visit for a minute, relate that you are helping a friend, and tell him that you seek to "...locate the father of a little girl born in December of 1958 in Asheville (or wherever)." Continue in your most non-accusatory voice and approach by telling him that you have reason to believe that the father of that child was very tall and of the same high school class as was he, the man to whom you are speaking.

Ask for his help in determining who that might have been. If he seems to have any information whatever, you should ask to talk with him further and in person, and to do so at HIS convenience. Since there were no further clues stated in the non-identifying information, if he assures you that he cannot help, nor has he any information, he likely is not your man, or at least will not ever tell you that he is.

In summary, during each contact with a classmate, male or female, your approach will be the same. You are doing genealogy, and because of the need for medical data you hope to find a woman who did not finish high school, would have graduated between 1948 and 1951, had a little girl, probably in late 1958 or 1959, and then seems to have disappeared. If none of those contacts prove helpful, and you have exhausted the possibilities within that fifty-mile radius, it may be that you are at a dead end in the area of the city of birth.

Assume now that, instead, it is you—the mother (or the father)—who seek the daughter given up those years before. Further, assume that you also have added your name to the state registry and in several of the Internet sites that provide contact lists. Pretend now that while those mechanisms were at work for you, you have failed in gaining access to the file through a court, that you learned nothing by inquiries at the hospital of the child's birth, and that the files of the county, state and social agencies revealed nothing.   Finally, no evidence was uncovered from the facility to which the child was taken after you surrendered her or from the lawyers involved, those having been revealed by the adoption record.

Your search area likely will be considerably smaller than that of a searching child. Since it often was and is the social agencies of the county of birth that have jurisdiction, and because there has always been a considerable demand for adoptable children, you should start with that county. Notice that this suggestion is not always applicable, especially where the adoption is through an attorney or charitable organizations such as Catholic Charities. Nevertheless, you must start somewhere, and the same county is as good as any place to commence. As before, all adoption records of any nature must be examined in the geographical area of the birth, especially the courts' orders having to do with such proceedings.

You too now must calculate the age at which the child would have gone to high school. If, as was Mary Elizabeth, your child was born in December of 1958, then he or she would have attended high school sometime during the years 1973 to 1976.   Once again, photos MAY help, so gather several of you as a teenager, those to be compared with all students revealed in the yearbooks for those years of the 1970s.

Examine those books for every school within your search area, and again look very carefully for any children who share your appearance or features in any way. Be sure to search forward and backward for at least three years from the year that you suspect your child would have graduated. Though such methods are highly prone to error, there are few other approaches open to you at this point.

If you find a likely prospect in a search for a girl, since she well may have married and now have a different name and be unidentifiable in any telephone directory, you should carefully note her full name, and go again to the courthouse marriage records for that county. There, search for a record of any marriage of that woman. If you find such records, you should seek out the telephone number and make the same call as was suggested above where the child was telephoning a man or woman who might be a parent. It is always helpful to also check the divorce records for those years after that marriage in order that you avoid seeking a married name that no longer exists. Here, as always, be sure to check the city directory, if there was/is one, whether you are searching for a male or a female.

If you find no marriage licenses for any women of her name and age there, then search the immediately adjoining counties for those same records. If you fail again, just as mentioned above in the discussion of searches by adopted children, go back to the yearbooks, gain the names of, and then search out classmates who might know something of the whereabouts of that young woman. If any of those folks remember her, ask if they know whether or not that girl had been adopted; this contact may have been told of that fact. If so, then you must seek her out in the same fashion as discussed below and in the preceding chapter. Remember too that the records of surrounding communities and local or nearby colleges are equally important avenues for investigation

As discussed in Mary Elizabeth's search for her mother, a newspaper ad may help greatly. Your ad should say something like, "You are, or may know of, my daughter, who was born at State St. Hospital, in Marion, OH, on Dec. 17, 1958. You weighed 8 lbs. 6 oz., and at birth your hair was light. Someone adopted you, we believe. I would like to make contact with you and will in no way interfere with your life. (Here reveal your address or telephone number or email address; make the contact easy for any reader.) As before, run that ad for a number of weeks in one or more papers of wide circulation within that county and those surrounding it.

Should you gain no information through those methods, we believe that you likely are at a very difficult roadblock. It may be that at this point, you can but wait for a contact, search for more on-line reunion sites, constantly update your name and address at the state registry, and be ever aware of changes in the law of your state.

Remember, while you may not be sure in what state the child was adopted, it is quite likely that some court in the state of birth had jurisdiction of your child and took some legal action not long after the birth. You need to search for such legal activity, no matter how unimportant such may have been. That being the case, and all else having failed, we heartily suggest that you seek out an attorney with adoption experience, negotiate his fee, and have him scour all records in that county and several surrounding jurisdictions for any evidence of your child and his or her disposition. He will be searching for any adoption proceedings in which the child was a female and was of the age that your child was.

Harsh as it may seem, that may be the end of your efforts until the law changes, there is some response to your registry notices, or you come across any clues or individuals that might know of or actually be your child.

FROM A NAME TO A PERSON

Throughout the following search suggestions and examples, remember that had you sought and gained an opening of the file by a court, in all likelihood you would have an address with which to work. That information would place you at the same point in your efforts as were Mary Elizabeth and Owen after they gained a copy of the original birth certificate.

Significantly, notice here that if you are searching in a state with open records, you will be in possession of not much more information than Owen, Barbara, and Mary Elizabeth have as a result of the acquisition of the birth certificate. As those three were required to do, you must now enter upon a search for a "missing person."

So, back to the search for Mary Elizabeth's mother. Recall that the birth certificate found in the files of Buncombe County revealed that the mother was named Barbara Hunt Parker, and that at Mary Elizabeth's birth Barbara had lived in Fayetteville, North Carolina. Those dual surnames revealed that Barbara likely had been married, and that the first surname, "Hunt," likely was her maiden name, the other, "Parker," being her surname resulting from a marriage prior to the date of the adoption.

So, when Owen arrived in Fayetteville, his first move was to check the telephone directory on the quite remote chance that Barbara had continued with those names and yet lived there. Having found no such listings, his next stop was the library. So, notice that while that address gained from the birth certificate was more than forty years old, it was a very important where, one of the most significant they would learn. By knowing she was in that city for any period of time, whatever activities she might have undertaken could have caused some record to be made of her stay there.

As do many, the Fayetteville library had the city directories for most of the years of the twentieth-century, and so Owen immediately checked in the 1958 volume for the address given for Barbara on the birth certificate.   Sure enough, at that Fayetteville address were listed four people; a man and a woman named Hunt, who appeared to be Barbara's parents, Barbara, there shown as aged twenty-five, and a four-year-old girl named Dianna. Owen was satisfied that he probably had found the correct family and persons.

He then checked the same directories for the preceding few years for both Barbara and for her parents. He found that the parents were listed in the directories for most of the preceding fifteen years, and that Barbara had lived with them throughout that period except for a couple years after 1950. Of significance to his search, during the year following the birth of Mary Elizabeth—1959—Barbara was shown as "Barbara Parker." Thus, he confirmed that she had once married and that almost surely there would be a marriage certificate somewhere in the area records, perhaps a divorce or other involvement with the law, and maybe more recent addresses.

And then too, since a four-year-old girl child was present, that prior marriage must have taken place before 1955 (1959 minus four years). Owen concluded that the child almost surely was a child of the marriage to the Parker man. So, that Dianna Parker might one day become a target in his search for the woman who was her mother, since that same

woman was Mary Elizabeth's mother. He made careful note
of Dianna's name, age, and probable birth year. So, Mary
Elizabeth had a half-sister, that knowledge providing another
emotional high for her.

He also learned from the occupations listed for those in
the directories that her father had worked as a "painter," and
that Barbara had been employed during 1958 and in 1959
variously as a "clerk" and as a "teller" in a local bank. He
thought that fact noteworthy, since Mary Elizabeth had been
born in December of 1958, meaning that very shortly after
her birth Barbara had returned to her employment at that
bank.

Because she had worked for a bank before and after the
birth, Owen felt safe in presuming that, whatever else she
may have been, Barbara was quite likely presentable, honest,
probably clean and neat of person, and had succeeded in
maintaining her deep secret, or so it seemed. Notice that the
image of Barbara was becoming ever clearer. It was likely
that the station in life that she seemed to have enjoyed as a
young woman, in part, would guide their future search; she
had not been a derelict.

Remember that Barbara had not finished high school.
Just as our hypothetical child did above when seeking her
unidentified 6', 3" father, off to the library and yearbooks
Owen went. If Barbara continued at her education, long
enough to be a sophomore or junior in high school, her
photograph would likely appear in the high school annual.
Sure enough, an hour or two of scanning the annuals
revealed that Barbara (her name still yet "Hunt") had been a
junior in a local high school in 1950. Notice, that if that
library had not collected such yearbooks, he would have
visited all the high schools in the area, and there asked to
examine those annuals for the years during which she would
have been in school.

There he found a picture of the pretty teen-aged and
innocent Barbara. When compared with the several
photographs that he had gained from Mary Elizabeth for
comparison purposes, though the resemblance was not
striking, there were many similarities. What a wonderful
discovery this was to be for Mary Elizabeth who, remember,

knew only the eye color, weight and height of that mysterious young woman who had given birth to her. From this little discovery, so commonplace for most if us, not only did Mary Elizabeth have the name of the woman who had borne her, she had a picture of that woman who also, for whatever reason, had made the decision to give her up.

What was the drama that caused Barbara to so act? Was it social pressure, had her parents failed to offer their support if they had even known, or did some authority determine that she was an unfit mother? What series of events could have caused the powerful natural bond between a mother and her child to be interrupted or severed? Mary Elizabeth did so hope that she would have an opportunity to ask her.

A MINDSET FOR REUNION

As Mary Elizabeth contemplated the new likelihood that she might some day visit with that mother, she knew that although that woman had given her up, it was important for her to remain compassionate. She might well be called upon to give and receive love and remain open to explanation as to why the long separation had been thought necessary by whoever was involved. By maintaining that attitude, she could allow a measure of grace to enter into a future relationship, as well as develop a greater capacity to be receptive to the reasons that brought the events that had so bound her away. In the earlier passages of this book, we challenged you to raise your level of consciousness. We hope that Mary Elizabeth's trepidation at that moment causes you to come to know how important it also may be for you to find deep understanding and compassion within your soul. It all is so very important.

WHERE DID THEY GO?

Still yet, pleasurable as those discoveries had been, the question loomed. Where had the family gone when they disappeared from the records of Fayetteville those years earlier? Since Owen had learned from the birth certificate that Barbara had been born in Newport News, Virginia, his first choice was to investigate the possibility that the family, for whatever reasons, had returned to that city upon leaving Fayetteville in about 1961. So, his next where was that Virginia city.

His search in Newport News revealed that Barbara's parents, in fact, had lived there for a few years before Barbara's birth in 1932. He then checked that local courthouse for tax, deed and mortgage records, voter registrations, and deaths in case either parent had died there. Having found no records of any such activities, and having checked in the same courthouse for lawsuits and criminal charges filed by or against those parents, he decided any further search in that county would not be fruitful, at least then.

He did remain aware, however, that those parents might have been returned to that early home for burial. Still, he did not search the cemeteries, since his first priority was to find Mary Elizabeth, not the graves of her parents.

Finally, when still in that courthouse, he checked the deed and tax records for ownership of land, by any Hunt or Parker families who might appear and be associated with Barbara and her Hunt parents, or to her yet unidentified Parker husband. While those names were and are common, no familiar names, addresses, or occupations seemed to be present. Owen was satisfied that the family had not returned to that Virginia community after having lived in Fayetteville.

So, back to Fayetteville he went. Just as he had done in Asheville and in Newport News, and as you must do during your visits to each of your *wheres*, a courthouse visit was required. After a search of the criminal records that revealed no charges ever having been filed against Barbara or anyone with either of those surnames, he went to the probate (wills and estates) division and to the records to be found there.

There he found the death of a woman who well might have been Barbara's mother, and drove out to the cemetery where that woman was buried. When he arrived there he found her grave and to his relief, he realized that she would have been too old to be Mary Elizabeth's mother. Had that cemetery been of such size as to have a "sexton" he could have inquired there, as well.

A DEAD PARENT

So, that headstone was not Mary Elizabeth's mother, but it might have been. Indeed, you may find that spot of earth that serves as the final resting-place of your own parent. We suspect that you will experience a measure of sadness in that event, however upon that discovery you must realize that the headstone is not the end of your search. There was and remains much, much more of that person than a place in the ground. While you no longer can ever have the opportunity to meet and speak with that parent, at least not in this lifetime, there is much to learn, much heritage to uncover, and the discovery of a grave is but a first step in a new, thrilling, and somewhat different search. In fact, your new efforts will be less tedious than those that brought you to that solemn place.

First, gather every scrap of information from the headstone, cemetery sexton, caretaker, or the church, in case it is a churchyard where the parent was buried. Then go to the local newspaper and search the obituaries in all papers published from the date of death for as much as six weeks afterwards. Copy completely whatever obituary is found. Go to the funeral home or mortuary that had charge of the remains, learn who paid for the funeral and burial, and locate the minister who performed the services. To the extent you can, contact all relatives named there or those gleaned from the mortuary records.

Go to the county courthouse; ask for a copy of the parent's death record. In your state, those records may be housed at the state capitol and available only by mail or telephone. Do your best to visit with the physician who signed that certificate and with anyone else whose name appears on it, especially the widower or widow, of course. Be sure to attempt to contact all children of the deceased whose names you find from any source, especially the obituary.

You also probably will have the last address of the deceased parent from the obituary column. Drive out there, look around, take pictures, talk to neighbors, and there learn if any relatives of the deceased person live nearby. After these simple efforts, you will have a number of leads, and a life story will have commenced to come together. In the years that follow, and as a result of these simple steps, you will have ready access to the family history and genealogy of that person, all of which is equally precious and is yours to savor and appreciate. Just as surely, as if you had visited with that deceased parent, the door to your heritage will swing open. Enough, then, of those who have died.

FROM TOWN TO TOWN

We left Owen at the cemetery looking at the grave of a woman of the same name, yet who was not Mary Elizabeth's mother. He returned to the courthouse and to the divorce files. From a genealogical standpoint, here, as always, the court records were critical to the continuation of his search.

Since Barbara had been about twenty-five when Mary Elizabeth was born and the birth certificate had revealed what probably was her married name, Parker, Owen suspected that she might have been married or divorced, or both, in Fayetteville, in that county, or at least not far away. Good fortune was with him, for in the very first index the court clerk provided, there was a record of her divorce. In that entry, it was revealed that the court had granted a divorce, gave Barbara custody of Dianna, the daughter of that marriage, listed the name of her Parker husband, and set forth the judge's order that the father pay monthly support to Barbara for little Dianna.

As you must, Owen then asked to review and copy the entire case file. Therein, he made a very important discovery. Some months after the divorce the ex-husband had failed to pay the support ordered by the judge, Barbara had complained and sought a court order, and thereupon the court issued an order to an Illinois Sheriff directing that support arrearages be paid at once.

Bingo! If Owen now could locate that ex-husband or his family in Illinois, perhaps those people might have knowledge of the whereabouts of the child, Dianna, by then in her thirties, and thereby—by locating that child—he might find Barbara, as well. He decided to return home, reconsider the facts he had learned, and gain what the Internet might provide.

While searching the Internet, and through the expertise of Mary Elizabeth's eldest son, they found a telephone number of that ex-husband in Illinois. Notice that had the father moved at anytime within that forty years, perhaps even out of that state, then it would have been necessary to go search the records of that Illinois community for him, his death, marriages, etc., and some clues as to his family and his whereabouts.

TO CALL OR NOT TO CALL

But, why hunt those people now? Since Barbara had disappeared from the records of Fayetteville after that divorce, that ex-husband was the best lead then at hand. A decision, then, to follow the trail, would mean a telephone call to the ex-husband. Owen knew that, unless asked, it was not his place to make that very important call.

Since for all they knew, this ex-husband might have been further involved with Barbara than the bare-bones court record had revealed, and considering that he might feel much bitterness by reason of differences with Barbara, those unknown to Owen, Mary Elizabeth had to exercise great care. So, though it was difficult for her to put off that call, she decided to consider the matter thoroughly, discuss it with Mike, and they agreed that Mike would make the call to that ex-husband on the following day.

Remember, in the ABCs of problem solving we suggested that you seek assistance with the tasks you are unable to complete by yourself. Mary Elizabeth did not feel comfortable calling the ex-husband so it was decided that Mike would do it for her.

As she contemplated that first call to someone who likely was (or had been) acquainted with Barbara, she suspected that it might be the first of several or even many calls to come. Perhaps very soon would come the day when she would find her mother.

As Providence would have it, that contact went very well and was one of the most rewarding moments of the entire search. Though Barbara's ex-husband had died some years earlier, his second wife and widow, Mrs. Parker, knew that some years earlier Barbara had remarried and had then lived in Orlando with her second husband. She related that at their last contact Barbara's husband was named Griffith. How exciting it was to uncover such valuable information. Owen and Mary Elizabeth now had another where, plus a more recent surname for Barbara. Mary Elizabeth hoped that she would be in touch with her birth mother by the afternoon.

Unfortunately, this "new" information was more than twenty years old. Though that last address was of that vintage, the widow Parker also told that Barbara's daughter, Dianna (by Mr. Parker) had married, had moved from Orlando, and that she and her husband had then moved on to still another Florida city. So, although Barbara's whereabouts remained undiscovered, Owen and Mary Elizabeth had a twenty or so year old *where* for her, had a more recent married name, and had an even newer married name and address for Barbara's first daughter, Dianna— Mary Elizabeth's half-sister.

DANGER IN CALLS

So, why not simply phone the daughter? There might be several reasons. Perhaps Barbara had never told Dianna of the illegitimate Mary Elizabeth, and if that were the case, would the daughter be distressed or even angry to suddenly learn that she had a half-sister? Would she contact Barbara and in anger demand to know what this search was all about? Would she tell Barbara that Mary Elizabeth was searching and that trouble might result? Remember, Barbara, Dianna, and her extended family knew nothing of Mary Elizabeth's station in life, or even of her existence. Would that daughter feel that Mary Elizabeth was seeking more than contacts and information, such as money?

There were no answers to any of those questions. After much consideration of the unknown problems that a contact might bring about, Mary Elizabeth and Owen decided against that idea. There would be no calls to the daughter until all other hope of contacting Barbara was gone. Back to the search for Barbara.

Though neither the forename nor the surname of Barbara's husband was at all common, the Internet revealed a dozen or more households bearing that same combination of names and then residing in Florida. However, none of those people lived in Orlando. Nevertheless, Owen called all of those numbers, and found that none of those answering were acquainted with either Barbara or her former or latest husband.

Next, Owen and Mary Elizabeth thoroughly searched telephone numbers across the South, on the theory, be it correct or not so much so now, that most of us do not move great distances when we do move and, that having failed, he then searched the entire United States. He and Mary Elizabeth gained numerous telephone numbers for similar names, called each, asked again if they had any knowledge of Barbara or that husband, all again to no avail.

OLD ADDRESSES

Mary Elizabeth felt—even knew, by then—that she and Owen were ever closer to finding Barbara. Still, in her quiet moments, she felt a measure of uneasiness over the arrival of that day and as to what words she would say when she heard her mother's voice for the very first time.

The Internet telephone directories having been exhausted without benefit, off to Orlando Owen went. His first stop was the old address for the daughter and her husband that the Illinois widow had provided to Mary Elizabeth. His intention was to view that residence of many years before, the neighborhood, and the people in order that their station in life might be measured, while maintaining the total secrecy of his purpose in being there. A knock on the door of a neighbor of that house revealed that the resident there had no knowledge whatever of any of the parties or of anyone else who seemed likely to be involved.

As you must, Owen then undertook a search of the neighborhood, hoping to find anyone who might remember any of the people related to or associated with that daughter, Dianna, or to Barbara. As pure luck (or Providence, if you choose) would have it, another immediate neighbor and his wife vaguely remembered the young couple and also recalled the name of the aged mother of that young husband (that daughter's mother-in-law). Another quick check of the local telephone directory provided a telephone listing for that woman, she too a widow and then ninety-two years old.

The next call required much thought, just as you should give thought to all of such contacts. Remember that this woman was the mother-in-law of Barbara's first daughter, Dianna. Should she be contacted, considering that she likely was in frequent, if not close contact with her son and Dianna? Would this contact reveal to all (except Barbara, that is) that Owen was searching for Barbara? If so, would Barbara resent any contact with the daughter made before she herself had knowledge of the efforts being made to find her? Tedious questions, at best.

Owen chose to telephone the woman and make his best effort, again, to be honest with her, yet to reveal nothing other than that he was doing genealogical search. The call was a success, and that elderly woman revealed that Barbara had been widowed from that second husband and once again had married. The woman also revealed the name of that third husband and the last address for Barbara known to that woman. That address was in a Georgia city a hundred or so miles away.

AN ADDRESS; WHO ELSE LIVES THERE?

So, Owen had a five- or six-year-old *where* in the form of an address. He drove that distance, checked into a motel, and began a new phase of the search, if, if Barbara yet lived there, that is. The telephone directory did indeed reveal a listing for a person bearing the same name as that of Barbara's latest husband. A city map purchased from the local Chamber of Commerce provided the location of that residence. Once again, it was time for serious thought before action was taken.

Owen telephoned Mary Elizabeth. "I am within four blocks of Barbara's home!" he told her. Mary Elizabeth remembered the pause she very much needed and took; it was more a gasp than a respite! Owen brought her up to date of the events that had taken him to that Georgia city. Mary Elizabeth was utterly delighted to be so close to actually knowing something of that woman who had borne her those decades earlier.

But wait. Not only did Owen and Mary Elizabeth yet know very little about the character of Barbara, they had even less information concerning that third husband. Who and of what character was he? What would be his attitude at the prospect of having an unknown stepdaughter appear at his door? Had Barbara told him of her indiscretion and the resulting child of those forty-plus years earlier? If she had not, what harm might a contact bring for Barbara, for this man, and for whatever extended family they might have? Should Owen make the call, if one was to be made, or should Mary Elizabeth do so, or even Mike? Under the circumstances, would a personal visit to Barbara's door be more appropriate than a call? Very difficult questions and ones with which you may one day be confronted.

What to do? Do you first study and observe that individual and his or her family? How do you judge the character of the person located or of those around him or her in order that your approach be most likely to succeed? Do you then call, write, visit, or have an intermediary make the first contact?

Anxious and excited though she surely was Mary Elizabeth and Owen made the decision to first learn all possible about this couple from a distance and to do so without revealing the investigation to anybody. So, Owen first went to view the house, the automobiles of the couple, and the neighborhood generally. His inspection revealed that the couple seemed to have regard for the appearances of their house and property. They appeared likely to be of Southern middle class, probably had no small children about, as revealed by the absence of playthings about the property, and seemed to maintain their belongings in keeping with the other residences of the pleasantly modest neighborhood.

That evening, Mary Elizabeth placed a call to her sister-in-law who lived in Florida, close to the address for Barbara's first daughter revealed to Owen by the mother-in-law. It truly is a small world, she found.

The sister-in-law not only knew of the daughter but also had taught school with her in previous years. She described her as a pleasant and kind person, interested in her students and having several foster children in her home. Though a resemblance was not striking, the sister-in-law thought that there was a similarity. Most importantly, with the favorable character of the daughter somewhat assured, surely the mother could not be much different.

Early the following morning Owen returned, parked within view of the house, and watched, hoping to see people come and go, especially any man who might be Barbara's husband. As you must, Owen's surveillance in no way gave the appearance of skulking or stalking. He simply parked in a public parking spot clearly in sight of the house and remained in his car. Had anyone inquired of his reasons for being there, he was prepared to be truthful and reveal that he was seeking a missing person and was attempting to learn through mere observation how he might best approach whoever did reside there.

The two cars parked in the driveway had not been there the night before, were unpretentious, and not particularly well kept. No one came or went.

Several hours passed, and a clean late model car arrived, parked in the car port, and a neat, pretty, and matronly middle-aged woman got out and entered the house without knocking, quite as though she was the lady of the residence. Owen felt certain that he had seen Barbara.

Still though, he yet knew nothing of her husband. Several more hours of waiting revealed no further movements, though other women did leave the house and drive away in the two cars that had been there since early morning. He wondered who those people were.

A call to Mary Elizabeth resulted in a decision to extend the surveillance through yet the following morning, again in the hope that the husband might reveal himself. As with their earlier decision that no contact would be attempted with Barbara's first daughter back in Orlando lest Barbara learn of the search through that daughter, here too inquiry of neighbors might be risky, since they also might call and prematurely alert Barbara.

The day had been a long one for Mary Elizabeth. She was hesitant and uncertain about the course for which she alone would be ultimately responsible. Imagine her dilemma; after months of searching, contact with her birth mother was but a telephone call away, yet if she said the wrong thing—used the wrong words—the long and tedious efforts she and Owen had undertaken might have been all in vain?

What should you anticipate? How much more time and energy, if any, should you spend considering what might occur during that call? At what point does one stop observing and planning and follow one's instincts with a contact? We think the answer is that you should spend only that time required to observe the individual and her (or his) surroundings, some minimal time at the courthouse checking criminal and divorce records, and then take action. By such observations and those few records, you will know something of the station in life of that person, and we believe that further study and surveillance will produce little more of value. As did Mary Elizabeth, avoid the trap of wondering over and over, "What if?"

Upon Owen's return from the surveillance, she called him and told him that, after much thought and support from Mike, she had decided to wait no longer. Though Owen suggested that additional surveillance might reveal needed facts, they discussed what her approach and words might be, and hung up.

SO, DO IT

So, Mary Elizabeth had summoned that measure of confidence needed for the call. She had spent much of the day distracted from her other activities by the task that faced her. Little could she know how often even during that day had she been on Barbara's mind. She had decided that no one else but she should make such a sensitive call.

As she dialed the telephone, she had a distinct feeling, be it instinct, wishful thinking, hope, or otherwise, that this contact would go well. In the few moments that the phone was ringing on the other end, Mary Elizabeth felt anxious that perhaps she was ill prepared for such a call. Once again, she thought that her words might be inappropriate, and that as a result her mother would again reject her. Nevertheless, she could not deny herself this opportunity to do what she had dreamed of for years.

Chrysalis

The ringing of the phone startled Barbara. The day had been a long one. George had gone to bed early, shortly after supper, and Barbara had been sitting alone with her thoughts most of the evening. She was nearing seventy years old, had taught classes most of the day, and was weary, though pleased with her day. Her summer students were bright and eager to learn, though they often had too many of life's distractions interfering with their studies. Her heart went out to the single mothers who worked hard to overcome the odds and get an education in order to support their young families.

As she had many times, she looked over at the table where she was greeted by the beautiful, impish face of her youngest granddaughter. She smiled; she had been blessed with healthy, beautiful children and adorable grandchildren.

But still, that other recurring thought was too often there, and it lurked just beneath her consciousness. That thought was of that other little girl and this day that child more than ever concerned her. She did not know why she was overly concerned right then; yet she prayed that child was safe and well, wherever she was.

"Who would be calling at this hour?" She answered the phone and was greeted by the voice of a young woman who said, "Is this Barbara?" For a moment, it sounded like one of her daughters. But then again, they did not call her Barbara.

Mary Elizabeth did not know what to expect, but her initial reaction was that the voice on the other end was a pleasant one. From the moment Owen had called to tell her that he was in a motel only a few blocks from Barbara's home, she had wrestled with her decision about calling Barbara.

She had considered asking Owen or Mike to make that call yet her intuition told her that she alone was the one who must confront that situation. Upon his arrival from work that evening, Mike had agreed that she should place the call. Though he had worried that she might be disappointed by rejection or otherwise, still yet he encouraged her to not further delay the contact. He anxiously waited in the other room.

FIRST CONTACT

She was so afraid that she could scarcely dial the numbers. The call Mary Elizabeth made to Barbara was a classic of how such a contact should be made. She introduced herself by name, and then said, "I was born on December 1, 1958 in Asheville, NC."

Indeed, Barbara was caught off-guard and though she was tired from the day's activities she knew that this was not the usual call from a telephone solicitor. She was forced to attention by the date given and was at once taken back to the birth of that little girl.

In an instant she remembered holding that infant but briefly before it was taken from her. It was the last time she had seen the child, yet those fleeting moments had remained in her memory for then more than forty years. In a flash, she recalled the feel of the baby-soft skin against her lips as she tenderly kissed that tiny human being.

She had tried to breathe in the very essence of that, her beautiful offspring. She was then aware that there would be no newborn baby picture for her to carry in her wallet, no cards highlighted in pink to be sent to friends announcing the birth of this new little girl. Those few moments and the memory of it were all she had. How difficult the decision to give away a child was for someone so capable of expressing love. She came back to the reality of the voice on the other end.

Mary Elizabeth went on to say that she had been adopted as an infant. In a split second Barbara knew without a doubt how life changing this call was and would continue to be about. A new, different, and pleasurable future had come upon her in the space of three or four minutes. She was struck with emotion. For Barbara, there was but wonder at the moment; after forty-plus years her child was present; what a Godsend this call was for her.

For the rest of that surreal call, time moved in slow motion for both of them. For Mary Elizabeth so much rested on this very important call. It was such a sensitive matter to have to speak with someone about whom you had almost no knowledge, yet with whom she was bound for eternity by nature.

She knew nothing more about this woman other than that she was her birth mother, drove a late model Chevrolet, and had worn a bow in her salt and pepper hair that morning. She paused, waiting in case Barbara needed to catch her breath.

Barbara said, "Oh my gosh, oh my gosh."

"Please don't hang up," Mary Elizabeth thought to herself. For a long few seconds, she wondered if the phrase "Oh, my gosh" was a good omen, or not so. She had no intention of bringing any harm to this woman, and she hoped that Barbara would not panic and hang up the telephone for no better reason than that she was lost for words.

Mary Elizabeth continued, "I think you are my birth mother." At the time it seemed like a critical statement, though in fact it had really been quite unnecessary. Barbara already knew why Mary Elizabeth was calling her. What Mary Elizabeth could not have known was that Barbara had never forgotten the dates of the birth of any of her children, and surely not of this one.

A pause followed during which time Mary Elizabeth was unsure whether or not this had been welcome news. She took a deep breath, still shaking from the rush of adrenaline.

Barbara quietly said, almost as if to herself, "I've wondered for years what I would say at this very moment."

She had? It was an honest reaction to the situation in which Barbara found herself and what a wonderful revelation that was to Mary Elizabeth. Those words meant that Barbara indeed had thought of her over the years?" Her fond dreams had been realized. Barbara was her mother in fact and in thought, and she had only dared to hope for that reaction over these years.

If there had been an iota of panic in Barbara's voice, Mary Elizabeth did not detect it. She groped for clues as to what Barbara might be thinking at that moment. Her voice had revealed surprise, certainly. And there was more. There was relief in her mother's voice, and it washed over her, over the forty years of wondering and fearing the worst, though hoping and praying for the best.

The rush of emotions and delight in the reception caused Mary Elizabeth to have no response to offer at that moment, and so she waited for Barbara to speak again. And she did. Quite as though she had asked the question of herself many times and almost automatically, Barbara gently asked, "Have you had a good life?"

The only answer that would do for that question from a woman who for decades had earnestly hoped that she had made the correct decision was a firm "Yes." Mary Elizabeth told her that in fact she had been blessed many times over and had a good and strong life, complete with family and others who loved her and had so much helped to make her life worthwhile.

Mary Elizabeth experienced great relief that the call had not been terminated. She suspected that perhaps she now would be given the opportunity to talk with her for a while. She so much wanted to continue to hear the voice she had only imagined for so many years, and to begin to seek and find answers to some of the many questions she had pondered without answers so many times. Maybe she would even be "kept" this time around, she fleetingly thought.

This phone call was the beginning of a rewarding and pleasant relationship for Mary Elizabeth and Barbara, one which would include phone calls, letters, emails, and visits. Most importantly, though, for both, it was the development of a closeness based upon unconditional love, each for the other. From the beginning, and not by reason of anything she did to prove herself, Mary Elizabeth had been accepted by Barbara. Accepted first, by virtue of being a daughter and then later by reason of an ever increasing affection. She was a daughter of Barbara's the same as the others, her children were Barbara's grandchildren, and her husband was another son-in-law.

Barbara was equally accepted by Mary Elizabeth, her husband and her children, and by her husband's family, quite without regard to anything that had happened in the past. Mary Elizabeth was delighted to have this nice lady involved in her life then and forever more. Her children equally enjoyed meeting the new "family member"—their half cousins, aunts and uncles—and found no difficulties in incorporating those strangers into their lives.

Mary Elizabeth was proud of her family and the ways in which they had reacted. Still, their responses were not a surprise; she knew them well and had never a doubt but that their reactions would be as those were. They all found that each had been immensely blessed by this reunion. We hope you will experience much of that same joy, as will your loved ones.

So, Mary Elizabeth's fantasies had not found reality. She was not heir to a throne after all. She was a normal person and very much like everyone else. She had not found the "woman of her childhood dreams" conjured up from a lack of information, but, instead, she had found something so much better; a real, living person. It was truly wondrous.

Neither would she find a replacement for Mrs. Kurtz, the woman who had lovingly raised her, investing so much time and energy into their relationship. Her birth mother and whichever of her family members chose to be included were to be pleasant and loving additions to Mary Elizabeth's existence among those she had loved for all of the preceding forty years. She had discovered that reality was much more gratifying than was fantasy after all.

As had Mary Elizabeth, you have probably given much consideration to the prospect of your reunion. Just as Mary Elizabeth did, it is time for you to make that first contact.

Make careful decisions regarding what you will say and how you will compose yourself. Unless you have lived in a shell, throughout life you have honed the skills that you will need today. Rely on these skills. Try to approach the contact as the simple task of introducing yourself to someone new.

Reunited at last, Jane and Beth

Beth with all the girls in Jane's family

Further, it is time to stretch to your full height, to reach your full potential. Do not allow your success in the search to be taken from you by simple and unreasoned fear. Decide that you will move ahead despite that hindrance.

Fear is not a weapon against dragons. Instead, it is your preparation, confidence, devotion to your higher power, and love of yourself and others that will serve as your weapons. The journey now requires you to claim your reward, and with this contact, we suggest that your willingness to love and to accept others as they are today is your most critical tool in the effort.

We know of five methods by which to make the first contact. You might send a letter, make a visit, send an intermediary in your place, or you may ask someone else to place this all-important first call for you.

WRITING A LETTER

If you choose to write a letter, prepare yourself to be ignored and to gain no response. If that is the result, you will be no further along than you were before you sent that message; you yet will have no indication of the reasons for which that parent chose to ignore you. As a result of the failure to respond to you, you may ascribe meaning and motives that simply do not exist. Then too, someone else may intercept the letter, in which case you will not even know if that parent ever read or even knew that you had attempted to communicate.

In short, though a letter might result in response and eventual reunion, that process may take weeks or even months, while a call will reveal much in a very few minutes. If, on the other hand, there is no response, you may learn nothing whatever. So, should you choose to write, you should not infer anything from inaction.

MAKING A VISIT

Perhaps you think you are able to present yourself better in person than on the telephone or by letter, or perhaps you simply are emotionally unable to make a call. So be it. If then you choose to introduce yourself in person, make every effort to meet one on one with that parent or child and away from the home and family of that person. To do otherwise is to risk that there will be others present who will know nothing of the pregnancy, adoption, or of the years that have passed since those events.

For all you can now know, those yet unknown people will be mortified or have great and adverse influence over the meeting. Such outsiders may be dominating to a degree that your efforts and hopes will be for naught even before you have more than been introduced to the parent or child. We think it apparent that such a visit without adequate warning and opportunity for both parties may result in irreparable damage to what might have been.

SENDING AN INTERMEDIARY

Of your options, we think this possibility is next best to a call from you. But, your gamble—and a big one it is, indeed—in sending another person is that the personality, presence, appearance, or even the tone of voice of the intermediary may not be pleasing to the parent. There is yet another difficulty in sending another person; if rejection is at hand, you can never know whether or not you might have succeeded where you agent failed. After all, to the extent that nature has provided even only a primordial bond, the person sent to the task surely will not have that advantage. Again, a poor choice, we believe.

HAVING SOMEONE ELSE MAKE THE CALL

Only you know and understand your own emotions and should you feel that you simply are unable to face the fear brought by that first contact, perhaps you should consider an alternative. As with any other intermediary, you must be most careful about whom you choose to speak in your place. You must know that by choosing this course, you are risking all your effort and perhaps the entirety of your future relationships with that parent or child upon someone else's "people skills."

Thus, while understanding the emotions at play is difficult for this messenger who has not been intimately involved in your past, that distance from the turmoil actually may enable the spokesman or woman to handle the situation without substantial emotion. So, while here is a possibility for you, again you are but avoiding your fear. If that must be, we can only say choose carefully, for you may not have another chance.

MAKING THE CALL

Thoughts of these options had consumed Mary Elizabeth for many hours after learning that she was so close to reunion. At length, she concluded that she best would be able to express her intentions and feelings with a phone call and also, she thought, the personalities of both she and her mother might be expressed more accurately and sincerely.

Should you follow Mary Elizabeth's course and choose this option, enter into the call with the notion that you will succeed. Make the call with humility, soft tones, and a smile on your face. Presume that the call will be pleasant and that your attitude and personality will show through.

Be honest and unpretentious. Speak slowly, understandingly, distinctly, and gently, allowing that mother, father, or child the time needed to arise from the shock and surprise and become conscious of what truly is happening. Be aware that he or she may be completely taken aback and may not be in any sense prepared for such a call. You may wish to say, "I know this may be a surprise to you, and I do not mean to disrupt your life in any way."

Be very considerate of the circumstances of the person you are calling, having learned as much as you could from outward appearances and whatever evidence was available to you. The call should be confidential, if at all possible. Next, and very importantly, explain why you are calling; state that you suspect she had given birth on that date those years ago, and that if so, you may be that child of hers. Always ask if it is a convenient time to talk or if she would rather you call back at a somewhat later time that day or evening.

Just as you considered the matter during your search, you now must continue to bear in mind with every word you utter that the principal reason your birth mother may have chosen adoption was to keep her family from knowing and thereby avoiding the social pressures that would result. If so, and you can not now know that, you must not be the one to destroy that confidence and open that secret that she has maintained over the decades.

So, having decided to call, when likely will be the most appropriate time to do so? Obviously, you should not call the workplace.

We suggest that calling when it is most likely that they will be alone will be best. Ideally, those with whom the person lives are people who respect his or her privacy and yet likely will have a great interest in the subject. So, if at all possible, talk to her privately. Hopefully, if she (or he, of course) needs to excuse herself from those in close proximity, she will do so.

If in the course of the first few moments you become aware of tension or a problem created on the other end of the phone by the spouse or others present with her, or if you detect any reluctance whatever to talk, suggest that you call back in a while. Ask her or him to set the time for that return call, or ask simply, "Might I call an hour from now or perhaps at 5:00 this evening?"

If it is you who are being called, do your best to find a quiet, private place to speak. If you are in a delicate position with others nearby, simply say something such as "I will need to look that up. Could you call back at ___ O'clock this evening, please?" With the advent of cordless phones, however, speaking privately has become much easier. Whether or not you have answered with such, excuse yourself, pick up one and move to a private place.

SUMMARY OF A SEARCH

So, in review, be aware that the many steps taken and methods used had been successful for Owen and Mary Elizabeth; however no two searches are the same. Then too, just as you must, Owen and Mary Elizabeth did not for a moment relent in their efforts to determine the *wheres* for their search. At the same time, they joined all free search and reunion lists that were available to them, including those of the state social agencies that were involved. Had all such efforts failed, as suggested earlier, they would have sought a court order that the file be unsealed.

Upon the discovery of each *where*, all community and local sources, especially the library, courthouse, tax offices, and newspapers, were exhausted for further clues. When a neighborhood—a smaller *where*—was located, it was visited, and neighbors and any others who were native to or had knowledge of the immediate area and its residents were sought out and questioned. When those neighbors provided leads, Owen and Mary Elizabeth made any and all contacts suggested, and when they needed telephone numbers, they consulted the Internet and the telephone directories. They were secretive about their efforts at all times, and were never willing to give up.

It is important for you to remember that had Mary Elizabeth learned the name of her birth father from Barbara or any other source, the search for him would have been very much the same—a simple search for a missing person. The *wheres*, local inquiries, and record searches would have been the same or similar. In addition to the sources utilized for finding Barbara, at each where a search would have been made in the courthouse records for any registration for the draft and also at the registrar's (register's, clerk's) office for a military discharge. As always, most men (and women) who have served our country have found it wise to record their discharge papers.

It is important to understand that there will be a certain amount of time, energy, and expense required to accomplish your search. Though usually you will complete your efforts in weeks or months, you must realize that the effort may take as much as several years.

While the Internet and the available telephone and library records will provide sources, your search almost surely cannot be accomplished without you or someone in your behalf visiting most of your *wheres*. The reason is that the Internet, almost without exception, has only abstracts of vital statistics, and since the records of the last fifty to seventy-five years with which you will be involved have not yet been abstracted, the Internet will not often be of assistance.

Finally, throughout your investigation, you must be considerate of the personalities and attitudes of the persons whom you seek and those with whom you make contact. Here are people with whom you may have nothing in common and, while you may be disappointed upon uncovering such folks, you must find it within yourself to put those results in proper perspective; they have had lives that very much differed from yours. They may or may not welcome you and may require a longer period of acceptance than you find desirable. Their spouses and their children may welcome you or not, and all have their reasons.

In short, personalities of others will be different, and you must plan to be open and willing to accept those as they are. That will be especially true when you have reached the point of reunion. During reunion that openness extends to your willingness to be receptive to the many changes that you will encounter.

WHAT NOT TO SAY AND DO

The title you use when speaking to this new relative is unimportant compared to the gravity and difficulty of the search that you have completed. However, that does not mean that you should consider using the familiar such as the title "Mom" when greeting them. Remember that this new person is not the same person as she who was separated from you years ago. You both must be prepared to meet in the present.

As soon as convenient, prompt a discussion about what each should call the other, but there is NO hurry to do that. Likewise, your children should not be hurried into addressing that mother as grandmother or grandfather, and your half-siblings from that mother should be left to speak of you as they choose. Everyone involved should be allowed to choose the titles with which they are comfortable.

Do not require anything of the person with whom you, until recently, sought to be reunited. While you enter into the initial phase of reunion expecting nothing of the person whom you seek, know that you must expect a great deal of yourself. You must maintain your composure, leaving all thoughts of the past behind for the moment.

As to the father, neither of you can pretend that he did not exist. This may not be the time to discuss him, though. Your desire to learn of him at this time is probably only one of the reasons for your call. It may not hurt to mention that someday you will want to discuss him with her.

Do not hurry the person being called into a relationship. Reunion can be intoxicating for sure, but being needy can quickly repel others. Be aware that others in one or both families may not share your enthusiasm. At the same time, do not ignore others as this new relationship unfolds. Try to maintain a balance in your approach and remember that this is but one aspect of your life that requires attention.

Do not smother this new family member. Proceed slowly, taking small steps as you go along. Trust and follow your instincts. Expect nothing. Make no demands. We have suggested throughout that you be very deliberate and give consideration to all of the possibilities. We think it is necessary that you continue on that course.

Be flexible. Whoever the surprised party is may need time to adjust and to deal with reminders of the past. You have had time to prepare for this and he or she may not have.

ENDING THE CALL

As the call ends, should you feel a need and desire to pursue the relationship, simply ask, "When may we talk again?" Then too and despite your renewed fears, ask the same question if you feel you are being hurried off the phone. The response will be honest, we suspect, and serve your purposes.

If your desire is to not make contact again, do not prompt further contact. As always, be truthful with yourself and with that person.

WHAT NEXT?

Go slowly, and do not hurry the relationship by thinking that the years past may be recouped in a few days or weeks or even years. For the moment, you are charged simply with now enjoying the process. Make it a point to appreciate what comes your way. Revel in your accomplishments and enjoy the results, the fruits of your labors. Take time to enjoy your thoughts! Reflect upon the distance you have traveled, the dragons you have slain, the heritage you have opened to yourself, and the treasures that you have unearthed. Enjoy your relationship, be it one that flowers or falls short of affection.

Share your joy with others in order that they learn of the benefits of this reunion, be it temporary or for the balance of your life. Joy is contagious and others involved in an adoption triangle may feel yours.

There are some that think suffering is a necessary part of life. If you are one of those, suffer over these changes in life if you must, but do not drag others along with you. If you need support, look for a support group or perhaps share with a friend.

Then too, after all of your planning, emotional preparation, and hard work dedicated to reaching this Promised Land, you may discover that you have conflicting emotions. Indeed, you may experience periods even of some regret. Even if the relationship sours, both parties to this reunion need time to incorporate this new knowledge into their personalities and to differentiate that they forever more will be from who they otherwise might have been.

A child now has discovered his or her genetic background and may wish to spend time ascertaining what they have inherited from whom and what they have learned from their adoptive family and their life experiences. You may feel as though you are reinventing yourself. Give yourself as much space and time as needed; there should be no hurry.

Birth mothers may experience sadness for the years lost. So be it. The past is just that, and it is now a duty to do all you can to adapt to a different future.

Adoptive parents may feel confused over the sudden rush of emotions, and they too must realize that their world will never again be the same.   Here are opportunities for a broadened life brimming over with new relationships. Will all those new experiences be pleasant?   Of course not, yet whatever comes now will be what you cause it to be. There are struggles aplenty for all involved in both families. These are not dragons, but are merely little bumps in your road ahead.

In summary, proceed slowly, be flexible, pace yourself and do so in keeping with the needs of your new family to do the same. Take small steps. Follow your instincts, and allow all others to do the same. If you are one of those who have a one-, five-, or ten-year plan, discard such notions for the time being.   Whoever the surprised party is may need time to adjust and to deal with reminders of the past, and those will and should very much affect your future. So be it. You have had time to prepare for this eventuality, and that other person probably did not.

A NEW GROUP

Do not assume that your kinship by blood has anything to do with your personality or those of your new family. You may find that you are amazingly similar, but you should not so anticipate.   Remember that you are different from many others in your circle, and these new "blood relatives" may vary, as well.

Along with the introduction of a birth mother to your family and you to hers, thought must be given to the pre-existing family needs of each other. Undertake to consider how those new people will fit into your life and the lives of each member of your present family.

It is our nature to approach strangers in a manner dictated by our past experiences with newcomers, be those good or bad. For example, you formed new relationships with your in-laws if you married. They too were strangers who became new family members or not depending upon your impressions and treatment at the hands of each of those.

You did so, though they were family only related through marriage, and you were open to a greater tolerance to the end that you please your mate. You formed a new group. You will need to do the same here, and the reasons are about the same. Once again you have an elevated need to accept the shortcomings of others out of a heightened obligation to "make things work." Just as with your new in-laws where the incentive was to please your mate, the extra motivation here arises from the fact that you are "family" by blood. In both instances, you may or may not have chosen that group as friends, but the added dimension of family places them within your circle.

Consider how you have formed all of your relationships in the past, and put your best foot forward, being tolerant with these new relatives. You will be called upon to thread your way through the dynamics of a wholly new family group, and you must accept good will when it comes, be tolerant of ill-will where you must. Intend no offences. They can not understand your personality unless you make it known to them. To the extent that you become a part of that group is up to both you and them.

In some instances, you will have to wait to be welcomed into the fold, and everyone likely will not welcome you. Permit them to make the mistakes of not including you at once. Old habits are hard to break. Mary Elizabeth has a half-sister who for wholly unexplained reasons has not accepted her.

Remember that Mary Elizabeth was given up for adoption so that Barbara could keep her older sister, Barbara's oldest daughter. Though Barbara's other children accepted this "new" sibling into their group, the sister who was kept instead of Mary Elizabeth has refused to accept Mary Elizabeth. That is all right; she has reasons that arise from her past experiences and perhaps the future will see to a change in both parties sufficient to meet half way.

Remember, finding your birth parent or child once given away is not a matter that should be viewed as an offense. It is a neutral behavior. Any feelings regarding that act are based upon perceptions and impressions derived from the situation. You likely will not appreciate every member of this new family, and equally not all will appreciate you. Those feelings in others have a basis, perhaps jealousy or dislike that you interrupted the status quo. Whatever their reasons, you must realize that they have chosen to live in that way, and there are forces at play about which you can neither know nor change immediately. In the long run of it, do not waste time worrying about it. In short, be careful of your expectations.

However you have handled others including family and friends, who have been accepting of you, will serve as a roadmap for these new encounters. If you are introverted and approach relationships accordingly, then you likely will continue to do so and so too will they. You should be honest with yourself and be aware of your own patterns.

On the other hand, "If it ain't broke, don't fix it." If you have a style and personality that allows you to meet and develop pleasant relationships with others, then continue with those methods still again. You have no obligation to bend your life style and approaches beyond accepting these new people as decent and worthwhile folks with problems similar to your own.

Remember that you are forming a new and additional group and are not replacing a former one. Enjoy these new people and their ideas, with no strings attached, no baggage, and no history. You may find immense benefits if you allow this thought to take root and grow. Mary Elizabeth particularly enjoyed the company of two of her sisters, finding their sense of humor and approach to life delightful. Kinship (and a search) brought together women who have enjoyed each other immensely, who may otherwise, have never met.

After all of the talk of interpersonal relationships is said and done, there is yet one final thought. Do not compromise your integrity or your honor. Periodically, stand back and evaluate the relationships. You may find that you have come to a measure of tolerance never before experienced as a result of kinship, and you may overlook shortcomings that otherwise would be intolerable for you.

Likewise, if you suddenly find yourself in a relationship that is less than desirable, and you find you are spending a great deal of time and energy trying to make it work, then take time to reevaluate it. Consider if, for example, because of the energy expended on this relationship or lack thereof, you are missing other friendships that require less work and that prove to be more rewarding.

A marginal relationship may not be worth pursuing. You may need to plan an exit strategy particularly if your efforts are greater than the results. If it so evolves, you must decide what you will salvage. Heritage, family history, and the all-important knowledge of medical history are but a few benefits you have gained by the journey. If it is to be, you can wish them well, leave on friendly terms, and enjoy for the rest of life those benefits. Remember what that information later may mean to the generations that follow you. You will have gained MUCH!

Whatever the result, savor the moment. You will benefit from the quest and the contacts. If you did not already so feel, you will come away knowing that you are as worthwhile and fortunate as everyone else is.

Interestingly Mary Elizabeth was not for a moment aware of her feelings of insecurity until she accomplished that reunion. You may have the same thoughts. As did she, you will experience a connection through that person to the rest of the world in which you live. You will finally be able to put your questions of adequacy or equality to rest as that parent becomes alive and ever more real.

REJECTION

What if Barbara had said she did not want to talk to Mary Elizabeth? Our advice here is to try to keep her on the phone. Tell her you don't want anything from her except _____ (Tell her here what you want out of the relationship). If, rather than making an effort to extend the call, you would prefer to hang up by reason of her attitude, ask if you may call her back and learn when she will permit you to do so.

What if she (or he) hangs up or says that she never wants you to call again? While this may be disconcerting, don't be alarmed. While that is certainly not the worst thing that may happen, neither has it been your first major hurdle. In some cases it will not matter if you are a recipient of the Nobel Peace Prize, your birth parent or the child you found simply may not want to have an association with you. Do not delude yourself by thinking that she did not really mean to hang up on you. She did.

If that was the result, we suggest that you write your birth mother asking for health and medical information and her reason for placing you for adoption or whatever other information you feel compelled to know. If the child you gave over to adoption hangs up on you, consider writing a letter explaining your reasons for doing so, and write about the legacy that you wish to share with her. Close the letter by assuring her that you want nothing from her except that which she feels she can freely give and that you intend no further contact with her unless she so chooses. She has made her wishes known, and like it or not, you should respect that decision.

Should you choose to continue to mourn your loss and present yourself to your world as a victim or martyr, instead of being on about your life, that is your choice, though surely not a good one. You may have been deprived of the healing or closure that a reunion might have brought, yet salvage what you can from whatever time the encounter took. So, time will reveal such healing as will take place. Many are those birth parents and adoptees that found that a few months brought a change of attitudes for the better. So, wait, you have no other choice.

The last move is yours. When to say good-bye and place in the future any further attempts at reunion is for you alone to decide. When you make that decision to abandon the effort for now, move on and remember there are no victims here.

CHOICES THAT FOLLOW

During the course of her search, and though she shared her progress with several others, Mary Elizabeth revealed her intentions to very few other than to her husband and to her adult children. However, after having found her birth mother, she felt that her responsibility to share her findings extended to Mrs. Kurtz. It was, she felt, part of the process.

Whether or not Mrs. Kurtz found herself able to support her daughter throughout the search efforts, Mary Elizabeth knew that the day would arrive, be it sooner or later, when she would feel it necessary to tell her adoptive mother of the results. As it turned out, Mary Elizabeth felt that the appropriate time was the day following the first phone call to Barbara.

As she made the short trip to her childhood home and to Mrs. Kurtz, Mary Elizabeth savored the satisfaction that arose from having followed her path. No matter the attitude of Mrs. Kurtz and the future of their relationship, Mary Elizabeth here again was facing whatever might come.

She had that inner feeling that comes to us all when we know that we are doing the right thing, being true to ourselves, and facing our own dragons. She was secure in following her own conscience regardless of the consequences.

Although some adoptive parents find it easy to support their children, others may find themselves not knowing what reactions are appropriate. They may not be prepared for this entirely new family situation. However, Mary Elizabeth and Mrs. Kurtz had discussed the matter of a search over twenty years before, and then Mrs. Kurtz had affirmed her daughter's need to search, and had offered to help, should that day arrive.

That day, Mrs. Kurtz's initial reaction was favorable. She said that she understood that searching was important to Mary Elizabeth. She was gratified and much relieved by that support from Mrs. Kurtz. As she drove home that next day, Mary Elizabeth was elated and felt some measure of confidence that all was fine.

Tragically, within a few months after having been told of the search, Mrs. Kurtz began to reveal a much different attitude. She had grown disturbed over her daughter's search. She had increasing difficulty in accepting the notion of a search at all and felt threatened by the people Mary Elizabeth had found, whoever and wherever they were. Even though Mary Elizabeth had lovingly assured her that, indeed, she had been a fine mother, and that the search should have nothing to do with their mutual affection and love, she became upset and felt to a measure disdainful of Mary Elizabeth and her family.

She vowed not to talk to her daughter again about the search. On several occasions, however, she mentioned that she was having difficulty dealing with that fact, even though she was unable to explain how or why she so felt. Mary Elizabeth encouraged her to seek help from a support group or counselor if she could not come to allow her, Mary Elizabeth, to help in the process.

As difficult and painful as our lives become at times, we must take advantage of opportunities to grow. Mrs. Kurtz had wanted to cling to the old idea that she should never have had to be confronted with a search and its results or face the first mother of her child. She compounded that error by perpetuating the belief that the birth mother would never again see her child. The status quo was much easier and safer to maintain than reaching higher in order to grasp the reality of the situation and of her place in it.

In an attempt to deal with the hurt that she was experiencing, she rejected Mary Elizabeth and her entire family, no longer inviting them to spend holidays with her and refused invitations to participate in Mary Elizabeth's life, even at the holidays. How tragic and how different their lives might have been. Mary Elizabeth hoped there would be a turn for the better.

Hopefully, with time, Mrs. Kurtz will come to know that someone else will not replace the love she shared with her daughter for so many years. Embracing the new objective of allowing her daughter to grow, rather than withholding love, would ensure that the bond between them would be strengthened. The suffering Mrs. Kurtz inflicted upon herself and certainly upon Mary Elizabeth was unnecessary and surely should not have been a part of this process.

While reactions by such as Mrs. Kurtz are not the rule, her attitude seems to have been the only one of which she felt capable. The lesson of it all is that you must be aware that such problems may come into being. If you find a similar reception, we suggest that time might bridge that gap, if at all, and counseling again may be of assistance.

What of Mary Elizabeth? Her earlier fears of rejection by Mrs. Kurtz were confirmed. Mary Elizabeth thought it ironic that Mrs. Kurtz handled her own fear of rejection by rejecting Mary Elizabeth out of hand.

This part of the story is not being told to frighten you. There is an understanding to be had by all. Though uncomfortable, unpleasant and certainly not with the happily-ever-after for which she had earnestly hoped, Mary Elizabeth had learned that one of her worst fears was to be realized. Still though, she had survived rejection, found she could manage painful growth, and is yet alive, well, and now enjoys feelings of peace when telling the story.

It is important that you realize that the problems experienced by Mary Elizabeth and Mrs. Kurtz are neither common nor new and are only remotely related to the search. She came to understand that the reactions of Mrs. Kurtz and all others as well, whether good or bad, are caused by something within them and not anything that Mary Elizabeth had done or not done. There are not any victims in this story, just people with feelings and emotions who may or may not have the capacity or the desire to deal effectively with such challenges that life brings them.

As mentioned, the act of search and reunion is just that, an act or an event. It has no personality or existence of its own. It is not illegal, immoral, hurtful or wrong. Its meaning has the significance that someone attaches to it due to his or her unique perceptions of all the facts. As to those unusual perceptions, you have no duty or responsibility.

So, that part of the journey was difficult for Mary Elizabeth. Nonetheless, she knew that in the long run of life she had been immensely blessed. The chrysalis had begun to form the moth. In a short span of life, she had evolved from a woman so in fear of rejection that she trembled as she dialed the phone to a woman who had faced rejection and found that she had the skills needed to face those and even more dangerous dragons. She had learned that by looking into the face of her fears, she had become ever more able to confront and attack the unknown future and what it might bring.

She had grown spiritually as she relinquished her concerns to her Higher Power, believing firmly that God had a purpose for her. She had been the only child in her birth family of six children who had been given over for adoption and placed in another family, and for that she felt there was a reason. She began each day with the knowledge that the past is only that, and her todays and tomorrows would be benefited by her willingness to seek higher ground and to make sense of her life. She recalled the words of Marianne Williamson in *Everyday Grace*, "Every situation is a lesson in becoming who we are capable of being."[18]

Mary Elizabeth knew that she now could focus on becoming a better and more complete person rather than dedicating time and energy in finding out where she had come from. She further realized that she alone could control herself, her thoughts, and her reactions; no one else. She alone would decide how she perceived her adoption. She would make the effort required to rid herself of the thoughts of blame directed toward her and others. She could choose to give and receive love, all the while feeling the power and peace of forgiveness. She continued to be pleased that she had chosen to search and knew that she had only begun to realize the benefits to be derived from those difficult efforts.

She also had found another place where she belonged in the world. She searched until she came upon those people who linked her to the past. She began to experience a reawakening of who she was in relation to history and to the world around her. She began to remake herself and the way she was oriented to society.

One cold winter day she received a call from one of her birth sisters. Barbara's husband George had died, and there was to be a funeral held for him in that small southern town where Barbara lived. What a sad occasion, but at the same time an opportunity she would not want to miss. She would meet her birth sisters and brother. Their reunion was pleasant, as they seemed to enjoy each other's company.

---

[18] By Riverhead Books, a member of Penguin Putnam, Inc., New York, 2000, p. 42.

What was especially remarkable, however, was receiving a package from Barbara several days after her return home. In it was a picture taken after the funeral, of all five sisters, Barbara, her sister and Barbara's niece, the people Mary Elizabeth had been so curious about for so many years. And there she was, smack in the middle of all of them. Being with this family in reality and not only in her imagination was a dream come true.

Barbara was also receptive to the profound changes brought by the reunion. Though she was hardly aware of the feelings, she had waited across much of her life for that moment of closure. She had so wondered what had happened to her little girl. Being found by Mary Elizabeth had caused her to feel that she had done the best she could, and that the Almighty had seen to it that the child had grown into decency just as Barbara prayed she would. She asked that in her behalf Mary Elizabeth thank her parents and relay to them her relief that Mary Elizabeth had enjoyed a good and loving home.

Meeting Mary Elizabeth was a salve for Barbara's wounds. Shortly after the phone call she had stood before the congregation of her church and revealed to them the lost and found story of her and that daughter. It was something akin to confession for her to be able to reveal those secrets after all the years. She was so very pleased and relieved to receive comfort from those around her. She too, was free and ready to grow.

Shortly after her first visit with Mary Elizabeth, Barbara and her sister returned to that small house on Oak Street where she had lived with her parents prior to giving birth to Mary Elizabeth. She gazed at that old house and thought of the times she had spent there, some good and many not so.

She knew what else she had to do. Looking through the telephone directory, she came across the names of four of her old friends. They were friends with whom she had gone to church those four decades ago; friends who had no notion of the trauma she had experienced right before their eyes.

It was time for the telling. She was ready for whatever reaction they gave her and she was without fear at the prospect of baring her soul. Gone was the "bad girl" of her past. She also was firm in her view that giving up a child had not rendered her "undesirable," as one unworthy of the love and respect of others. No more years would be spent living with a cloud of regret hanging over her life. And most importantly, Barbara knew that the compelling need to be rid of the secrets was being met.

She shared her experiences with them. Over a long lunch in a friendly tearoom on the following day, she told them of the pregnancy she had concealed, even from them. She continued and revealed her surrender of that the baby to adoption, of the pain it had caused her for so very many years, and of the reunion which had brought her so much pleasure. No one had known of her secret until that moment, and every one of those women knew they could not bring back the past or alter it in any way. However, and at long last, on that day her friends could and did provide encouragement and loving support.

Barbara finally was at peace with herself, and though she had steeled herself to the possibility of further rejection, it had not come. Her old friends had indeed been just that. How utterly gratifying for her.

She felt other changes arising from her thoughts. New vistas began to open for her. There had never been a moment when she had forgotten or ceased to love that little girl. It came as something of a pleasant surprise for her to realize that mothers do continue to love regardless of the circumstances and the time passed. She also felt even surer that it is critical to peace of mind to give love wherever we are and without regard to the past.

But wait, amid all this joy and pleasant reunion, what of the birth father?

It was only with great reluctance that Barbara had revealed his name. Perhaps she had not forgiven him, perhaps there was more to the story than she was willing to tell, or maybe she had been concerned that harm might come to Mary Elizabeth. But she knew that this mature daughter sitting before her had a right to know.

MEETING THE FATHER

Shortly thereafter Mary Elizabeth made the decision that she and Owen would locate, meet, and talk with that father. Within a few weeks they were on their way to his Southern home.

She realized a certain peace and comfort on that warm October morning as they approached his house. The ocean glistened quietly in the background, and the trees along the roadside were laden with Spanish moss, so common to the area and so familiar to her.

The sunlight rained through the trees and into their eyes, causing them to blink from the brightness. The odor of the salt air, the feel of the tidal rhythms, the warmth of the sun on her skin, and the peaceful feelings she had known in falling asleep to the sound of the waves on the nearby shore, all would take on a deeper meaning this day.

It was little wonder that she had enjoyed the weeks she had been able to spend nearby across her lifetime. This was Mary Elizabeth's ocean, the one she had come to every summer for the previous forty years. Incredibly, she thought, she had found her birth father but a few miles from the very place where she had vacationed with her family every summer since childhood. Sometimes we find ourselves searching for years, only to end up where we started. How strangely ironic, she thought, that they could have been so very close in distance, yet truly a lifetime apart.

It all was beautiful, and her anticipation was almost electric. Still though, it had not been easy to reach this place. It was not the drive that had been difficult, but rather it was the emotional highs and lows with which she had grappled while on the way. As they drew closer to that man, she hoped that whatever the results might be, most of the remaining dragons would be vanquished, she would be near the end of her search, and the treasure so long sought would be at hand.

She had been incorrect in assuming that this would end her journey. She soon would learn that there was more to this aspect of her search than she could ever have imagined.

Photographs of Beth and her birth parents, Jane and Carl, at
very close to the same ages.

Carl and Beth at reunion

No matter what more this day might bring though, she did know that she was about to discover a part of her previously unknown heritage. She would soon learn of the history of those who came before her, extending back many generations throughout this beautiful section of the country. She would find that her affinity for this area (Tidewater North and South Carolina) might be more than happenstance. It might even be what some in that area have for centuries described as "ancestral memories."

She would learn that her paternal ancestors had settled here many generations before. No wonder she had felt such an affinity for the area; she loved the sights, the sounds, the smells, and the food. She had passed streets named for "her people" without even knowing of those ancestors. How proud she was, and how much she realized that she really was "home" there.

She and Owen arrived and were standing at his door. They knocked and he emerged. Much the same as it had been during her first visit with Barbara; it was truly awesome for Mary Elizabeth to see him for the first time. She searched his face for similar characteristics, for a smile, for any familiar feature.

Then she saw those eyes; brown and bright, just as were hers and those of her children. She was thrilled with those moments and soon came to know that he was a highly decorated army officer who had retired to the area where his grandparents had raised his mother. That pleasant meeting ended, and she came away absolutely delighted with the broad vista of heritage that he had revealed for her.

Their relationship seemed to progress well in the beginning and what seemed to be a true friendship began to develop. They stayed in touch through phone calls and letters. He came to visit her and her family and truly seemed proud to be able to watch and listen as Mary Elizabeth's eldest son spoke at an event on *Veteran's Day*.

No matter those pleasant beginnings, within just a few months he told her he would no longer maintain contact with her or her family. He had cast her aside, and once again she felt those terrible feelings of rejection. No one said it would be easy.

Despite that rejection, she realized that she had been able to experience not only a brief reunion, but also that she had uncovered medical history from his side of her lineage that might one day be invaluable. Then too, through who he was she had gained valuable information about her genealogical background, a most proud heritage for her descendants for all time to come.

That was treasure enough, she knew, since those facts would never have been known but for her search and were indestructible. Not only had her family been prominent and respected citizens at the time of the American Revolution, but one of them, in fact had signed the Declaration of Independence. Her children shared that pleasure, even though they too had, in a sense, been rejected.

Once more, it was apparent to Mary Elizabeth that this turn of events and the emotional reactions that came with that rejection had their genesis in events of the life of that father. His attitude came from within and not from anything Mary Elizabeth had said or done. She wondered if that loss of contact with her and her family had brought regret and remorse to him. In the future, any attempt to reestablish contact with her would be welcomed, albeit on her terms.

As of this writing, at his request, he and Mary Elizabeth were reunited briefly before all contact was discontinued again by the birth father. Their relationship is tenuous at best, still yet, it may one day develop further or it may not, but she has gained another treasure.

Mary Elizabeth cannot now know what the future holds, and you may experience the same or similar results. Whatever is, is, and thus you must stand ready and on guard against those dragons in your road ahead.

CONCLUSION

For Mary Elizabeth, and perhaps for you, it was as if she had been living in a cocoon for most of her previous life, always afraid to venture too far outside that cocoon and its safety and comfort. Much as that cocoon fell into disuse and finally disappeared so too did the insecurities about her place in life felt by Mary Elizabeth. Through the process and because she had remained receptive to the opportunities it offered for growth, she was able to emerge as the beautiful moth with wings to fly beyond the past and away from old ideas and restricted notions. So too will you.

As you encounter the faces of blood relatives and pore over albums of pictures of those who have gone before and yet were responsible for your very existence, the thoughts from your years without a heritage and history will be transformed. You have wanted what so many have taken for granted, and now that it is at hand there will yet be much to assimilate and many years ahead in which to do so.

Mary Elizabeth, with the support of Owen and many others, had found the treasure that had belonged to her, yet had remained quite out of her reach. Despite the many dragons, disappointing and tedious emotions, and difficult challenges that had appeared along her route to her treasure, she found that the benefits resulting from the search happily far outweighed those negatives.

Again, as it was for Mary Elizabeth, though you will have but little control as to the outcome of your reunions, you surely can write your own script as to how you will emerge from the process. Reunion is not only the beginning of new relationships, it also represents the dawn of a realization that you will not—indeed, can not—ever return to your previous life, yet as you did with the search, you surely may dictate the terms of your future.

Your existence, which to now has been punctuated by curiosity and desire to know of your family and their past, will be forever gone. As a chrysalis, growth is inevitable, however, if you are to develop into the beautiful moth of which you are capable, you must make the choice to do so. Your opportunity for phenomenal growth is at hand.

Realize that through reunion, no matter the extent of pleasure brought or not brought to you, the effects that adoption had upon you and you life will be forever altered. Those changes will occur as rapidly as you permit. The treasure you have gained will continue all the rest of your days and just as the moth may not again return to the chrysalis stage you are forever changed.

It is important that you acknowledge and rid your mind of one final myth. As children, we believe our perceptions are true, even when those miss the mark. For adoptees, the singular act of having once been given away often has far reaching effects. We suspect that it might happen again, and so we spend a lifetime of energy attempting to be accepted, to fit in, and to assure our position within our chosen groups.

However, when you find those to whom you are related by blood you come to know a common bond and realize that you are and forever will be a part of a true family; forever and ever, amen. You cannot be given back; will not be returned to the adoption agency or forced to be whom you were; and you will not ever again be constrained to think, as others have required. Ironically, though you really were required to earn these new relationships and your new family, in reality you have claimed what was already yours.

Ultimately, you likely will be able to permit, receive, and welcome the unconditional love of those previously unknown to you. You will feel a new peace within your being. You will know that no longer must you seek every day to earn the love of anyone. Now and in the future, you have but to give and receive as you choose.

If there is a lesson of life in it all, it is that by looking for someone else that you ended up finding yourself.

Importance Of Medical History
To Adoption Families

Now more than ever before family health history is important to the medical care of individuals. The family medical history is a record of the health, the illnesses, and the circumstances of death of persons genetically bound to you. In this setting, by "family" we mean "blood" relatives. These are the people who have contributed to your gene pool, which is the blueprint for your body's structure and function and reveals the strength and weaknesses of the body. Such a record is ordinarily obtained by a health care provider during an interview dedicated to the purpose of having what is considered to be a complete medical record.

Over the years, the importance of a family medical history has grown in specific and measurable ways. Such histories have moved from often being little more than interesting caveats to being of real significance for the patient and for her physicians. Health risks of an individual revealed by his family medical history are now much more defined and serve as markers for health care professionals; markers that aid in the determination of whether or not that patient should have tests and treatments beyond what might have been otherwise thought appropriate.

The diagnostic tests available to patients have improved at an ever-increasing pace, and the treatments available to alter the course of current or future disease processes are also more extensive and effective than in the past. It is apparent that the need to know a patient's family medical history is extremely important and also more now than in the past that revealed history will affect that person's medical care and health outcomes. In short, a patient's medical history is more important now that at any time in the past.

Moreover, this increase in the value of family medical history by physicians has outpaced changes in the legal and the adoption systems. The law, as well as the adoption system as it now stands, hinders, even to the point of prohibiting, adoptees from obtaining their very valuable medical history. Hence, if these systems do not encourage outright harm, they serve as a substantial barrier for adoptees in their need to gain access to that most vital information.

As in the past, virtually everyone knows that "the apple doesn't fall far from the tree," and that traits and tendencies are very often apparent in ethnicities and in family groups. Any court requested to open an adoption file, in order that the medical background of parents and relatives to be available as tools for medical purposes, surely should consider that reality.

Further complicating an adoptee's search for his family medical history is the fact that little is usually known concerning the health of relatives and ancestors, and what is remembered is likely non-specific or even incorrect. Serving as examples of the lack of accurate data, are the numerous people who relate that some relative died of "old age." Stories of death "from cancer of the stomach" of family members, instead, could have been cancer of the colon or even a bowel infection.

Death certificates are very blunt instruments, if being used to obtain medically relevant information. That bluntness is a result of the fact that the intensity and accuracy of diagnostic testing that we know today was lacking in the past and often the cause of death was an educated bedside guess by the caregivers. Often the causes were even less precise when the death was not witnessed. However, the search for the family medical history should not be slowed since all information may be useful. To the trained medical provider, even noting physical features and ages are extremely helpful to the development of a health risk analysis for a patient, adopted or not.

Two notable changes have occurred in recent years since many of the laws regarding adoption were set forth. First, knowledge of genetics has mushroomed. The human genome has been mapped and improvements in analytical methods have further defined the purposes of those fundamental elements and the effects of those on the human body. This science is moving forward at a very rapid pace. These advancements have led to the capacity to identify some of the many genes associated with both health and illness. Therefore, more information connecting family medical history with the genes and with how a person's health may subsequently be affected by such is being made ever more available.

Second, the nature of health care delivery for the vast majority of people has changed dramatically. When most elderly patients of today were young, neither they nor their family members visited their physicians unless they were "sick" and sometimes rarely even then. It was remarkable to find anyone who felt "well," and yet who also saw his or her physician routinely. There are many reasons why there are more "well" visits to health care providers than in the past. There is an ever increasing realization by the patient and the health care establishment that pre-emptive measures for the health of a patient likely will pay off later.

In earlier times, thoughts of taking expensive medications to ward off theoretical illnesses that might come in the distant future were not common in our society. Now of course, routine examinations and visits to health care providers are the norm. To illustrate, a recent discussion in a prominent medical journal focused on the difficulties had by physicians in finding time for "sick" patients, their hours being increasingly expended to preventive and maintenance health care visits by those who feel "well."

In cases of acute illness or injury, treatment often is administered without family medical history, since the immediate outcome of such care is more reliant upon the skills and tools immediately available to the health care provider. Still though, in matters of preventive or maintenance health care, knowledge of the family medical history is essential.

The discipline of medical genetics is vast and growing by the day, and there are many fine general and specific subject reviews available. What follows is an overview; a brief discourse on some of the common health problems that plague our patients and the current role that knowledge of that family medical history plays in care giving for those people.

The practical impact genetics may play with the average person and his primary care physician is apparent. Everything about our bodily structure, its function and susceptibility to disease or dysfunction, is a direct result of our genes and environmental influences on those genetic tendencies. In fact, essentially all cancers arise from gene defects, and most of those cancers occur from the interaction of those defects with the environment, thereby causing a susceptible normal cell to go awry.

The details of these interactions will be under even more intense scrutiny in the near future. Empirically, some families never seem to have cancers or early coronary disease, while other families are quite the opposite. Nevertheless, only approximately ten percent (10%) of cancers are felt at present to be directly inherited, the others being presumed to be sporadic mutations and (or) situations where susceptibilities meet opportunities.

The earlier a cancer occurs in an individual however, the more likely it is that there is a direct and causative gene defect. Significantly, for our purposes here, unless there is a family history to suggest a possibility of an inherited cancer, genetic testing is not advised to screen for such cancer genes. It should be apparent then that without the advantage of such historical data, prediction, prevention, and care for an adoptee are more difficult.

Physicians find that, aside from acute illness, the largest proportion of their time is spent in an effort to diagnose cancers and atherosclerosis (clogged arteries) early and whenever possible in order to alter a patient's risk to succumb to those diseases. Since, as said, these common problems are often a result of genetic and environmental factors, if the physician is aware of both types of risks for that patient, then that physician is more able to determine how aggressive the prevention measures, surveillance testing, and therapy for that individual should be.

Moreover, if a patient has a significant family history of a disease then it is more likely that their insurance carriers will cover some of these measures. In this fast paced world any warning flags that extra attention should be paid to the health risks of a particular patient are welcomed, and family medical histories very often provide those warnings of needed caution.

Be aware that breast cancer affects approximately one in nine women by the age of eighty. We know that women who have a positive family history of breast cancer are at greater risk to develop that disease. Of the ten percent (10%) with a strong inheritance tendency for breast cancer, approximately one-half (50%) have the BRCA 1 and (or) BRCA 2 gene mutations. These gene defects increase the risk of not only breast, but ovarian and colon cancer, as well. Women who carry BRCA 1 gene have an approximate lifetime risk of breast cancer of ninety percent (90%) and twenty percent (20%) by age forty. Fearsome statistics, for sure.

So, given a patient with a family history of breast cancer, generally the physician would alter the standard approach by advising more aggressive screening measures (mammograms and breast exams). Further, if she has had two close relatives with breast cancer, or has had one with a positive screen for the BRCA genes, then she too should be genetically tested to see if she carries the BRCA gene.

In short, with respect to cancer screening of many types, if a female is positive for BRCA then her health management should change drastically over that of the average patient. Again, gaining access to family medical history that an adoptee may not have is very important.

Ovarian cancer is a dreadful disease, and early detection is almost impossible, given the location and growth characteristics of such tumors. In fact, it appears that a positive family history of that disease is the most important risk factor identifiable for the development of that cancer. Again, any information made available that causes the patient and the physician to be aware of increased risk to develop such cancers will assist that patient greatly.

Given a patient with a positive family history of ovarian cancer, screening with a CA-125 blood test at least annually is advised, even though this test is not sufficiently accurate for the average female patient. Also, annual ultrasound evaluations of the ovaries and a pelvic examination are indicated. Such safeguards are not perfect, by any means, yet are an improvement over care for the average person.

Patients with ovarian cancer should be BRCA gene tested, and if the results are positive, then the relatives of the patient should be tested, as well. If one of the relatives of that person is positive for the BRCA gene, then the risk of ovarian cancer is so high that removal of the ovaries from the apparently healthy relative should be considered after appropriate consultation with a physician. Again, these alterations in care are not usually done if the family history is unknown, as usually is the case with an adoptee.

While a routine colonoscopy for early colon cancer detection is useful for everyone over the age of fifty, the risk of colon cancer is doubled in cases where there is a history of the disease in even one of the immediate relatives. The stronger the family history, the more aggressive should be that surveillance. Therefore, if your physician knows that you have a strong family history of colon cancer then he will likely advise early and more frequent testing. Parenthetically, it is more likely your insurance company will agree to reimburse for such procedures.

Also deserving of mention is another common health problem. Coronary artery disease is a major killer in this country, and there are many risk factors, both environmental and genetic. Those risk factors are known to affect the outcome of any individual so afflicted. Modifying these risks appropriately and screening closely for evidence of occlusion developing in the major blood vessels of the heart, periphery, and in those leading to the brain are the goals of therapy. When and how aggressively a physician treats a patient with medications or advises a screening program for coronary disease depends upon his clinical suspicions based upon a compilation of risk factors.

If that patient has a family history of early coronary disease, then despite whatever he or she may have done to lower risks, aggressive treatment, including medications, is likely indicated. The same plan of early and aggressive therapy holds true for patients with a family history of diabetes and obesity. Once again, the need of an adoptee to obtain such information is very significant.

A family medical history also may indicate that the physician should look for unusual illnesses that are often rare and are difficult to diagnose. Testing of the general population for these ailments is usually not indicated since testing of a mostly unaffected group will lead to too many falsely positive tests and great expense. However, once ascertained through the family history that an individual is a member of a group that has a high likelihood of a rare disease then testing is effective and indicated.

As an example, a physician friend was pregnant, and when her obstetrician inquired about her family medical history she mentioned that her mother had died suddenly after she was born. Her astute clinician then checked her blood for an inherited blood clotting disorder and, indeed, found her to have this condition.

By reason of her genetics she lacked essential proteins that are natural anticoagulants, and so she tended to clot quickly. In retrospect, her mother likely had this genetic defect and probably died from a pulmonary embolism (blood clot to her lungs). The life of the physician friend was probably saved through knowledge of her family medical history and by the diligence of the physician who sought out that knowledge, since the patient was placed on appropriate medications immediately thereafter, and especially prior to the blood-clotting tendency created by pregnancy. An adoptee without knowledge of her family medical history would not have been able to so benefit.

Access to information concerning genetic roots for the purposes of good health care is now a necessity and no longer an option. If there is family history out there containing medical information that may be pertinent to health, and yet the law and the system refuse access to that information, then the law and regulations certainly need to be changed to so provide. If change by the legislature and courts is not in the offing, then at least for the immediate time those in charge of such files must be made aware of and seriously and fully consider the implications to the health of an adoptee.

If an adoptee is in a position to inquire of their medical history, then effort should be made to gain knowledge of any still births and miscarriages within that family. The adoptee should surely ask about early deaths, unusual illnesses, or the appearances of diseases at young ages. Also to be investigated specifically are family cancer types and the occurrences of diabetes and heart disease. And finally, the adoptee should know of his or her ethnic origins and of any intermarriage within the family.

Today, unlike in the past, many more illustrations could be given of the importance of family medical history as those relate to the practical health care of individuals. However, what have been provided here are but the more common examples that are seen by heath care practitioners on a daily basis. If further information is desired, again, there are many references available as to medical genetics supporting the need for family medical history. Suffice it to say that any quest for medical information about family heritage should be encouraged and should evolve from a mere curiosity to a necessity.

Conclusion

"What we seek to achieve is the enlightened mind,
the illumined attitudes of acceptance and release, the
ultimate conviction and capacity to cast out fear
through our ability to love."[19]

As Mary Elizabeth watches her 10-year-old daughter at play, the child seems as though born into royalty, exuding confidence and composure, and preparing to conquer her world. Unlike Mary Elizabeth as a child, her daughter is not hampered by who she perceives herself to be and freely relies upon her strengths and confidence to reach whatever young goals she chooses. She is unaware of the ease with which her life flows; that comes naturally.

As she looks on, Mary Elizabeth vows that she will guide that child in such a fashion that the daughter will not bring upon herself those heart-rending personal problems that Barbara and Mary Elizabeth were called upon to confront. As parents, we are charged with a responsibility to nurture and protect our children, sons and daughters alike, even if one day that means assisting them in making the choice to keep and raise their own child despite raised eyebrows that society might have because of the circumstances of the birth.

More importantly we must impart to our children the knowledge early on that being a parent entails great responsibilities. Perhaps the lives of Barbara and Mary Elizabeth would have been very different had her parents been comfortable or had they found it necessary to bring matters of human sexuality to her attention. This is not an argument for sexual freedom but instead it is a plea for

---

[19] Marianne Williamson, *Illuminata* (Riverhead Books, New York, 1994), p.49

communication particularly with those we love. Reproduction is a part of life and discussion of such must be also.

Our children must know that our love does not end with an unfortunate and perhaps unwanted birth. For, if we place higher value upon the expectations of society than we do integrity and honor of ourselves, we may one day find ourselves searching for a grandchild given over to adoption, and worse yet, learning that there is not a child to find, what with the ease of abortions.

But society really is us. And we have brought about changes that two generations ago would not have been tolerated. We have seen mothers support their daughters as they attempt to raise their babies without a mate. Then too, we have seen open adoptions and reunions occurring with greater frequency. As parents we can continue our efforts to remove the limitations that we as a society have placed upon others and ourselves.

The law is dynamic and fluid, and it responds, albeit slowly sometimes, to the times. Since our demand to have access to heritage and history now is greater, we may expect that the law will respond to those new approaches. For now, there are search methods in place and those often may be conducted with some measure of success. All efforts to locate such as adoptees and birth parents revolve around the *wheres* of the lives of those sought. While in the course of a lifetime we may leave record of ourselves in many places, a very high percentage of those references will be stored in those records located near our residences.

So it is that the searcher must ever be conscious of where and when the person being sought may have left a mark. Beyond that consciousness and the realization that by searching you are doing nothing wrong, the balance of your efforts will be simply hunting down the offices and depositories in which records have been or are maintained.

Since a newborn is not capable of leaving a record of itself, the state in which that adoptee was born will be your first *where*, followed by the county of birth, and then hopefully the precise location and address. With rare exception you will visit those *wheres* at an early date, there to search every index and record that may be found pertaining to the first hours, days, and weeks of that child's life.

You are now equipped with the information needed to make adoption search and reunion more palatable. Jonathan Livingston Seagull's unlimited idea of freedom teaches us to believe in "...one's body being nothing more than thought itself."[20] We hope we have provided you with the material needed to help you seek your own truth and to examine and question the ways you have thought about adoption. We have found that there are no rulebooks and this book is certainly not meant to be perceived as such. If it helps, we are pleased.

We have attempted here not to minimize the problems faced by various members of the adoption triad. The road of search may be a tedious one but it is our opinion that it will only be as difficult as you allow it to be. We have suggested that the methods described here have been proven effective. Question every thought and motivation along the way though, just to be sure you have chosen your path well. Seek solutions. Seek peace. We hope our words bring you comfort and assist you with your search.

Adoptive parents indeed benefit from the birth mother's decision of long ago not to parent their child. Through the adoption process, they had the privilege of raising a child despite the fact that nature did not permit that. As a result they gained a once in a lifetime opportunity and the unique privilege of nurturing and introducing into their world a young human being. What providence did not permit, unknown birth parents and society provided.

Will your resistance to a search by your child as a result of your own insecurities impede her journey? Or will your relationship with her grow stronger because you have understood and shared her adventure? Remember that the decision to search by your child does not mean that you have in any way failed in your efforts to raise that person properly. An adoptee's anticipation of rejection from a birth parent should not be compounded by the possibility of rejection from you as well. Adoptive parents can now know that they

---

[20] *Jonathan Livingston Seagull,* op cit., p. 121

need not be afraid of losing their child or of being replaced. Many of those parents with whom we have spoken have supported their grown children during and after a search just as they have in life. They have indicated that their lives have remained unaffected for the most part by their child's search and reunion.

Giving a child over to adoption does not condemn you to a lifetime of suffering because you do not know how the child has fared. You must not remain in limbo, unable to reconcile the past and unwilling to embrace the future. Birth parents can enjoy knowing the child they lost. Contrary to your attitudes about her birth at the time, if now you are sought out, will you be able to welcome her into your life? You may find that emotionally, you have now grown sufficiently as to be able to do so, without concern for how others perceive either of you.

Adoptees can bring resolution to the question of who they are and from where they came. There is the likelihood of happiness for those who seek to find it. It is a personal journey. Those who search surely are deserving of happiness, nonetheless, they must expend the effort to seek it out and then allow themselves to receive it. Remember, there is no limit to the number of people one is capable of loving and enjoying.

Now, our story has been told, and we hope you have come to the realization that not only will you be rewarded for increased awareness and understanding, but so too will those around you. Remember again the story of the gulls. It is time to allow the knowledge you have gained to benefit others. "Fletcher Lynd Seagull, do you want to fly so much that you will forgive the Flock, and learn, and go back to them one day and work to help them know?"[21]

Just as those people at your side may benefit from your efforts, you should take advantage at every turn of the experience and advice of others. Just as did Mary Elizabeth you should seek out your Higher Power for such assistance as you may find there. Know also that you were created to receive and give unlimited love; to and from more than one or

---

[21] *Jonathan Livingston Seagull*, p. 90.

two parents, siblings, aunts, uncles, and grandparents. Allow these feelings of joy to replace the old ones of fear, anger, blame and pain.

All those involved in adoption are finding that though we are unable to change the past, we know that the march of history, just as it has affected us, will in the future be affected by us. As we move from feeling that we are victims of a system to being champions of change, we also must look about and enjoy the lives that we have forever changed and made better.

When the story of your life is written, how will you be portrayed? What is the legacy you will leave to those who come after you? It should be, "Seek what belongs to you and never give up."

What is described these days as "closure" will be in your hands, and you surely will have earned it. Or as Marie Curie said, "We must have perseverance and above all confidence in ourselves. We must believe that we are gifted for something, and that this thing, at whatever cost, must be attained."[2]

Good Luck.

Beth and Paul

---

[2] *Wisdom for the New Millennium* (Exley Publications, New York, NY 1999) no page number

Index

Addresses
  old, as clues, example, 195
Admonitions
  early, are persuasive, 35
Adopted
  meanings of word, 51
Adoptees
  1st call, example, 223, 227
  addressing 'new' parents, 227
  adoptions alter life, 14
  advantages of adoption, 33
  are different, 50
  are taught secrecy, 135
  assume obligations, 137
  aware of being different, 50
  belong to adoptive parents, 124
  biological heritage lost, 67
  birth date as important, 183
  birth parents may find, 23
  birth records, critical, 194
  birthright was severed, 14
  change ideas of their birth, 56
  coping with myths by, 22
  desire to know heritage, 15
  destructive feelings of, 140
  did not choose conception, 40
  dilemmas of, 137
  dispel procrastination, 144
  early advice considered, 35
  early ideas of secrecy, 135
  equality with parents, 157
  erroneous perceptions of, 48, 146
  errors in blame by, 46
  facing need to search, 138
  features of, heritage, 68
  feelings of inadequacy, 22

  finding courage to search, 147
  have 2 sets of parents, 118
  hearing preparations by, 201
  hesitant to inquire, 106
  hurdles confronting, 135
  if rejected, what?, 147
  imagination of, example, 19, 62, 134
  imagination, example, 66
  lost heritage discussed, 22
  love for adoptive parents, 44
  mind-set changes needed, 144
  need medical info, 99
  need to fabricate past, 17
  need to search by, 65
  no reason to explain, 68
  non-adoptee differences, 21
  not indebted to parents, 136
  part of birth parents, 113
  past status is not now, 49
  preparing for rejection, 97
  presenting evidence by, 202
  presumptions about, 15
  rejection, 146
  rejection as an enemy, 145
  revelation of 1st child, 64
  same as others?, 21
  search preparation example, 134
  search reasons questioned, 68
  search requires maturity, 60
  search, including others, 153
  search, myth of discontent, 23
  search, tell adoptive parents?, 157
  search, telling children, 78
  search, who to tell, 75

About the Authors

Beth Sherrill was the only one of six sisters and brothers given over to the adoption system. With the help of Paul, the co-author, she found her birth parents. Beth has her bachelor's degree in Human Services, worked as a counselor within that field for five years, and now owns and operates her own business. With her husband of twenty-one years, she is raising their four children in their small town in Tennessee.

Paul Drake, JD, has done genealogical research for more than fifty years, teaches and lectures on the subject frequently, and has published several popular guidebooks for uncovering ancestors, all published by Heritage Books. He is a father of three and a grandfather of seven, and lives with his wife and their little dogs in Crossville, Tennessee.

ML   2/05